# S1-S2 GEOGRAPHY

## KENNETH MACLEAN & NORMAN THOMSON

Hodder Gibson

2A Christie Street, Paisley, PA1 1NB

# Acknowledgements

The publishers would like to thank the following individuals, institutions and companies for permission to reproduce photographs in this book. Every effort has been made to trace ownership of copyright. The publishers would be happy to make arrangements with any copyright holder whom it has not been possible to contact.

Action Plus page 128 (7.29), American Stock/Archive Photos page 85 (5.25), AP pages 81 and 83 (5.18 and 5.20), Borders Tourist Board page 55 (4.20 and 4.22) Charles Tait Orkney 1160 page 67 (4.51), Corbis pages 31, 36, 38, 42, 44, 45, 57, 58, 59, 60, 69, 71, 76, 77, 79, 80, 81, 84, 88, 92, 93, 97, 108, 112, 113, 114, 115, 121, 123, 138, 142, 147, 149, 151, 155, 163, 165, 167, 168, 170, 171, 173, 175, 177, 178, 179, 180, 184, 185, 186, 187, 188, 189, 190, 192, 194, 195, 197, 198, 199, 200 and 202 (3.9, 3.21, 3.27, 3.33, 3.38, 3.40, 4.28, 4.31, 4.33, 4.38, 4.55, 4.56, 4.59, 5.9, 5.10, 5.13, 5.14, 5.16, 5.17, 5.23, 5.24, 5.32, 5.38, 5.39, 5.41, 6.2, 6.7, 6.32, 6.40, 6.42, 6.43, 6.45, 6.46, 6.48, 7.13, 7.20, 7.54, 8.3, 8.4, 8.12, 8.17, 8.21, 8.28, 8.43, 8.47, 8.49, 8.51, 9.2, 9.4B, 9.7, 9.11, 9.15, 9.17, 9.18, 9.19, 9.22, 9.23, 9.28, 9.29, 9.30, 9.32, 9.33, 9.36, 9.38, 9.39, 9.41, 9.41, 9.45, 9.47, 9.51, 9.53, 9.54, 9.57, 9.58, 9.59, 9.60 and 9.64), David Jones (image number PA740310) page 86 (5.29), Ian Jones (Telegraph Group Ltd) page 99 (6.10), Life File pages 66 (image number EX/627 EE), 109 (image number AX/386 KH), 115 (image number AX/46 C1), 169 and 203 (4.48, 6.36, 6.49, 9.4A and 9.66), Mary Evans Picture Library page 86 (5.29), NASA page 72 (5.1), Panos Pictures page 43 (3.36), Science and Society Picture Library page 87 (5.31)
Science Photo Library pages 4 (image number H407/232 IMLD40), 34 (image number EO76/194WOR030, 35 (image number EO70/379UDU01W) and 41 (image number EI55/100SPY07E) (1.1, 3.16, 3.17, 3.19 and 3.32)
Scottish Natural Heritage pages 63 (Lorne Gill, 4.42) and 105 (Patricia and Angus Macdonald, 6.26).

All other photos supplied by the authors.

This product includes mapping data licensed from Ordnance Survey® with the permission of the Controller of Her Majesty's Stationary Office. © Crown copyright. All rights reserved. Licence no. 100019872.

The characters were drawn by Richard Duszczak Cartoon Studio
The illustrations were drawn by Peters & Zabransky Ltd

The authors wish to thank Andrew Johnston of Hilton Farm, Perth and Nick and Liz Down of Little Callestock Farm, Cornwall.

Orders: please contact Bookpoint Ltd, 130 Milton Park, Abingdon, Oxon OX14 4SB. Telephone: (44) 01235 827720. Fax: (44) 01235 400454. Lines are open from 9.00–6.00, Monday to Saturday, with a 24 hour message answering service. You can also order through our website www.hodderheadline.co.uk.

Note about the Internet links in the book. The user should be aware that URLs or web addresses change regularly. Every effort has been made to ensure the accuracy of the URLs provided in this book on going press. It is inevitable, however, that some will change. It is sometimes possible to find a relocated web page by just typing in the address of the home page for a website in the URL window of your browser.

British Library Cataloguing in Publication Data
A catalogue record for this title is available from the British Library

ISBN 0 340 846 712

Published by Hodder Gibson, 2a Christie Street, Paisley PA1 1NB
Tel: 0141 848 1609; Fax: 0141 889 6315; Email: hoddergibson@hodder.co.uk

First Published 2003
Impression number    10 9 8 7 6 5 4 3 2
Year                 2009 2008 2007 2006 2005 2004
Copyright © 2003 Kenneth Maclean and Norman Thomson

Typeset by Pantek Arts Ltd, Maidstone, Kent.
Printed in Italy for Hodder Gibson, 2a Christie Street, Paisley PA1 1NB, Scotland, UK.

# Contents

## One approach to geography

This is a geography book. Along with other books, atlases, maps, television programmes, newspaper reports, the Internet and fieldwork visits, it should help you with the study of geography in S1 and S2.

People have different ideas about geography. One famous Scot – **Sir Patrick Geddes** – suggested that geography was about **Place**, **People** and **Work** in different parts of the world. Studying different places, people and work helps us to understand the many **landscapes** which we see around us, on our travels and on our television screens.

### *Life and work of Sir Patrick Geddes (1854–1932)*

Patrick Geddes (Figure 1.1) was born in Ballater, Aberdeenshire in 1854. His early years were spent in Perth because his parents had moved to a cottage on Kinnoull Hill, which overlooks the town. When he was old enough, he attended Perth Academy. The school was then beside the open parkland of the North

**Figure 1.2A**   Pupils sketching the River Tay from Kinnoull Hill

Inch, on the west bank of the River Tay. He was happiest when he was exploring the woods and quarries on Kinnoull Hill (Figure 1.2A) tramping across the Perthshire countryside, and conducting experiments in a laboratory, constructed by his father, in their garden.

Upon leaving school, he worked in a local bank, but his goal was to be a scientist. After a lot of study in London, and travel in France and Mexico, he became a lecturer at Edinburgh University. He was later appointed Professor of Botany at Dundee University, in 1889. By then he had many other interests.

**Figure 1.1**   Sir Patrick Geddes (1854–1932)

**Figure 1.2B**   The Geddes family cottage

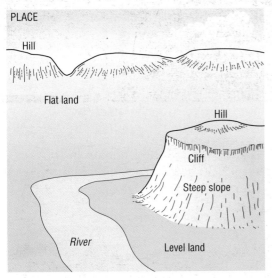

Figure 1.3A   Place

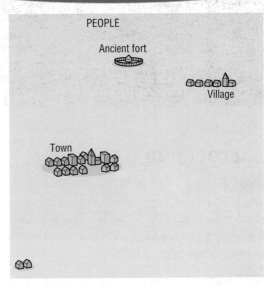

Figure 1.3B   People

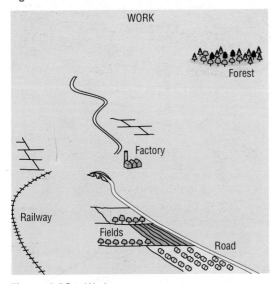

Figure 1.3C   Work

**Figure 1.4**   Countries and cities visited by Sir Patrick Geddes

He is remembered today because:

★ of his ideas about town planning. He wrote reports on towns and cities including Dunfermline, Dublin, Tel Aviv and Chennai. He believed in keeping and improving older parts of towns rather than bulldozing them (Figures 1.5 and 1.6)

★ of his many books and exhibitions. He showed the importance of studying Place, People and Work. One of his famous projects involved the Outlook Tower beside Edinburgh Castle (Figure 1.7). On its different floors, there were exhibits showing Place, People and Work in Edinburgh; Scotland; Europe and all around the world.

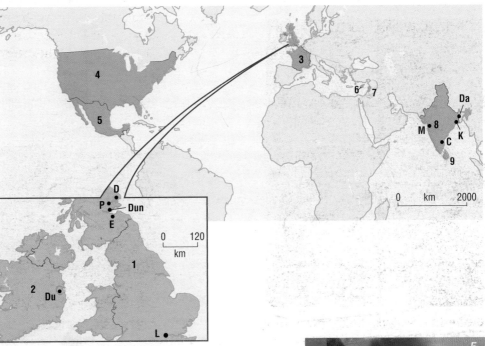

**Figure 1.5** Renovated housing in Edinburgh

**Figure 1.6** Converted church (now housing)

Today, it is popular with tourists who visit its 'Camera Obscura' a large periscope which projects views of central Edinburgh

★ of his ideas about environmental education. Books are useful but it is better to go outdoors and learn for yourself by carrying out fieldwork (like the pupils in Figure 1.2).

Patrick Geddes died in Montpellier, in the south of France in 1932. He had set up a Scots College there to spread his ideas.

**Figure 1.7** Edinburgh's Outlook Tower

## ASSIGNMENTS

1 Read about Sir Patrick Geddes and look at Figure 1.3. It has three incomplete drawings. Using a piece of tracing paper:
  a) Carefully copy the top drawing and the word Place.
  b) Then fit the tracing over drawing B. Copy the drawing and the word People.
  c) Finally, fit the tracing over the third drawing. Copy the drawing and the word Work.

2 Some of the places visited by Geddes are shown in Figure 1.4. With the help of an atlas, name
  (i) the various countries numbered 1–9.
  (ii) the cities shown by their first letter.

3 Complete this table by filling in examples of Place, People and Work. You should choose from the list below.

| Place | |
|---|---|
| | population (growth, migration), villages, towns and cities |
| Work | |

farming   mountains and hills   coastlines
industry   tourism   river valleys   volcanoes
deserts   transport   tropical rain forests

4 Why is Patrick Geddes famous?

5 Look at Figures 1.5 and 1.6. Why might Patrick Geddes have approved of the changing uses of these buildings?

# Chapter 2

# Atlas and Map Skills

## Different views of the earth

The earth is a sphere, but not a regular sphere shape. It is not completely round. It bulges out in some places, especially around the **equator**. It is flattened at the two **poles**. It looks more like a clementine than an orange.

The bulges are caused by the **rotation** (spinning) of the earth from west to east. It spins faster at the equator than it does at the poles. This is what causes the bulging around the middle of the sphere at the equator.

The equator is the earth's circumference. If you were to travel round the equator, you would travel a distance of 40,000 km. The equator divides the earth into two halves, the **Northern** and **Southern Hemispheres**. The distance between the two poles is just under 20,000 km.

## Mapping the earth

### Globes

The sphere-shaped earth is best represented by a globe because this shows more or less the correct

★ shapes

★ proportions

of the land masses (the **continents**) and the oceans.

If you look at a globe, you can see very different views of the earth, depending on which part of the globe is being studied. Most of the earth's surface is water (Figure 2.1) yet, from one viewpoint (Figure 2.2), the earth may appear to be almost all land. A third viewpoint from above the South Pole (Figure 2.3) would show a globe which is all ice and sea.

### Maps

Map-makers (**cartographers**) have made maps of the earth in different ways:

★ originally by projecting an image of a globe, or half a globe, on paper

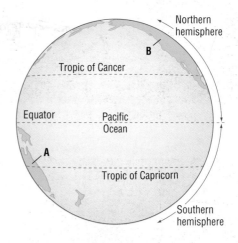

**Figure 2.1**   Water world

**Figure 2.2**   Land world

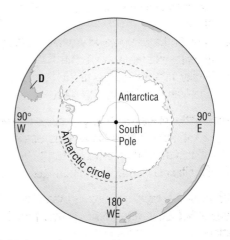

**Figure 2.3**   Ice and water world

★ then by using mathematical formulae

★ now by using computers.

Trying to show the globe on a sheet of paper is like drawing the world on an orange and then trying to pull the peel off and flatten it. This is impossible to do without the peel tearing or breaking (Figure 2.5).

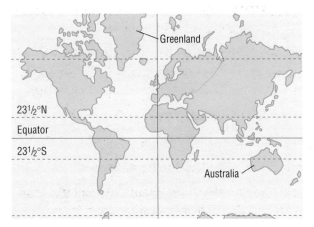

**Figure 2.4**  Mercator's map of the world

Over the last 400 years, many different types of world maps have been devised. All world maps have weaknesses. Continents and large islands may be

★ the wrong shape *or*

★ the wrong size in relation to each other.

Figures 2.4–2.6 show three very different maps of the world. Notice how the shapes and the relative sizes differ from map to map. Figure 2.4 is a good map for navigation; Figure 2.5 is an attempt to flatten a globe on a sheet of paper; while Figure 2.6 was specially drawn to show the correct relative sizes of the continents, especially Africa.

## The continents

There are seven major land masses or continents – **Asia**, **Africa**, **North** and **South America**, **Antarctica**, **Europe** and

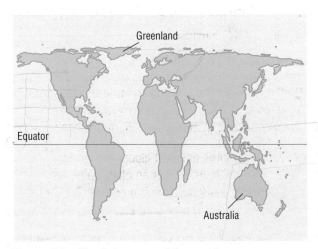

**Figure 2.6**  The Peters map of the world

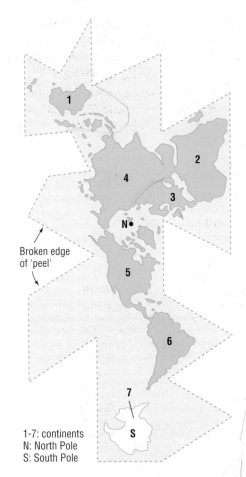

1–7: continents
N: North Pole
S: South Pole

**Figure 2.5**  Fuller's map of the world

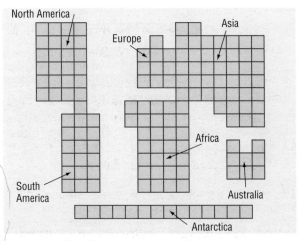

**Figure 2.7**  Relative sizes of the continents

**Australasia**. Figure 2.7 shows their relative sizes. Notice that

★ Europe is joined to Asia (together they are sometimes called **Eurasia**)

★ Australasia consists of Australia and New Zealand. If all the small islands of the Pacific are added, the name **Oceania** is used.

## ASSIGNMENTS

**1** a) Where does the earth bulge outwards?

b) What causes this bulging?

c) At which two places on the earth is it flattened?

**2** a) What is meant by the earth's rotation?

b) In what direction is the earth rotating?

**3** a) Which line of latitude divides the earth in two?

b) What is a hemisphere?

**4** Is most of the earth's surface land or water?

**5** If you were looking down on earth from a spacecraft, over which part would the earth appear to be (i) mostly land (ii) mostly sea?

**6** Study the three different globes in Figures 2.1–2.3. With the help of an atlas, name the continents marked A and B on Figure 2.1; C on Figure 2.2, and D on Figure 2.3.

**7** Look carefully at the unusual map of the world in Figure 2.5. Name the continents numbered 1–7.

**8** Study Figure 2.7.

a) Name the largest and the smallest continents.

b) Which is larger – North or South America?

**9** Australia is two and a half times bigger than Greenland. On which of the world maps in Figures 2.4–2.6, does it appear much smaller?

**10** On which of the world maps does Africa appear to be much longer and thinner than it should be?

**11** a) Which of the world maps in Figures 2.4–2.6 shows all of Antarctica?

b) Give a reason why most world maps do not show Antarctica, or only its northern fringe.

# Where on earth?

## Locating places: latitude and longitude

All places on the earth's surface can be located precisely according to their latitude and their longitude. Lines of **latitude** (from west to east) and **longitude** (from north to south) can be drawn on globes and maps.

**LATITUDE** is the distance north and south of the equator measured in degrees (°).

The maximum distances in latitude from the equator are at the two poles at 90°N and 90°S. On a globe (Figure 2.8), lines of latitude are

★ circles parallel to the equator

★ always the same distance apart

except for latitudes 90°N and 90°S.

Latitudes 90° North and South are points – the North and South Poles – rather than lines.

**LONGITUDE** is the distance east and west of Greenwich, London, measured in degrees.

Since the earth is a sphere, it spins through 360°. The maximum distance in longitude from Greenwich is 180°, both east and west. A line of longitude may also be called a **meridian**. The one which passes through Greenwich is called the **Prime Meridian**. The Prime Meridian divides the earth into the Western and Eastern Hemispheres.

On a globe (Figure 2.9), lines of longitude

★ are 110 km apart at the equator but

★ converge on the two poles.

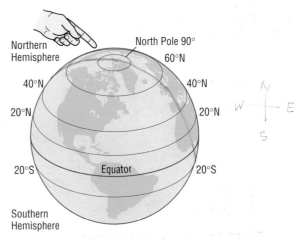

**Figure 2.8**  Lines of latitude

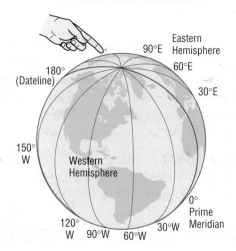

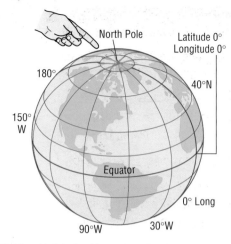

**Figure 2.9** Lines of longitude

**Figure 2.10** A global grid

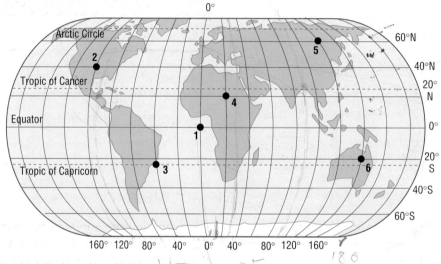

**Figure 2.11** The world: latitude and longitude

W ← | → E

The lines of latitude and longitude can be used to form a grid on both globes and maps (Figure 2.10). This helps to locate places exactly on the earth's surface.

If a ship gave its position as being on the equator and on the Prime Meridian (Latitude 0 degrees; Longitude 0 degrees) it would be in the Gulf of Guinea, off the coast of West Africa (Figure 2.10).

The grid formed by the lines of latitude and longitude varies on world maps. One example is shown in Figure 2.11 above. Look in your atlas for other types.

Scotland is closer to the North Pole than it is to the equator, and it lies entirely west of the Greenwich Meridian.

The grid on the map in Figure 2.12 can be used to locate places in Scotland in two different ways

★ using latitude and longitude

★ using the letters and numbers.

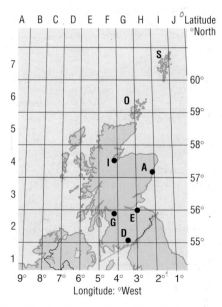

**Figure 2.12** Scotland's latitude and longitude

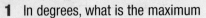

## ASSIGNMENTS

**1** In degrees, what is the maximum
   a) latitude?
   b) longitude?

**2** a) What is a meridian?
   b) Which is the Prime Meridian?

**3** What is meant by a 'hemisphere'?

**4** Which continents are located in
   a) the northern hemisphere?
   b) the southern hemisphere?

**5** Which two continents are partly in the northern hemisphere and partly in the southern hemisphere?

**6** With the aid of an atlas, name one country in each of the hemispheres:
   a) the northern   c) the western
   b) the southern   d) the eastern.

**7** Look at Figure 2.11. Point 1 is the Greenwich Meridian – Latitude 0° (the Equator) and Longitude 0° (the Greenwich Meridian). With the aid of the grid on this map, give the latitude and the longitude of the places numbered 2–6.

**8** Look at Figure 2.12 and, with the aid of an atlas, complete the following table and give the approximate latitudes and longitudes.

|  | Glasgow | Aberdeen | Shetland |
| --- | --- | --- | --- |
| a) Latitude |  |  |  |
|  | **Orkney** | **Arran** | **Harris** |
| b) Longitude |  |  |  |

## TO TAKE YOU FURTHER

# (1) Longitude and time

The earth is rotating (spinning) from west to east as it revolves around the sun. Along each meridian, the sun is seen

◆ rising on the eastern horizon

◆ setting on the western horizon.

It takes the earth 24 hours to complete one full rotation. There are 360 degrees of longitude, so

◆ in one hour, the earth spins through 15 degrees

◆ in six hours it spins through 90 degrees

◆ every 15 degrees of longitude makes a difference of one hour in time.

Therefore, for example,

◆ in Bangladesh, at 90° East, the sun rises and sets six hours earlier than at Greenwich

◆ in Guatemala, Central America, at 90° West, the sun sets and rises 6 hours later than at Greenwich.

There are 24 time zones in the world (Figure 2.13). In theory, each time zone should have absolutely straight north-south boundaries, but

◆ these are altered to match political boundaries

◆ the International Date Line (which is both 180° East and West of Greenwich) zig-zags through the Pacific Ocean. This makes sure that all of the islands within a particular country are kept within the same time zone.

South America, Africa and Australia all have three time zones. The continents in the northern hemisphere have a greater west-east extent. More time zones are needed. There are six in North America and twelve in Eurasia. Russia has nine of these twelve time zones.

Countries make their own decisions about time zones. For example,

◆ Iceland should be 1 hour behind Greenwich Mean Time (GMT), but has chosen to use GMT

*continued* ➤

**TO TAKE YOU FURTHER** *continued*

◆ China should have three time zones, but has chosen to have only one. The whole country, from 75° East to 120° East, takes its time from its eastern coast. All of China is therefore 8 hours ahead of GMT.

## ASSIGNMENTS *TO TAKE YOU FURTHER*

**1** a) Give another word for 'rotating'.
   b) In what direction does the earth rotate?
   c) How long does it take the earth to complete one rotation?

**2** How long does it take the earth to rotate through
   a) 30 degrees
   b) 75 degrees
   c) 120 degrees of longitude?

**3** Study Figure 2.13 carefully.
   a) How many world time zones are there?
   b) Name two continents where the time is
      (i) ahead of Greenwich Mean Time (GMT)
      (ii) behind GMT.

**4** Name the country which needs nine time zones.

**5** Looking at the information provided, calculate the time in zones X, Y and Z when it is mid-day (12 noon) GMT.

**6** Read the text about Bangladesh and Guatemala again. Find them in your atlas. When it is 4 pm at Greenwich, what time will it be in:
   a) Guatemala?
   b) Bangladesh?          16pm

**7** Look at Figure 2.13 again. If a match in the 2002 Football World Cup kicked off at 4 pm in Japan, what time would it be shown live on television in Britain?

**8** a) What is the longitude of the International Date Line (IDL)?
   b) Why does the IDL zig-zag from north to south?
   c) Is it better to cross the IDL from west to east or from east to west?
   d) Explain your answer.

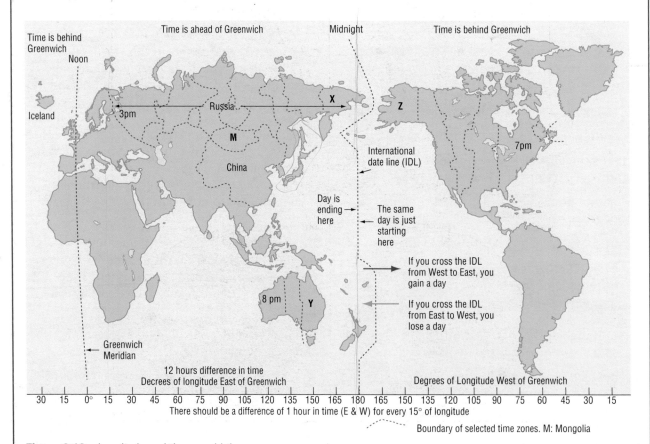

**Figure 2.13**   Longitude and time: world time zones

**TO TAKE YOU FURTHER** ▶

# (2) Night and day

We already know that the earth is rotating as it revolves around the sun. As a result,

◆ half of the earth will be lit up by the sun, so there will be daylight

◆ the other hemisphere will be in shadow, so there will be darkness.

Figure 2.14 shows what you would see if you were able to hover in space and look down on the North Pole for 24 hours continuously in late March or late September. You would see the Greenwich Meridian spinning into daylight and then back into darkness. Every latitude has 12 hours of daylight and 12 hours of darkness during these two months.

However, the earth is tilted on its axis, so that in late June and late December the length of night and day is very unequal (Figure 2.15). In late June

◆ in the Northern Hemisphere, day is longer than night

◆ in the Arctic, the sun does not set

◆ in the Southern Hemisphere, night is longer than day

◆ in the Antarctic, the sun does not rise.

In late December, the opposite applies.

**However, at the equator, there are always 12 hours of daylight, and 12 hours of darkness.**

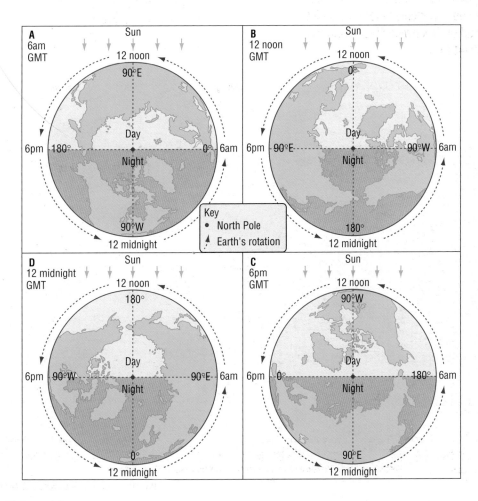

**Figure 2.14**   Night and day

*continued* ➤

**TO TAKE YOU FURTHER** *continued*

**ASSIGNMENTS TO TAKE YOU FURTHER**

1 Look carefully at Figure 2.14 which has four parts. Find the Greenwich Meridian (0° longitude).
   a) In the first part, is the sun rising or setting at Greenwich?
   b) In the third part, is the sun rising or setting at Greenwich?

2 Look at Figure 2.15.
   a) Is the earth's axis perpendicular or tilted?
   b) What effect does this have on the length of night and day?
   c) In which months does this occur?
   d) On 22 June, which hemisphere has long days and short nights?
   e) Where would you rather be on 22 June, the Arctic Circle or the Antarctic Circle?
   f) Explain your answer.

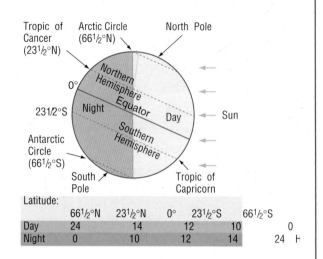

| Latitude: | 66½°N | 23½°N | 0° | 23½°S | 66½°S | |
|-----------|-------|-------|-----|-------|-------|---|
| Day | 24 | 14 | 12 | 10 | | 0 |
| Night | 0 | 10 | 12 | 14 | | 24  H |

**Figure 2.15**  Varying length of day and night: 22 June

# Features of a good map

Maps are a good way to convey a great deal of information about any part of the world. All maps should have the following information:

★ a **title** which tells you exactly what the map is trying to show

★ a direction symbol (**compass**) which points north

★ a **scale**, which can be expressed in three or four different forms

★ a **key** or legend, which tells you exactly the meaning of the colours and symbols.

Title and key are absolutely essential, but

★ on some atlas maps, usually world maps, the scale may not be given

★ a direction symbol may not be given.

If north is not indicated on a map, it can be assumed that it is at the 'top' of the map.

On larger-scale maps (maps of smaller areas), the scale and the direction must always be shown. Figure 2.16 is an example of an atlas-style, world map, which has a clear title, and a full key. North is shown, but no scale is needed, because distances are not important on this map.

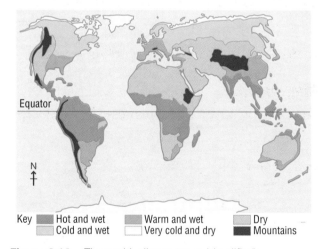

| Key | Hot and wet | Warm and wet | Dry |
|-----|-------------|--------------|-----|
| | Cold and wet | Very cold and dry | Mountains |

**Figure 2.16**   The world: climate types (simplified)

Figure 2.17 is an example of a map on a much larger scale than the first map. Scale is shown in two ways:

★ by a line (linear) scale

★ visually, by showing Scotland on the same scale.

The short title explains exactly what the map shows and there is a clear key. There is a direction arrow.

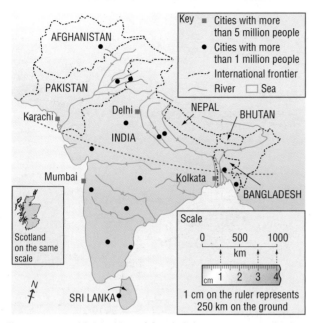

**Figure 2.17**  Major cities of South Asia

★ a statement

★ a visual comparison.

Linear scales are used on two of the maps (Figures 2.17–2.18) and a visual comparison is given on Figure 2.17. The scale could be expressed in two other ways

★ as a fraction, for example, 1:25000. This means that 1 cm on the map represents 25,000 cm on the ground

★ as a statement, for example, 4 cm on the map represents 1 km (on the ground).

**Points to remember: the larger the map scale**

★ **the smaller the area which can be shown**

★ **the more detailed the map.**

Figure 2.18, the final example, is a map of the smallest area, and is therefore on the largest scale. Scale and a direction arrow are essential in this case. The key is short but precise, and the title again explains the purpose of the map:

★ why the map was drawn

★ what information you can obtain from it.

## Map scales

The scale of a map can be expressed in four ways

★ a line scale

★ as a fraction

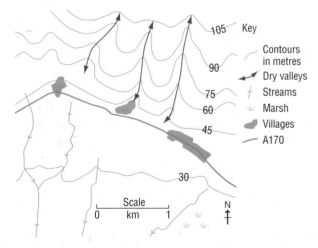

**Figure 2.18**  Village sites near Pickering, North Yorkshire

### ASSIGNMENTS

1  Why is a map title important?

2  What does a map key tell you?

3  If there is no direction symbol, where should you assume north to be on the map?

4  How many ways are there to show scale on a map?

5  Look at Figure 2.17. Which two ways are used to show the scale of the map? Which is the more helpful?

6  Study Figure 2.18. Using the scale, measure the distance in km from west to east across the map.

7  If there are two maps, one at a scale of 1:100000, the other at 1:25000, which will be the more detailed?

8  Look at the three maps in Figures 2.19–2.21.
   a)  Draw a line scale for each map.
   b)  Measure the area of each map in square km.

**Figure 2.19** Map A

*Source*: Ordnance Survey
sheet 72 (Landranger)

**Figure 2.20** Map B

*Source*: Ordnance Survey sheet 343
(Explorer)

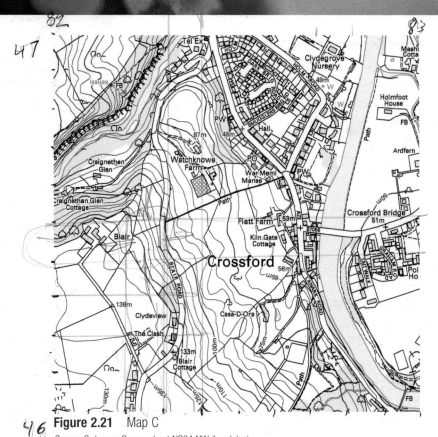

**Figure 2.21** Map C

*Source*: Ordnance Survey sheet NS84 NW (Landplan)

## Maps of different scales

Crossford, a small village in Lanarkshire, is shown on page 16 on three Ordnance Survey (O.S.) maps of very different scales:

A – 1: 50000 (the smallest scale)

B – 1: 25000

C – 1: 10000 (the largest scale).

The three maps were published at different dates, so the information shown will differ.

★ All three maps are in full colour

★ Map C shows individual buildings and gardens within the village, and the names of roads

★ All three maps use symbols to distinguish between deciduous and coniferous trees

★ Maps B and C show the boundaries of farm fields by thin black lines

★ All three maps show where tomatoes and flowers are grown under glass on market gardens – these glasshouses are shown as rectangles with diagonal lines.

★ Map B provides a great deal of information for tourists, for example, the green arrows show the Clyde Walkway.

## Grid squares and grid references

We have already found out that lines of latitude and longitude are used to locate places on the surface of the earth. On atlas maps, these lines may form a grid. The lines which form the grid are identified

★ as lines of latitude – the lines which run from west to east

★ as lines of longitude which run from north to south.

For example, if you look back at Figure 2.12, the map tells you that

★ Orkney is 59° north of the equator, and 3° west of Greenwich

★ Shetland lies between 60° and 61° north of the equator, and between 1° and 2° west of Greenwich.

The lines of latitude and longitude form a grid on the map in 10 columns (identified by letters) and 7 rows (identified by numbers).

These can be used to give a **grid reference**, for example, F4 is the reference for Inverness ('I' on the map).

## The National Grid system

There is a complete grid reference system, the National Grid, for the O.S. maps which cover Great Britain. Figure 2.22 shows the grid squares for Scotland.

The squares are formed by lines which are measured in terms of distance from the starting point south-west of Land's End.

★ Going East: North–South lines which mark these distances are called **Eastings** and

★ Going North: West-East lines which mark these distances are called **Northings**.

## Grid references on O.S. maps

When you look at any one of the 204 O.S. maps at a scale of 1:50000 you will see that

★ it has a grid, formed by blue lines, of 1 km squares

★ the Eastings and the Northings are numbered in blue in the margins of the map. The numbers may sometimes also appear on the grid on the map.

# Using grid references

## Four-figure grid references

Figure 2.23 shows the simple rule which applies when using map references of O.S. maps on any scale:

### Eastings come before Northings.

To find the reference of the grid square in which the church is located: find the vertical grid line (Easting) to the left of the church. Read its value from the margin.      **Answer: 20**

Find the horizontal line (Northing) below the church. Find its value.      **Answer: 28**

Combine the two values to give a four-figure reference for the grid square in which the church is located.      **Answer: 2028**

**When giving the reference of a grid square, always give the reference of the South West corner.**

Figure 2.24 shows, in simplified form, a small section of the 1:50000 map sheet on which the village of Crossford can be found (look back at Figure 2.19).

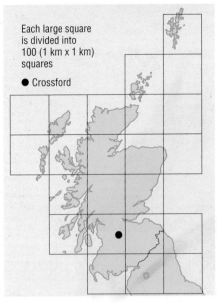

**Figure 2.22**  Ordnance Survey grid squares used in Scotland

**Figure 2.23**  A four-figure grid reference

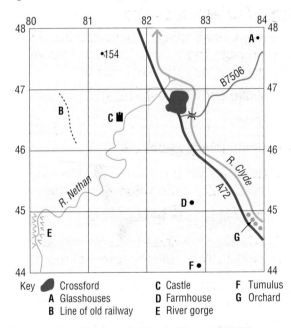

Key
Crossford     C Castle        F Tumulus
A Glasshouses         D Farmhouse     G Orchard
B Line of old railway     E River gorge

**Figure 2.24**  The Crossford Area (Scale 1:50000)

It shows an area of 16 square km. The eastings are numbered along the top and bottom, and the northings along the sides. Selected features shown are identified in the key.

Using a simple four-figure grid reference, the location of the village of Crossford can be given as grid square 8246.

## ASSIGNMENTS

**1** Give the reference of the grid square in which you would find
   a) a spot height 154 m
   b) a farmhouse
   c) an orchard
   d) the line of an old railway

**2** Name the features you would find in the following grid squares: 8044; 8347; 8146; 8244.

**3** Give the reference of the grid square in which you would find a bridge over the River Clyde.

## TO TAKE YOU FURTHER

# Six figure grid references

In some cases, giving a four-figure reference may not be sufficient. Using a six-figure grid reference is more precise. It locates places in an area of 1 square km within 100 metres. This is easier to do on a 1:25000 map (see Figure 2.25). The values of the Eastings and the Northings are given in the margins. In addition, the distance between any two eastings or northings is shown as divided into tenths (every 100 metres).

To give a six-figure reference, for example, for the summit of Wood Hill (Figure 2.25)

◆ First find the value of the Easting as before, in this case **20**
◆ Then measure in tenths the distance of the summit from the Easting, in this case **5**
◆ Add this number to the first to give a three-figure reference for the Easting **205**

◆ Find the value of the Northing **33**
◆ Measure in tenths the distance of the summit from the Northing, in this case **4**
◆ Add this number to the first, to give a three-figure reference for the Northing **334**
◆ Put the two parts together to give the six-figure grid reference for Wood Hill **205334**

The same rules apply with 1:50000 maps, but there is no help in the margins to measure the tenths. You must therefore estimate, or measure with your ruler (2 mm = one-tenth in this case).

## ASSIGNMENTS TO TAKE YOU FURTHER

**1** Study Figure 2.25. Give six-figure map references for the two farms: (i) Posso (ii) Glenrath.

**2** Study the 1:10000 map extract Figure 2.21. The scale can be expressed as 10 cm to 1 km. You should use your ruler to measure the tenths.
   a) Give six-figure map references for: Crossford Inn; Blair Cottage; Manse.
   b) Name the features which are located at: 824466; 823462; 827469.

**3** Draw your own map to show the situation of Crossford. Draw it on the same scale as Figure 2.24 Copy the grid. Draw in the courses of the two rivers, the A72 and the area covered by the village. Do not show anything else. Do not show the values of the grid lines. Instead, letter the columns A–D, and number the rows 1–4. Crossford should be in square C3. Give the reference of the squares in which the River Nethan flows (i) north (ii) into the River Clyde. Give your map a title. Draw a line scale. Add a simple key. Insert a north point.

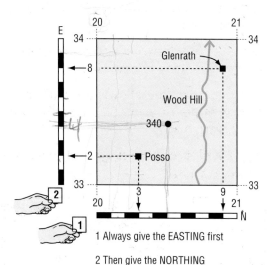

1 Always give the EASTING first

2 Then give the NORTHING

**Figure 2.25** A six-figure grid reference (1:25000 map)

# How maps show height and relief

## *Height*

On large scale maps such as those produced by the Ordnance Survey, height is shown by

★ **spot heights**

★ **trig points**

★ **contours.**

All heights are shown in metres.

**Spot heights** are points on the landscape where the height has been accurately surveyed (Figures 2.26 A and B). Printed in black or brown, they are found

★ on the tops of hills and mountains – the **summits**

★ on lower, flatter ground to show the height of a valley floor or plain.

**Figure 2.26A** A spot height on a summit

**Figure 2.26B** A spot height in a valley

**Trig points** (or **stations** or **pillars**) are shown by a blue dot inside a blue triangle, with a precise height beside it (Figure 2.27). They mark the vantage points which surveyors first used to map an area with their theodolites. Triangulation pillars of stones (now of concrete) about a metre high were built on summits. Theodolites were placed on the top of these to measure angles to other points in a series of triangles.

**Figure 2.27** A trig point

These measurements fixed places accurately in relation to each other. Other vantage points used on low ground included

★ church spires

★ chimneys

★ lighthouses.

In some cases, towers or masts were built.

'Trig point' is derived from 'triangulation point'. They are much less common than spot heights on O.S. maps. In the area of North-East Fife shown in Figure 2.28, there were only 12 trig points as compared to almost 100 spot heights. Figure 2.28 also gives an indication of the triangulation system used in North-East Fife.

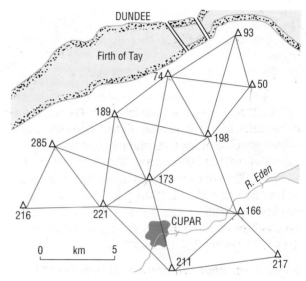

**Figure 2.28** Trig points in North-East Fife

**Contours** are brown lines on O.S. maps which have been drawn to join places of **equal height above sea level**. Notice that:

★ it would be impossible to show contours for every metre difference in height

★ heights, in metres, are printed in brown on the contours

★ contours are drawn at a vertical interval of every 10 metres or 5 metres

★ some contours are shown in a darker brown, either at every 50 metres or at every 25 metres.

*Always check the map key for information about the contours.*

**Figure 2.29** Types of slope: contour maps

Figure 2.29 shows

A: The contours are equally spaced, so the slope is even.

B: The contours show that the slope begins very steeply, then levels out (a **convex** slope).

C: The slope begins very gently, then becomes much steeper (a **concave** slope).

★ If there are no contours, the area is flat

★ the fewer the contours shown in an area, the gentler the slope

★ the greater the number of contours shown in an area, the steeper the slope.

Figure 2.30 shows cross-sections of these slopes.

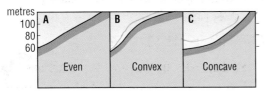

**Figure 2.30** Cross-sections of slopes

## Rocks

You will find that O.S. maps also show where rocks are found. Symbols are drawn in black on top of the brown contours to show

★ cliffs/crags

★ rock outcrops

★ scree.

For example, in very steep, rugged areas, the use of the rock symbols gives precise information (Figure 2.31) about what you would find there.

## Relief

'Relief' is a word used to describe the height and the shape (the **landforms**) of a landscape. On the small-scale maps in an atlas, the relief is shown in a very general way by using graded colours and shading (see p. 24).

On larger scale maps, such as those produced by the O.S., relief is shown by

★ the patterns formed by the contours

★ the frequency of the contours

★ the rock symbols and spot heights.

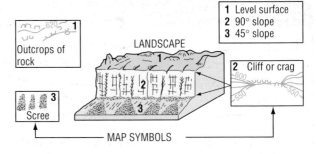

**Figure 2.31**   Rock features: scree/rock outcrops/a cliff

With practice, you should be able to identify simple landforms from the patterns made by the contours and the symbols used (Figure 2.32).

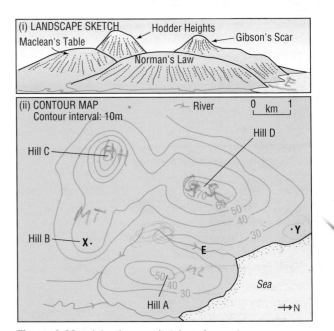

**Figure 2.32**   A landscape sketch and a contour map

## ASSIGNMENTS

**A** Look at Figure 2.32. The sketch has been drawn from ground level looking across the landscape. The contour map is a plan view of the same landscape looking down from above. The contour map can be compared directly with the landscape sketch.

  **1** What is the contour interval (the difference in height between any two contours) on the map?

  **2** Decide what height the spot heights X and Y are. Choose from the following options: 26m; 34m; 71m; 67m; 48m.

  **3** At what height do the two rivers rise? Choose from the following options: less than 30m; 30–40m; 40–50m.

  **4** In a table, match the four hills A–B on the map with the hills named in the sketch. Give the height of each hill.

**5** Which hill is steepest? Give a reason for your choice.

**6** Which hill would be easiest to climb? Give a reason for your choice.

**7** Which hill has a (i) conical top (like an ice-cream cone) (ii) flat top?

**8** Which hill is situated (i) farthest north (ii) farthest south?

**9** River valley E is shown on the contour map. It cannot be seen on the sketch. Can you explain this?

**B** **1** What is a (i) contour (ii) concave slope (iii) convex slope?

  **2** What is (i) a cliff (ii) scree?

  **3** What is meant by the **relief** of a landscape?

# Contour patterns showing simple landforms (Figure 2.33)

Scale 2 cm = 1 km

**1** No contours; highest point 25 m. A flat, low area or plain with a slow-flowing stream.

**2** An area with only one contour (30 m) forming a circle. A plain with one very low, rounded hill or **knoll**.

**3** Only one contour forming a branching shape. A plain with a stream flowing in a broad, shallow valley.

**4** Two contours, far apart. A difference in height of about 20 m. A gentle slope.

**5** Three contours forming a circular pattern, with a height difference of over 20 m. A round-topped hill.

**6** Many contours, close together, with a height difference of 130 m. A very steep slope.

**7** A large area over 350 m without a contour. A high, but flat area or **plateau**, with steep sides.

**8** Three undulating contours forming "Vs'". Highest land in north. Two streams flowing south in deep valleys, separated by an area of higher ground or **spur** (S).

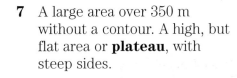

**9** Many contours, close together, forming a narrow "V" pointing south-west. Highest in north-east. Steep slopes on either side. The highest area is a long, narrow **ridge** (R).

## ASSIGNMENT

Study the contour diagrams in Figure 2.33 very carefully. Then look at the contour map in Figure 2.34. Nine features are lettered A–I on this map. The heights are different but the contour patterns are similar.
In a table, match the features A–I with the landforms 1–9 shown in Figure 2.33.

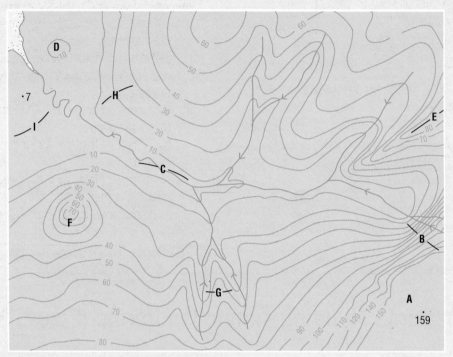

**Figure 2.34**   A contour map

## TO TAKE YOU FURTHER

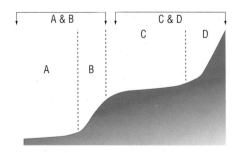

**Figure 2.35**   Cross-section of a hill

## ASSESSMENTS TO TAKE YOU FURTHER

**1** Look at Figure 2.35. It is a cross-section or profile of a hill (as seen from the side). The section is divided into four parts labelled A–D.
If this hill were shown on an O.S. map, on which parts would the contours be
a)   close together?
b)   far apart?
Show your answers in a simple table.

**2** Is the slope A–B concave or convex?

**3** Is the slope C–D concave or convex?

*continued* ➤

**TO TAKE YOU FURTHER** *continued*

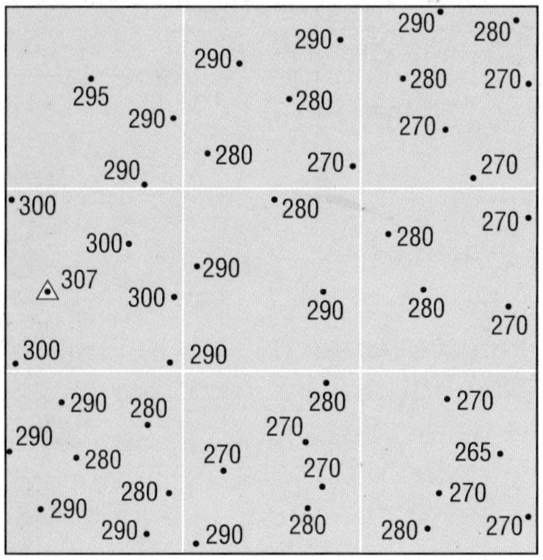

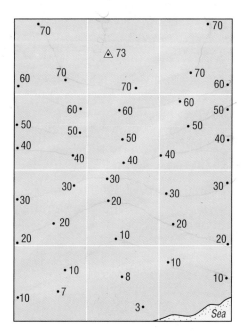

**Figure 2.36A**

**4** Study the diagrams in Figure 2.36. They represent areas which have been surveyed, and spot heights and trig points have been accurately measured in metres. A 1 km grid has been drawn on each map. In your notebook, for each diagram in turn:

a) draw an accurate grid.

b) plot the spot heights and trig points in pencil.

c) add any additional information given such as the sea.

d) then draw a contour map by joining points of the same height.

e) try to identify these features from the contour patterns:
steep slope; plain; spur; river valley; summit.
Print the names of these features neatly on the map, and draw in the river courses.

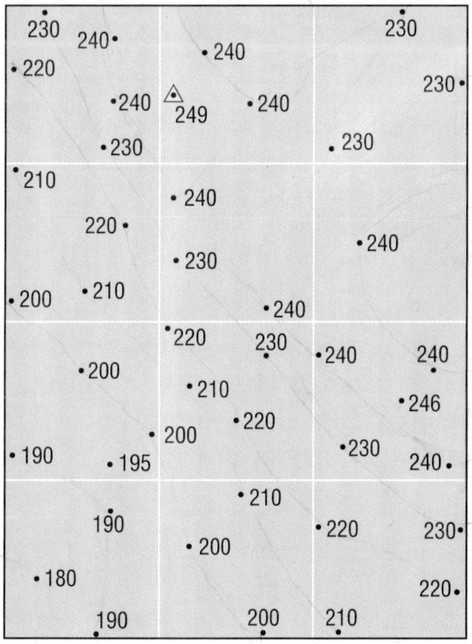

**Figure 2.36B**

**Figure 2.36C**

# Using an atlas

An atlas should contain four or five important sections

★ At the front there should be a **contents** page. This gives you a page number for each map.

★ This may be followed by some pages which tell you how to use the atlas. There may be a general key and information about **scale**.

★ Most of the atlas should consist of maps, on different scales, and drawn for different purposes. The information is given in a special kind of shorthand which the mapmakers (**cartographers**) have devised. This shorthand uses symbols and colours which are explained in a **key** on each page.

★ Most maps will be **physical** (or **relief**) maps which show the height of the land (Figure 2.37). Height is shown by graded colours such as green, yellow, shades of brown, purple, grey. Shading may also be used to show steep mountain areas. The rivers and lakes are shown in blue. The depth of the sea can be shown by shades of blue. Physical maps may also show the main towns, the main roads and railways.

★ Other maps could simply show the countries in the world, or states in part of the world, by using different colours. Such a map is called a **political** map (Figure 2.38) They may also show the main cities, roads and railways.

★ There may also be special maps which give information about climate, vegetation, population, land use, and the main products.

★ There is always an **index** at the back of the atlas. This will give you information about places, listed alphabetically, shown on all the maps. In some atlases, the index is divided into two parts. There is one for places in the British Isles, the other for the rest of the world. The index will give you the page on which the place is shown, a grid reference and/or its latitude and longitude. This information will help you to locate the place precisely on the page.

| Place | Page | Grid Reference | Latitude (in °) | Longitude (in °) |
|---|---|---|---|---|
| Glasgow | 12 | 4D | 55 N | 6 W |
| Antofagasta | 19 | 6D | 23 S | 70 W |

★ There could also be a section giving statistical information about individual countries.

**Remember: Atlas maps are simple and selective. They cannot show everything, but they can provide much useful information about any country.**

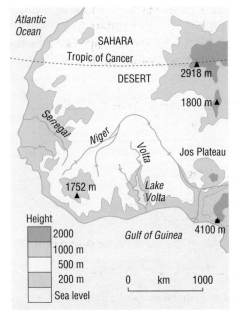

**Figure 2.37**   Physical map of West Africa

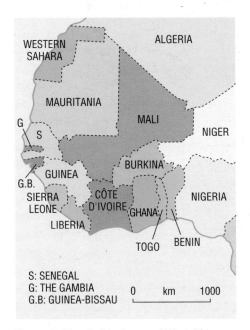

**Figure 2.38**   Political map of West Africa

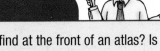

## Starting out

Always start by looking for the country on the contents page. If you cannot find it, you should then look at the index. This will give you the main page on which the country is shown. It may be shown on a smaller scale on other pages, but with extra information.

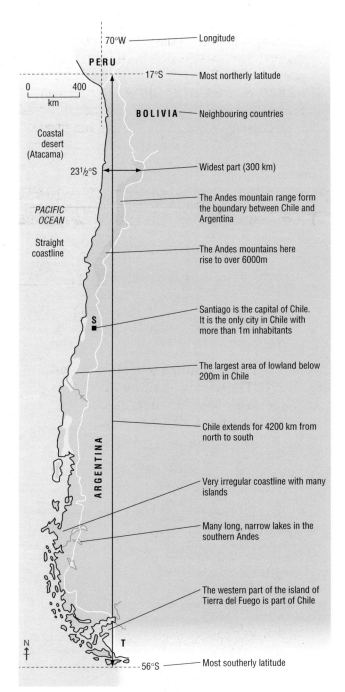

- Longitude
- 70°W
- **PERU**
- 17°S — Most northerly latitude
- 0    400 km
- **BOLIVIA** — Neighbouring countries
- Coastal desert (Atacama)
- 23½°S — Widest part (300 km)
- The Andes mountain range form the boundary between Chile and Argentina
- *PACIFIC OCEAN*
- The Andes mountains here rise to over 6000m
- Straight coastline
- S — Santiago is the capital of Chile. It is the only city in Chile with more than 1m inhabitants
- The largest area of lowland below 200m in Chile
- Chile extends for 4200 km from north to south
- **ARGENTINA**
- Very irregular coastline with many islands
- Many long, narrow lakes in the southern Andes
- The western part of the island of Tierra del Fuego is part of Chile
- N
- T
- 56°S — Most southerly latitude

**Figure 2.39**    Chile

## ASSIGNMENTS

1 What list will you find at the front of an atlas? Is the index found at the front or the back?

2 What will the contents page tell you?

3 What are listed in alphabetical order in the index?

4 What important information is also provided in the index?

5 What does a cartographer do?

6 What are the differences between (i) a political map and (ii) a physical map?

7 Using your atlas, draw up a table to show the latitude, longitude and population size of Aberdeen; Birmingham; Detroit; London; Los Angeles; Manchester; Phoenix.

Figure 2.39 shows how much information you should find about Chile in a simple atlas such as *Philip's Foundation Atlas*. Notice that, because of its unusually narrow shape, an atlas map of Chile can only show a limited amount of information. Study Figure 2.39 carefully before attempting the two assignments which follow.

## Any country: basic facts

On the map page on which you find the country, first look at the type of map. In most atlases, this will be a physical map. Then look at the key and the scale of the map. Look at the grid formed by the lines of latitude and longitude.

You should then be able to find the following facts from the map:

★ its range of latitude

★ its range of longitude

★ the maximum distances from west to east, and from north to south

★ the names of adjoining seas and oceans

★ some of the features of the coastline

★ the names of neighbouring countries

★ the height and form of the land

★ the names of mountain ranges, plains etc.

★ the height and names of the highest peaks

★ the names of the main rivers, and the direction in which they flow

★ the names of large lakes

★ the name and the size of population of the capital city

★ the names and size of population of other large cities.

From maps of different scales and types on other pages, you may be able to find something about the country's

★ climate

★ natural vegetation

★ land use.

Most atlases now have detailed sections of several pages devoted to different maps of the British Isles. Some atlases have detailed sections on other countries such as Italy, Brazil and Nigeria.

There may also be useful facts and figures about countries in special tables.

## Atlas work: USA and India

Several of the topics later in this book use examples from the USA and India – Chapter 5, Chapter 7, Chapter 8 and Chapter 9.

Using your atlas to complete these exercises will give you a good background to these topics.

### ASSIGNMENTS

1 Study Figure 2.40, the outline map of the USA. With the aid of an atlas

   a) measure the distances A–B and C–D in km

   b) name the detached American state (1)

   c) measure the distance from X–Y in km

   d) number the lines of the latitude (2–7)

   e) number the lines of the longitude (8–10)

   f) name the neighbouring countries (11–12)

   g) name the areas of sea (13–15)

   h) name the highest peak (19) and give its height

   i) name the rivers (20–23)

   j) name the lakes (24–26)

   k) name the valley (27) and give its height

   l) name the volcano (28)

   m) name the desert (29)

   n) name the state (30)

   o) name the large cities (31–35)

   p) name the capital (36).

2 Study Figure 2.41, the outline map of India. With the aid of an atlas

   a) measure the distances A–B and C–D in km

   b) number the lines of latitude (1–3)

   c) number the lines of longitude (4–5)

   d) name the neighbouring countries (6–12)

   e) name the sea areas (13–15)

   f) name the mountain (16) and give its height

   g) name the plateau area (17) and its mountain edge (18)

   h) name the rivers (19–21)

   i) name the river feature (22)

   j) name the desert area (23)

   k) name the earthquake area (24)

   l) name the large cities (25–30)

   m) name the capital (31)

3 (i) Copy and complete the following table.

   (ii) Which is the more crowded country?

   (iii) Which country has the greater proportion of its population living in large cities?

| Country | Area (square km) | Population (millions) | Number of cities with over 5 million people | Number of cities with over 1 million people |
|---------|------------------|-----------------------|---------------------------------------------|---------------------------------------------|
| USA     | 9373             |                       |                                             |                                             |
| India   | 3288             |                       |                                             |                                             |

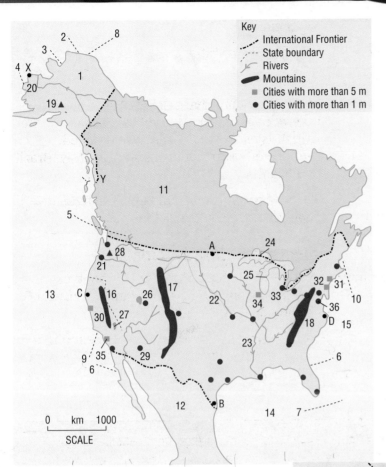

**Figure 2.40**   Outline map of USA

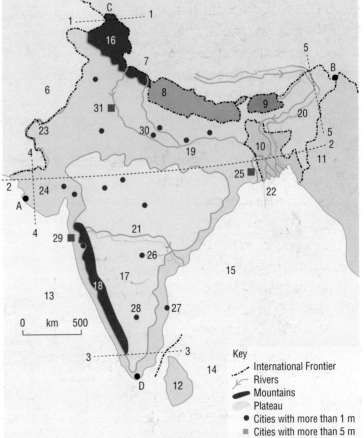

**Figure 2.41**   Outline map of India

# Chapter 3

# Weather, Weather Hazards and Water

## Britain's varied weather

### Weather and climate

People talk about the weather. Often, it is the opening topic of conversation. People watch daily weather forecasts, but there are no daily 'climate forecasts'. This is because weather is about **day-to-day changes** in the atmosphere: it includes changes in temperature, rainfall, sunshine and wind. Climate, however, is about the average weather conditions. It deals with average temperatures, average rainfall, average amounts of sunshine and average wind speed and direction. These have been measured over many years.

Compared to many places in the world, the British Isles have a climate that is mild and damp. It is also very changeable, making it difficult to accurately forecast (Figure 3.1).

Conditions vary from one part of the British Isles to another. Figure 3.2 shows:

**Figure 3.1**  A heavy summer rainstorm

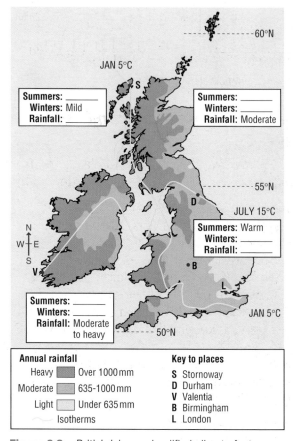

**Figure 3.2**  British Isles – simplified climate features

★ the average distribution of rainfall. (Spot the differences between west and east.)

★ the differences between summer and winter average temperatures. (Spot the differences between west and east, north and south.)

As well as the map, four climate graphs are shown in Figure 3.3. Figures for Birmingham are shown in this table:

| Climate data for Birmingham (163 m above sea level) | | | | | | | | | | | | |
|---|---|---|---|---|---|---|---|---|---|---|---|---|
| | Jan | Feb | Mar | Apr | May | June | July | Aug | Sept | Oct | Nov | Dec |
| Average monthly temperatures in ° Celsius | 3 | 4 | 6 | 8 | 11 | 15 | 16 | 16 | 14 | 10 | 7 | 5 |
| Average monthly rainfall in millimetres | 74 | 54 | 50 | 53 | 64 | 50 | 69 | 69 | 61 | 69 | 84 | 67 |

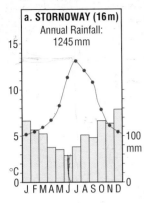
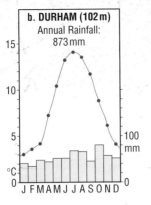
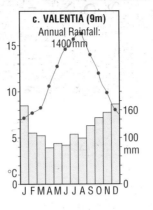
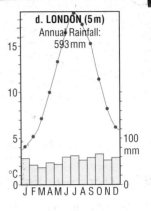

**Figure 3.3** Sample climate graphs

## Why temperatures vary in the British Isles

Temperatures vary from place to place, and from season to season. Temperatures are affected by:

★ **Latitude** – the closer a place is to the equator, the warmer it is. At the equator, the sun's heat is concentrated on a small area (X on Figure 3.4). At the poles, however, the sun heats a large area (Y on Figure 3.4). In winter, the midday sun is lower in the sky. Its rays are spread over a wider area, keeping temperatures lower (P on Figure 3.5). In summer, the midday sun is higher. Its rays are concentrated on a smaller area, keeping temperatures higher (Q on Figure 3.5)

★ **Altitude** – the higher we rise above sea level, the lower the temperature becomes. Mountains and hills are cooler than lowlands. A rough figure is that the temperature drops by 1°C for every 100 metres in height. Figure 3.6 shows the different average January temperatures for Fort William and the summit of Ben Nevis, Britain's highest mountain

★ **The sea** – in winter, places close to the sea are warmer than places inland. In summer, places close to the sea are often cooler and inland places are warmer. This is because the sea heats up slowly in the summer and cools slowly in winter. Inland, the land heats up quickly in summer and cools rapidly in winter. Western coastal areas are also kept warmer because of a warm current of water called the North Atlantic Drift. The prevailing south-west winds that pass across this current are warmed by it (Figure 3.7).

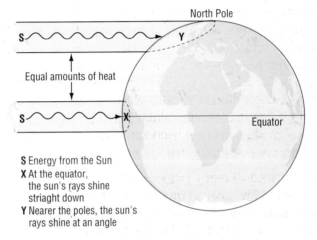

**S** Energy from the Sun
**X** At the equator, the sun's rays shine straight down
**Y** Nearer the poles, the sun's rays shine at an angle

**Figure 3.4** Latitude and temperature

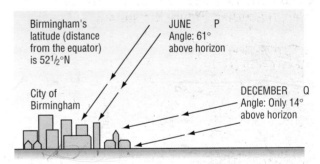

**Figure 3.5** Birmingham: changes in the angle of the sun's rays

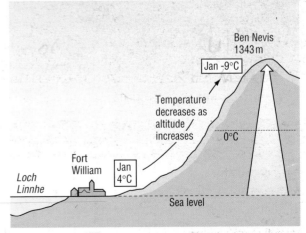

**Figure 3.6** The effect of altitude on temperature in Fort William

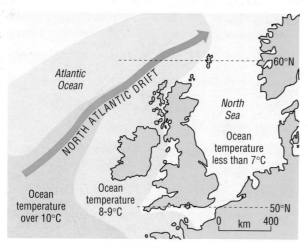

Figure 3.7    North Atlantic Drift

## Useful words

**Atmosphere** – a 900 km high blanket of air covering the earth

**Prevailing wind** – is the usual direction from which wind blows. In the British Isles, it is from the south-west

**Range of temperature** – the difference between the maximum and minimum temperature

**Isotherm** – a line joining places of equal temperature

### ASSIGNMENTS

1   Briefly, explain the difference between weather and climate.

2   Look at the four climate graphs in Figure 3.3. Giving figures and months –
In summer: Which place is the warmest? Which place is the coolest?
In winter: Which place is the warmest? Which place is the coldest?

3   Which place has the highest rainfall? Which place has the lowest rainfall?

4   Complete the four descriptions in Figure 3.2 using the following words to help you:

cool  cold  mild  warm  heavy  moderate  light

5   Draw a climate graph for Birmingham using the Figures in the data table. Give your graph a title.

6   Using your answers to question 2, explain the temperature differences in the British Isles.

### TO TAKE YOU FURTHER

## Air masses and the British Isles

Britain's changeable weather is also influenced by air masses. An **air mass** is a huge area of air with similar temperatures, humidity and pressure that starts life, for example:

◆   over a cold dry **continental** area, like Siberia, in winter

◆   over a warmer but damp **maritime** area, like the mid-Atlantic Ocean in winter.

The air mass, warm or cold, damp or dry, then flows towards the British Isles. Figure 3.8 shows five air masses flowing towards the British Isles. Each air mass is different and brings its own type of weather conditions, depending on the season. Tropical air masses are more common in summer, polar air masses are more likely in winter. However, the British Isles are a 'battleground' of air masses and they can come at anytime.

### Air masses and people

Different activities are affected by particular air masses.

### ASSIGNMENTS TO TAKE YOU FURTHER

1   Briefly explain what is an air mass.

2   a)   How many air masses affect the British Isles?
     b)   Why is the British Isles called a 'battleground' of air masses?

*continued*  ➤

**TO TAKE YOU FURTHER** *continued*

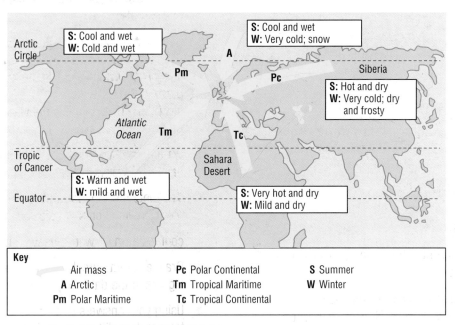

**Figure 3.8** Air masses affecting the climate of the British Isles

**3** Using the information on Figure 3.8, make a large copy and complete the table below:

| Air mass | Summer features | Winter features |
|---|---|---|
| Arctic maritime | Rarely occurs | |
| Polar maritime | | |
| | Hot and dry | Very cold and usually dry |
| Tropical maritime | | |
| Tropical continental | | Rarely occurs |

**4** Look at the 4 photographs in Figure 3.9.
   a) Match each of the four photos with the following air masses:
   arctic
   tropical continental
   polar continental
   polar maritime.
   b) Give reasons for each of your choices.

**5** Which two air masses do you think most frequently affect weather in the British Isles?

**6** Which two air masses do you think least frequently affect weather in the British Isles?

**Figure 3.9** Air masses and people

# Rainfall, highs and lows

## What is rainfall?

Rainfall is the main type of precipitation. Precipitation includes hail, sleet, snow, frost and dew. Rainfall occurs when:

**A** moist air rises;

**B** moist air cools as it rises;

**C** water vapour condenses into water droplets which form clouds (cooling air cannot hold much moisture);

**D** the droplets form raindrops (or, if cold enough snow, hail or sleet) and fall to the ground.

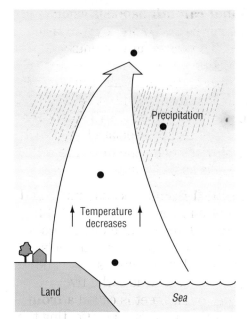

**Figure 3.10**  How rain forms

## Types of rainfall

Air laden with moisture rises in three different ways. This results in three types of rainfall:

★ **Relief rainfall** (Figure 3.11) occurs when moist air is forced to rise over mountains. As it rises it cools, condenses, clouds form and rain falls over the high ground. Figure 3.12 shows that the land on the sheltered side receives little rain. This is called a **Rain Shadow** area. Western parts of Britain and Ireland are more mountainous than the east. These uplands have heavier rainfall than the sheltered lowlands of the east

**Figure 3.11**  Heavy cloud over mountains

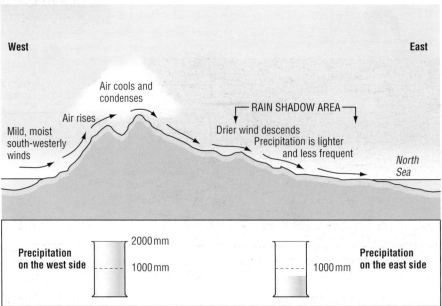

**Figure 3.12**  Relief rainfall in Great Britain

★ **Convectional rainfall** happens when warm, moist air rises rapidly from a warm land surface. The warm air currents are called convection currents. The result is short but heavy thunderstorms. Such rain is typical of hot, sunny days and it usually falls in the late afternoon. Figure 3.13 shows the towering type of cloud associated with such rain. If the air rises high, the moisture freezes and falls as hailstones

★ **Frontal rainfall** results because warm and cold air do not mix very well. Figure 3.14 shows that the lighter warm moist air rises over heavier cold air. The warm air cools, water vapour condenses, clouds form and rain results. The place where the two different types of air meet is called a **front**. This is the main type of rainfall affecting the British Isles because fronts are the meeting place of warm tropical air and cold polar air.

# Hopeful highs

## High and low air pressure

The earth's atmosphere is over 900 km thick and presses down on the earth's surface. This downward force is called **air pressure**. Air pressure is affected by:

★ altitude – air pressure is greatest at sea-level and decreases as you climb a mountain

★ temperature – the warmer the air, the lower the air pressure; the colder the air, the higher the air pressure.

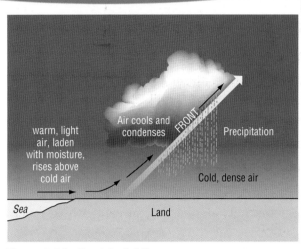

**Figure 3.14**   Frontal rainfall

Changes in the atmosphere cause the British Isles to receive either:

★ areas of high pressure called anticyclones or

★ areas of low pressure called depressions (page 35). Figure 3.15 shows that high and low pressure bring different types of weather. The diagram also shows that wind blows from high pressure areas to low pressure areas.

## High pressure and anticyclones

Anticyclones are usually associated with good weather conditions. Figures 3.16 and 3.17 show typical features of an anticyclone covering the British Isles. Often they last for several days and bring settled weather. The cross-sections (Figure 3.18) show that there are differences between summer and winter weather conditions.

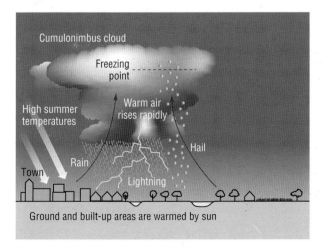

**Figure 3.13**   Convectional rainfall

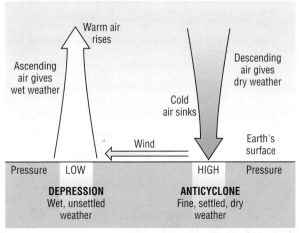

**Figure 3.15**   High and low pressure and wind

**Figure 3.16** Satellite photo of Britain in Summer

In both summer and winter, anti-cyclones can bring clear skies over Britain.

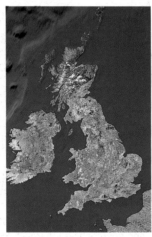

**Figure 3.17** Satellite photo of Britain in Winter

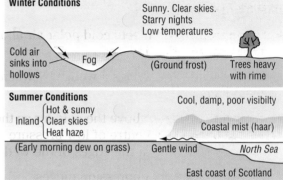

Isobars are widely spaced

This anticyclone covers all of the British Isles

H
1036
1032
1028
1024

Gentle winds blow clockwise round the high pressure (**H**)

**Winter Conditions**

Sunny. Clear skies. Starry nights. Low temperatures

Cold air sinks into hollows · Fog · (Ground frost) · Trees heavy with rime

**Summer Conditions**

Inland { Hot & sunny / Clear skies / Heat haze

Cool, damp, poor visibilty

Coastal mist (haar)

(Early morning dew on grass) · Gentle wind · North Sea

East coast of Scotland

**Figure 3.18** Typical features of an anticyclone

## Useful words

**isobar** – a line joining places of equal pressure

**millibars** – unit of pressure shown on weather maps

**evaporation** – the process by which water becomes water vapour

**condensation** – the process by which water vapour becomes tiny drops of water

## ASSIGNMENTS

1 Read the section on 'What is rainfall'.
   a) Name four types of precipitation.
   b) What is the main type of precipitation?

2 Copy Figure 3.10. Match the sentences labelled **A** to **D** with the correct bullet point from the diagram.

3 Read about the 3 types of rainfall.
   Three of the following sentences are correct. Make a copy of the correct sentences.
   ◆ Winds blow from low pressure to high pressure.
   ◆ The west of the British Isles is wetter than the east.
   ◆ Relief rainfall occurs when moist air rises over highlands.
   ◆ Convectional rainfall is associated with heavy thunderstorms.

4 With the help of a simple diagram, answer either a or b:
   a) What is relief rainfall and why does it it happen?
   b) What is convectional rainfall and why does it happen?

5 Read about air pressure and anticyclones.
   Copy the following, choosing the correct highlighted words.
   Anticyclones are areas of **high/low** pressure. They are shown on weather maps with **closely/widely** spaced isobars. Wind speeds are **light/strong**. Skies are usually **cloudy/clear**. This means cold, **frosty/snowy** conditions in winter and **hot/cool** summers.

**TO TAKE YOU FURTHER**

# Low pressure and depressions

Frontal rain affects the British Isles as part of a **depression**. Depressions are huge areas of low pressure bringing rain, cloud and unsettled weather. On a satellite photograph they show up as enormous swirls of cloud (Figure 3.19). They are often mentioned on weather reports, especially in winter. On weather maps, symbols used to show fronts in a depression appear as upside down 'V's. (Fronts are shown on Figures 3.19–3.20). Depressions affecting the British Isles often develop when:

◆ warm tropical air meets cold polar air above the western Atlantic Ocean

◆ the warm air then forms a wedge between the cold air

◆ the warm air rises above the cold air as the wedge becomes a centre of low pressure and rain develops at the edges of the wedge

◆ the wedge-shaped depression moves eastwards to the British Isles.

Figure 3.20 shows that the two lines separating cold air from warm are called the **warm front** and the **cold front**. When a depression moves

**Figure 3.19** Satellite photograph of a depression over Iceland approaching the British Isles

from west to east across the British Isles, it brings a sequence of weather as it passes over particular places (see Figures 3.21 and 3.22).

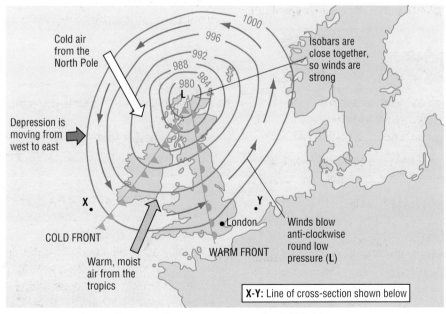

**Figure 3.20** Typical features of a depression over the British Isles

*continued* ➤

**TO TAKE YOU FURTHER** *continued* ➤

**Figure 3.21**  Continuous rain in London brought by a warm front

**ASSIGNMENTS** *TO TAKE YOU FURTHER*

1  Read about low pressure and depressions. Copy the following, choosing the correct highlighted words.
Depressions are very **large/small** areas of **high/low** pressure. They bring **settled/unsettled** weather. On weather maps they appear as upside down **'W's/'V's**. They form as **warm/cold** air rises over **warm/cold** air. A typical depression passes over the British Isles from **east to west/west to east**. Rain first falls as the **warm/cold** front passes then as the **warm/cold** front passes.

2  Describe in detail the changes in weather as the depression shown in Figures 3.20 and 3.22 passes over London.

3  After group discussion, draw up a table to show how (i) an anticyclone, and (ii) a depression may affect the following:
farming   tourism   recreation
typical daily conversation   the landscape

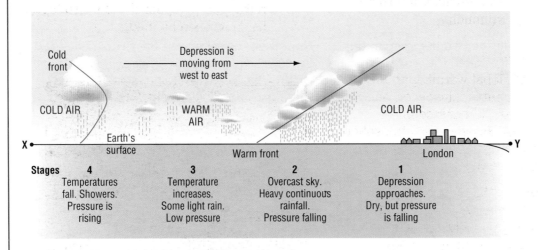

**Figure 3.22**  Cross-section of a depression

# Global warming

## *Changing climate*

Ever since the atmosphere developed millions of years ago, climate has been changing. It is only 10,000 years since the end of the last Ice Age. Today, many scientists believe that the world is becoming warmer. This **Global Warming** is seen as a major problem.

## *Greenhouse effect*

Over the past 100 years, global temperature has risen by 0.6°C. In the next 50 years, scientists predict a temperature rise between 2°C to 6°C (Figure 3.24). It is believed that this global warming is caused by the 'greenhouse effect'. Figure 3.23 suggests that the earth's atmosphere acts like a giant greenhouse.

36

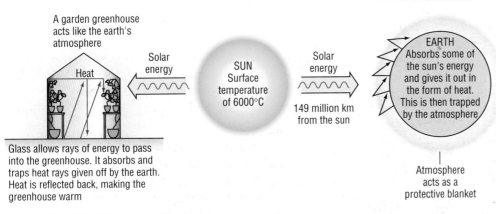

**Figure 3.23**   The 'Greenhouse Effect'

★ **A greenhouse**: allows heat in, traps some of it, lets plants ripen early

★ **The atmosphere**: allows heat in, acts like the glass in the greenhouse and traps heat using various greenhouse gases, keeps the earth from freezing.

Without the greenhouse effect, the entire earth would have a much colder arctic type climate. The average temperature would be around −23°C. Many scientists now worry that the 'greenhouse effect' is too efficient and that the earth is warming up too much.

## Greenhouse gases

The exact causes of global warming are complicated. Most scientists, however, believe that it is mainly due to an increase in the amount of greenhouse gases in the atmosphere. The increase in these heat-absorbing gases is the result of human activity.

★ **carbon dioxide** is the most important. This gas has increased because
  ◆ we are burning more fossil fuels such as coal, oil and natural gas in power stations and factories.

◆ Trees naturally store carbon dioxide. Figure 3.25 also shows that clearing and burning large areas of rainforest add to the amount of carbon dioxide in the atmosphere.

★ **methane** levels also have increased because of
  ◆ increased rice cultivation and the growing numbers of 'windy' cattle and waste disposal dumps
  ◆ CFC gases from aerosol sprays and refrigerators. Officially CFC production has now been banned.

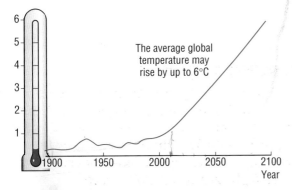

**Figure 3.24**   Temperature change 1900–2100

The average global temperature may rise by up to 6°C

**Figure 3.25**   Sources of greenhouse gases

## Results of global warming

Whatever the causes, global warming seems to be a fact of life. The 1990s were the warmest years on record. Global warming will have important effects on climate and people. A lot depends on where people live. One thing is certain: the poorer countries, for example, Bangladesh will be worst affected because they are too poor to protect themselves.

Some likely effects include:

★ Weather becoming more unpredictable and stormy, for example, stronger hurricanes along the Atlantic coast of North America (Figure 3.26)

★ Some crops benefitting from warming but, in some areas, for example, the Sahel, drought will reduce crop yields. Food shortages may result

★ New pests and diseases, for example, malaria, spreading. Warm, humid conditions will encourage more midges in Scotland (Figure 3.27)

★ Various plants and animals, for example, polar bears, penguins and the mountain gorilla disappearing

★ Rising sea levels caused by melting ice caps will mean flooding of low-lying coastal areas such as the Nile delta, Bangladesh, and islands, for example, the Maldives.

# Solving the problem

In an ideal world, the emission of greenhouse gases needs to be reduced. We should use fossil fuels more efficiently and increasingly switch to renewable energy resources such as wind, water and solar power. Countries need to co-operate on such issues. Even countries which may benefit from global warming live in a world where the misery of others affects all of us.

Unfortunately, some countries are reluctant to cut greenhouse emissions. For example:

★ The USA is not keen because its large companies argue that the living standards of the world's richest country would fall. The companies also would lose a lot of their profits

★ China is determined to develop its industries and depends on coal as an important source of energy.

**Figure 3.27**   Possible victims of global warming

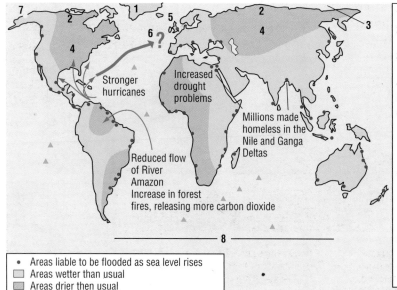

Stronger hurricanes

Increased drought problems

Millions made homeless in the Nile and Ganga Deltas

Reduced flow of River Amazon Increase in forest fires, releasing more carbon dioxide

1 Melting ice caps
2 Longer summers damage permafrost
3 Sea ice 15% thinner than in 1950
4 Decline in crop yields
5 Longer growing season
6 British climate becomes colder as the North Atlantic Drift weakens because of increased rainfall
7 Shishmaref, an Inuit village whose inhabitants have voted to move to a new village 8 km inland as the climate warms up
8 Break up of ice sheets e.g. Larsen ice sheet in Antarctica. Increase in the number of icebergs

• Areas liable to be flooded as sea level rises
☐ Areas wetter than usual
☐ Areas drier then usual
▲ Increase in sea level of 88 cm by the year 2100

**Figure 3.26**   Possible consequences of global warming

## ASSIGNMENTS

1 Copy the following sentence selecting the correct highlighted words:

   The sun's heat is trapped by greenhouse gases, for example, **oxygen/carbon dioxide**. These keep the earth's temperatures **higher/lower**. Greenhouse gases are **increasing/decreasing**.

2 Match the six diagrams in Figures 3.25. with these causes of global warming: aerosol sprays and refrigerators; 'windy' cattle and waste dumps; burning fossil fuels in power stations and factories; increased rice cultivation; rainforest destruction; car exhaust fumes.

3 a) Give two reasons why global warming results in rising sea levels
   b) What are the other likely effects of global warming?

4 Either: What are the likely good points about global warming? Or: Why is it difficult to get countries to agree about ways to prevent global warming?

## TO TAKE YOU FURTHER

# Alternative energy

Many countries have agreed to cut down their production of greenhouse gases. This can be done by:

◆ reducing energy consumption (Figure 3.29)

◆ gradually switching to alternative energy sources. Some of these are shown in Figure 3.28. They include renewable energy sources such as wind, waves, tides and solar energy. At present only around 3% of British energy production comes from renewable sources. It is hoped that by 2010 this figure will have risen to 10%. It is suggested that Scotland will be able to supply a lot of 'green' energy. Thanks to its position on the windy north-west fringes of Europe, Scotland is well placed to produce wind and wave power.

## Wind power

Figure 3.30 shows a wind farm at Dun Law in the Borders. A **wind farm** is a group of **wind turbines** usually sited on exposed hilltops. The most ambitious Scottish scheme will also be the largest project in Europe – the proposed farm of 300 turbines at Barvas Moor on Lewis. Wind farms have several advantages:

◆ they use a free source of energy

◆ they create no waste or greenhouse gases

◆ they are renewable – so long as there is wind.

But there can be fierce opposition from local people and even environmentalists. People have

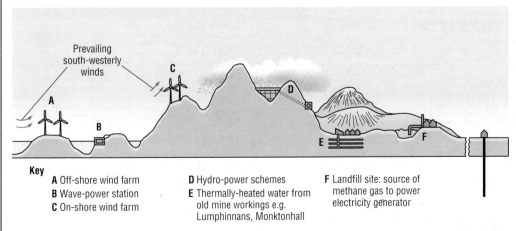

**Key**

A Off-shore wind farm
B Wave-power station
C On-shore wind farm

D Hydro-power schemes
E Thermally-heated water from old mine workings e.g. Lumphinnans, Monktonhall

F Landfill site: source of methane gas to power electricity generator

**Figure 3.28**   Alternative sources of energy in Scotland

*continued* ➤

### TO TAKE YOU FURTHER *continued*

objected to a proposed scheme at Edinbane on Skye because:

◆ the plan involves 28 turbines, each almost 90 metres high, in an area of attractive scenery

◆ the turbines are noisy – like 'a boot in a tumble drier'.

**Offshore wind power** is another possible source of energy. Groups of up to 30 turbines are proposed for sites up to 8 km offshore, for example, in the Solway Firth. These windfarms should be exposed to more wind and have less effect on scenery.

**Wave power** is another possibility. A wave power plant has been built on Islay. The problem, however, with all wind, wave and solar power sources is that they cannot guarantee continuous electricity 24 hours a day, all year round.

**Hydropower**, however, is much more reliable and has been used since the first small scheme was installed at Fort Augustus in 1890. Money is now being spent on:

◆ upgrading many of the existing hydro-schemes such as Pitlochry

◆ building new, small-scale schemes such as in Assynt.

Clean, cheap and suited to Scotland's wet upland area, hydropower supplies 11% of Scotland's electricity.

Two recent energy alternative resources include:

◆ using waste such as methane gas from landfill sites and farm manure

◆ tapping geothermal heat by pumping water into derelict mines.

### ASSIGNMENTS *TO TAKE YOU FURTHER*

1 Using Figure 3.29, suggest various ways in which energy consumption can be reduced.

2 Write a short account of the good and bad points for a wind farm being built near your house.

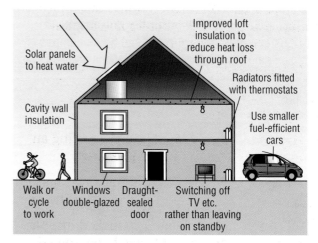

**Figure 3.29**   Reducing energy consumption

**Figure 3.30**   Wind farm at Dun Law

# Cyclones and flooding

## Cyclones and tornadoes

Cyclones are tropical storms which bring:

★ immensely strong winds up to 250 km per hour

★ torrential rainfall

★ huge surges of sea water which flood coastal areas.

Figure 3.31 shows that cyclones form over the tropical oceans and can cover long distances. They die out as they move inland but they are hazards to life and property, especially in poorer countries. Figure 3.31 also shows that tropical storms have different names, for example, hurricanes, typhoons, willy-willies and cyclones.

Tornadoes are related to non-tropical storms. They are very violent whirlwinds with rain and thunderstorms, but are much smaller than cyclones. They develop over land, not over the sea. Most tornadoes occur in the USA, especially 'twister alley' in the Great Plains, and they can be very destructive.

## Formation of tropical storms

In a typical year there are around 80 tropical storms, mainly in late summer and autumn. Tropical storms form when:

★ the sun heats the ocean up to 27°C

★ sea water **evaporates** forming large amounts of **water vapour**

★ the water vapour rapidly rises creating an intense area of **very low pressure**

★ a huge spiral of rising, swirling air forms and rotates around a calm centre called the **eye**

★ more and more moist air is sucked into the spiral, condenses and forms huge, towering clouds that eventually release millions of tonnes of rainfall.

## Tropical storms overhead

Once they are formed, tropical storms move away – anticlockwise north of the equator; clockwise to the south. Figure 3.32 shows that tropical storms are giant and funnel-shaped with violent winds on the outside, thunderstorms, and enormous towering clouds releasing torrential rain. Figure 3.32 shows a tropical storm passing over an island, for

example, in the West Indies, or off the coast of southern Bangladesh. As it passes over:

★ violent winds up to 250 km and driving torrential rain lash at the coast

★ storm surges with waves up to 9 metres wash over the coast.

Then people may be deceived and think that their suffering is all over when

★ a period of calm results as the eye of the storm settles over them.

But

★ later, the next edge of the storm strikes, causing further damage.

Tropical storms can leave a trail of death and destruction. Although early warning systems have been installed, their impact can be severe in poorer countries because:

★ buildings are more likely to be poorly constructed

★ cash crops on which the country depends can be destroyed, for example, bananas in Dominica

★ governments and people cannot always afford to prevent future damage.

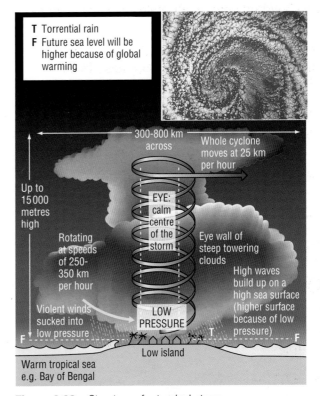

**Figure 3.32**  Structure of a tropical storm

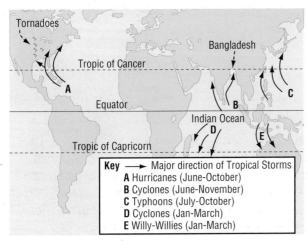

**Figure 3.31**  Tropical storms and tornadoes

# Floods in Bangladesh

## Background to Bangladesh

Bangladesh is about half the size of the UK and is home to almost 140 million people. It is one of the world's most crowded countries. Figures 3.33–3.34 show that most of the country is prone to flooding. It is formed by the **delta** of the Ganga and the Brahmaputra (see page 57). This is the world's largest delta and is criss-crossed by many river channels. Thanks to the annual floods brought by the monsoon rains, Bangladesh has fertile soils and rich fisheries.

However, Bangladesh is one of the world's poorest countries. Only 14% of the population live in cities, mainly in the capital, Dhaka. The rest of the population live and work on the land. Most of the land is owned by a few wealthy landowners. Many Bangladeshis:

★ own only a tiny plot of land, or are landless

★ live on land that is likely to be severely flooded.

## Causes of flooding in Bangladesh

Although flooding is a regular annual event, there have been six severe floods since 1988. Figure 3.35 shows there are two main causes of flooding:

★ exceptionally heavy monsoon rains cause the river levels to rise more than usual. In 1998 around a thousand people died, two-thirds of the country was flooded and a quarter of the population were driven from their homes

★ storm surges, up to 9 metres high, caused by cyclones, flood coastal areas and off-shore islands. 140,000 people perished one night in 1991 as a cyclone swept in from the Bay of Bengal.

It is the poor who suffer the most. They are most likely to:

★ be drowned

★ be made homeless

★ lose their crops

★ suffer from cholera and typhoid by drinking water from contaminated wells.

**Figure 3.33**   Rural flooding in Bangladesh

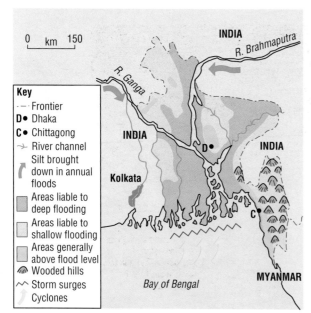

**Figure 3.34**   Bangladesh

Key
- - Frontier
D● Dhaka
C● Chittagong
↣ River channel
Silt brought down in annual floods
Areas liable to deep flooding
Areas liable to shallow flooding
Areas generally above flood level
Wooded hills
Storm surges
Cyclones

---

### Surviving the 1998 flood

"Our houses were full of water, some were broken down as the mud walls were washed away. Some of us went to live on the high roads, some made banana tree rafts to sleep on. But most of us had been ready and had built a platform in the roof of our homes and we lived up there. We cooked on our portable clay stoves. It was a great struggle to look after the children. We had to watch all the time that they didn't fall off the platform into the water below. Lots of people got snake bites as the snakes tried to get out of the water too. We had to go by banana raft to get food. We had built a bank of water hyacinth for our cattle to go on so they survived. Our husbands had no work as the land was flooded. GUP (a local self-help organisation) gave our husbands food in return for repairing the damaged bridges and roads. They gave us quick growing seeds so that we had them to plant and grow food as soon as the water went."

from article by Jo Jones (*Christian Aid*)

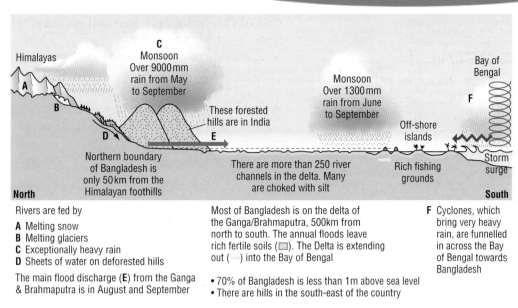

**Figure 3.35** Flooding and Bangladesh

The labels within the figure read:

Himalayas

**C** Monsoon Over 9000 mm rain from May to September

These forested hills are in India

Monsoon Over 1300 mm rain from June to September

Bay of Bengal

**F**

Off-shore islands

Storm surge

Northern boundary of Bangladesh is only 50 km from the Himalayan foothills

There are more than 250 river channels in the delta. Many are choked with silt

Rich fishing grounds

**North** **South**

Rivers are fed by

**A** Melting snow
**B** Melting glaciers
**C** Exceptionally heavy rain
**D** Sheets of water on deforested hills

The main flood discharge (**E**) from the Ganga & Brahmaputra is in August and September

Most of Bangladesh is on the delta of the Ganga/Brahmaputra, 500 km from north to south. The annual floods leave rich fertile soils (▢). The Delta is extending out ( ) into the Bay of Bengal

• 70% of Bangladesh is less than 1m above sea level
• There are hills in the south-east of the country

**F** Cyclones, which bring very heavy rain, are funnelled in across the Bay of Bengal towards Bangladesh

## *Dealing with floods*

Figure 3.36 shows some of the ways in which Bangladeshis deal with floods. As the extract suggests, people in the villages work together to:

★ design houses with raised areas where people and small animals can safely stay if flood water is not too high

★ raise the land around their houses and community buildings such as mosques and schools

★ plant trees to keep the soil together

★ strengthen embankments around islands and very low-lying areas.

The Government assists by:

★ building flood shelters

★ developing early warning systems, including satellites, broadcasts and volunteers cycling around and using megaphones.

However, it can be difficult to accurately forecast the exact timing and direction of cyclones. Many people are loath to leave their homes, sometimes believing that storms and floods are the will of God. Also, in this mainly Muslim country, some families are reluctant to allow women and men to mix in the shelters.

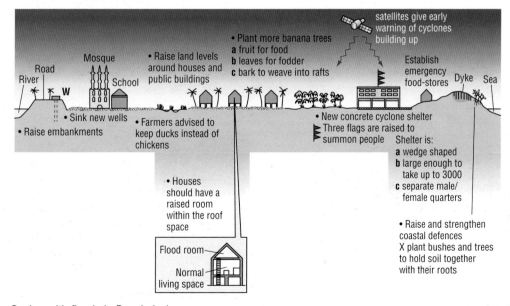

**Figure 3.36** Coping with floods in Bangladesh

1   Look at Figure 3.31. Use an atlas to complete this table

| Name of tropical storm | Area affected | Time of year |
|---|---|---|
| | Indian Ocean | June–Nov/ Nov–March |
| Willy-willies | | |
| | Caribbean Sea/ West Indies | |
| | | July–October |

2   Look at Figure 3.32 and read about tropical storms. Copy and complete these sentences, choosing the correct highlighted words:
   ◆   Tropical storms start over large areas of **warm ocean/ warm land**.
   ◆   Tropical storms develop in areas of very **low/high** pressure.
   ◆   The calm area in the centre of a tropical storm is the **eye/eye wall**.
   ◆   The whole tropical storm moves towards land at **250/25 km** per hour.
   ◆   Tropical storms **increase/decrease** in strength when they move inland.

3   Give three ways in which a tropical storm can cause damage in a low-lying, coastal area.

4   Suggest three reasons why much of Bangladesh can be affected by severe flooding.

5   Imagine you live on a small island off the coast of Bangladesh. Write an account describing
   (i)   a cyclone striking your island
   (ii)  the damage caused
   (iii) the action your community take after the event.
   Illustrate your answer with diagrams.

6   Look at Figure 3.36. Write a paragraph explaining what is being done to reduce the impact of flooding in Bangladesh. How easy is it to carry out these measures?

7   In spite of the seasonal flood danger, why do so many Bangladeshis continue to live in such areas?

# Flood control on the Yangtze

The Yangtze River is one of the world's longest, deepest and fastest-flowing rivers. It is one of several major rivers in China which have caused major flooding over the centuries (Figure 3.38). The Yellow River (Hwang-Ho) has been called 'China's Sorrow' because of the results of its frequent floods.

Until the mid-20th century, little could be done about the flooding by China's rivers. Since then a number of mega-dams has been built. The largest of these by far is the Three Gorges Dam on the Yangtze River (Figure 3.37).

The Yangtze rises on the plateau of Tibet more than 6,000 km from the sea. Figure 3.39 shows the main features of its journey from Tibet to the delta at its mouth. The Yangtze and its

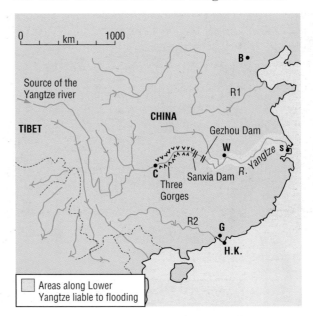

**Figure 3.37**   Location of the Three Gorges Dam

**Figure 3.38**   Flooding on the Lower Yangtze

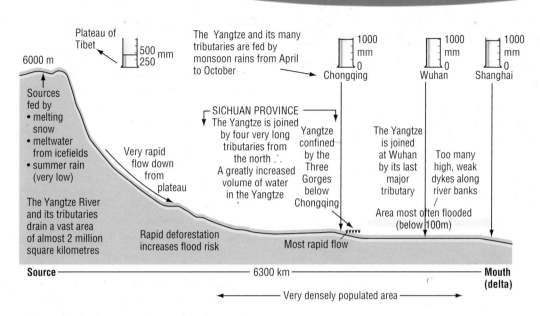

Figure 3.39   The Yangtze River ('Chang Jiang' – the long river)

Figure 3.40   The Three Gorges Dam

many tributaries drain a vast area of almost 2 million square km. From Sichuan Province downstream it is very densely populated, especially below the Three Gorges. It is this area which has been most affected by flooding. The lower end of the Three Gorges seemed to be the ideal location for a mega dam.

After many years of discussion and planning, the dam was completed in 2002 (Figure 3.40). It was a tremendous feat of engineering, but it would seem that its consequences will not all be for the good (Figure 3.41). Government officials see only the positive aspects, but local people who have lost their houses and their land in the creation of the reservoir think very differently.

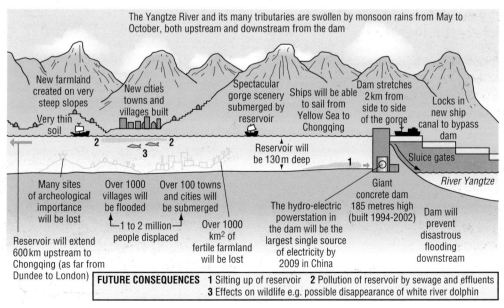

Figure 3.41   Consequences of the Three Gorges Dam on the Yangtze River

## Views on the dam

### The Government View:

*"We have made the Lower Yangtze safe from flooding. We will reduce pollution levels by reducing our use of fossil fuels. The electricity generated by the dam will attract new industries. Chonqing will become a seaport."*

### The Displaced Farmer:

*"The reservoir has drowned too much farmland. They have terraced new land for us, but the soil is thin and stony. There isn't enough land for all of us. I will have less than half the area I had before. One-seventh of a hectare is not enough to grow enough food to feed my family."*

### The Displaced Townsperson:

*"We are not happy. Many promises were made when we were told that we would have to leave Zigui and move to the new town. In the end, we were only given £46, which did not cover the cost of the move. When we got here, we were given a flat to rent, but there is no work here. There are no factories yet in the new town. Prices in the shops are much higher. We are much worse-off now than in the time before the dam."*

Environmentalists point out that the dam will not necessarily prevent flooding. The last major tributary joins the Yangtze at Wuhan. It is also at its highest level during the monsoon season. Their greatest concern is that the Yangtze will become a 'poisoned' river above the dam.

Work on the Yangtze is not yet completed. There are now plans to to divert some of its headwaters northwards to supplement the flow of the Hwang Ho and its tributaries.

### ASSIGNMENTS

1 Study Figure 3.37. With the aid of an atlas, name (i) the sea into which the Yangtze flows (ii) the cities along its course marked C,W and S (iii) the other two major Chinese rivers marked R1 and R2 (iv) the other Chinese towns marked B,G and HK.

2 Study Figure 3.39. (i) How high is the source of the Yangtze? (ii) Which of the following words would best describe the source? cold/hot  icy/boggy  wet/dry  grassy/wooded. (iii) Which are the flood danger months along the Yangtze? What is the total rainfall during these months? (iv) How high is the land through which the Yangtze flows below the dam? (v) How will the land be protected from flooding?

3 Figure 3.41 Why do you think environmentalists have stated that they fear the Yangtze will become a poisoned river?

4 Look at Figure 3.41 Give two reasons why the tourist trade might be harmed by the building of the dam, and two reasons why it might benefit from it.

5 In small groups, carefully read the views of the government official and the two displaced people. Also take into account the views of the environmentalists. Discuss the different views before coming to a group decision on whether or not the building of the dam will have more advantages than disadvantages. Give evidence to support your decision.

# Chapter 4 Landforms and Land Use

## Never at rest

The earth's crust consists of three different types of rock: sedimentary, igneous and metamorphic.

**Sedimentary** rocks are formed from the compressed remains of other rocks

**Igneous** rocks are formed within the crust from the cooling of molten material

**Metamorphic** rocks have been changed and hardened by

★ great heat from molten rocks within the crust *or*

★ great pressure from earth movements

### Examples of rock types

Sedimentary – Sandstone, chalk, clay, limestone

Igneous – Granite and basalt

Metamorphic – Marble, slate and schist

## Characteristics of rocks

Some rocks are relatively soft, others are relatively hard. Some rocks are **permeable** – they allow water to drain through them very easily. **Impermeable** rocks such as clay are virtually waterproof and the water remains on the surface.

All rocks are formed of minerals, for example, granite is formed mainly of feldspar, mica and quartz.

All rocks are constantly being worn away, and the landscape is therefore changing. Some rocks wear away more quickly than others. Others are much more resistant, but will wear away through time. Wearing away is most rapid in warm, wet climates.

All rocks, even the hardest, have weaknesses which increase the wearing away. Some common causes of weakness are:

★ cracks and joints in the rock
★ minerals in the rock which are more easily broken down such as feldspar in granite and calcite in limestone
★ highly permeable rocks, for example, limestone, chalk or sandstone.

| PHYSICAL | CHEMICAL | BIOLOGICAL |
|---|---|---|
| In this type of weathering the rocks | In this type of weathering the rocks | In this type of weathering cracks in the rocks are widened by |
| • Disintegrate<br>• Become smaller and smaller | • Crumble away<br>• Are dissolved | • Plant roots<br>• Burrowing animals |
| How does this happen? | How does this happen?<br>Rain (a weak acid) trickles down through joints | How does this happen? |

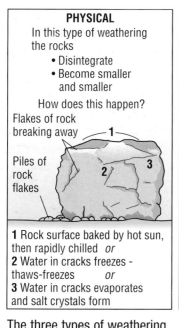

**1** Rock surface baked by hot sun, then rapidly chilled *or*
**2** Water in cracks freezes - thaws-freezes *or*
**3** Water in cracks evaporates and salt crystals form

**1** Former ground surface
**2** Granite rock outcrop
**3** Present ground surface
**4** Depth of softened granite washed away

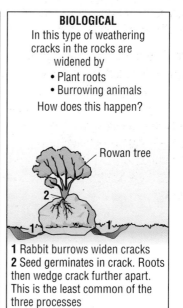

**1** Rabbit burrows widen cracks
**2** Seed germinates in crack. Roots then wedge crack further apart. This is the least common of the three processes

**Figure 4.1** The three types of weathering

# Wearing away the landscape

The landscape is being continually worn away. This is because of two processes: weathering and erosion.

**Weathering** is the breaking up of the rocks in the earth's crust.

There are three types of weathering (Figure 4.1)

★ **Physical**

★ **Chemical**

★ **Biological**

Physical weathering is caused by rapid temperature changes and the freezing and thawing of water in cracks in the rock.

The surface of the rock expands, then contracts and finally cracks. Vertical cracks are enlarged.

**Figure 4.2**   A scree slope

In both cases, fragments fall from the rock surface. They accumulate around the rock, or slide down slopes because of gravity. **Scree** slopes are formed in this way. (Figure 4.2)

Chemical weathering affects a variety of rocks. Chalk and limestone both crumble and can be dissolved by water. Bare limestone plateaus, scored by deep grooves, are one result (Figure 4.4). Underground limestone caves are also formed in this way.

Biological weathering is caused by plant roots and animals burrowing, widening cracks.

Weathering has been going on for thousands of years. The evidence is under our feet. Soil is mainly finely weathered rock.

## Eroding the landscape (Figure 4.3)

However, the landscape is also being changed by erosional processes. These include

★ running water (rivers or the sea)

★ the wind, especially in desert areas

★ ice in glaciers or ice-sheets.

The wearing away of the landscape in these cases is known as 'erosion'. Since the rivers, the sea, the wind and the ice are all moving, the eroded material is carried away or **'transported'** and eventually dropped or **'deposited'**. Through time, the waste material can itself be compressed to form new sedimentary rocks.

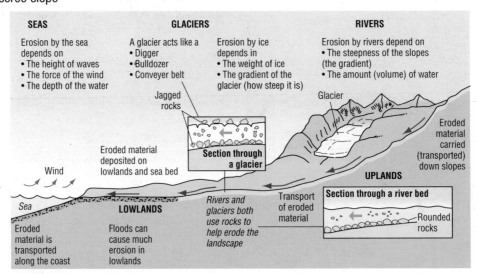

**Figure 4.3**   Never at rest: the changing physical landscape

**Figure 4.4** A limestone pavement

**Figure 4.5** A chalk upland

## Different landscapes

Some rocks, such as sandstone, may form a landscape of either lowlands or uplands. Other rocks, such as clay, only form a lowland landscape. Many rocks, such as granite, form only upland landscapes, that is hills, plateaus and mountains. Their height and shape vary.

### ASSIGNMENTS

1  (i)  Name the type of rock which was formed
    a)  from compressed sediments
    b)  by cooling of molten rock
    c)  by pressure or great heat.
  (ii)  Name two rocks of each type.

2  What is meant by 'weathering'?

3  Explain how rocks are weathered by
    a)  rapid temperature changes
    b)  plant roots
    c)  rain trickling down through cracks.

4  What is meant by 'scree'?

5  Is weathering faster or slower in (i) hot, wet or (ii) cold, wet climates?

6  Write a short account of what is involved in biological weathering (Figure 4.1).

7  Describe the ways in which erosion differs from weathering.

## The rock cycle: recycled rocks (Figure 4.7)

Since the formation of the earth, rocks on the earth's surface have been weathered and eroded. Rock fragments were washed down by rivers and deposited in lakes and swamps, and on the sea bed. These fragments varied in size, from tiny grains to pebbles and accumulated in layers. Shells, animal bones and plants often fell into the sediments. Many are preserved as fossils.

Then, gradually,

★ rock fragments were cemented together

★ the bottom layers were compressed into rock by the weight of sediments above them

★ much later, earth movements raised the new rocks above sea level. For example, the Himalayas were raised over 8000 m above sea level

★ the horizontal layers were often folded like the Himalayas and the Alps

★ the processes of weathering and erosion began once more

★ rock debris was again carried down to the sea, lake or swamp bed.

In other words this process is continuing today, but it will be many millions of years before the debris of today becomes solid rock.

## How do we know this has happened?

Geologists have found evidence in many places. One example is Capitol Reef in the desert south of Salt Lake City, Utah (Figure 4.6). The 300 m wall of this deep canyon shows four distinct layers of sedimentary rock:

★ the oldest, at the base of the cliff, was formed from sediments in a swamp

★ the thick layer of shale above was formed on the bed of a shallow sea

★ the third layer was formed from sediments on lake beds and swamps

★ the youngest rocks form the highest layer, but they have been compressed from ancient desert sand dunes.

The sediments from which these rocks were formed were mostly deposited during the age of the dinosaurs. The remains of many dinosaurs have been found in other locations nearby. These dinosaur 'quarries' are a major tourist attraction in Utah today. The area round Capitol Reef became a national park in 1971 because of its geological importance.

The sandstone at the top of Capitol Reef has been weathered, so there is scree just below this top layer. Although this is a desert, with only 175 mm rainfall each year, there are heavy summer downpours during thunderstorms. These have deeply eroded the shale layer.

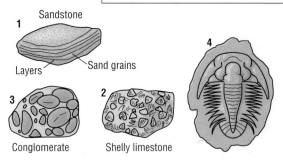

**Key**
1 Fine-grained sandstone
2 A shelly limestone
3 A conglomerate with large rock fragments
4 A limestone containing a trilobite fossil

**Figure 4.7**   Recycled (sedimentary) rocks

### ASSIGNMENTS

1 Name the type of rock formed from
  a) compressed (i) mud (ii) grains of sand (iii), silt
  b) rock fragments cemented together
  c) the remains of sea creatures

2 Look at Figure 4.6. which shows the layers of rock at Capitol Reef. What evidence is there that the climate has not always been a desert?

3 Read the text carefully. Draw a circular diagram to summarise the rock cycle, using the following key words in the correct sequence:

   compression; weathering and erosion; transportation; uplift; deposition; folding

**For more information about Capitol Reef National Park, visit www.nps.gov.**

# Rocks and the landscape

Cornwall is the most remote part of England (Figure 4.8). It is a **peninsula** jutting south-westwards into the Atlantic Ocean. It has a rugged coastline, with the most famous cliffs being at Land's End. It has a crumpled landscape, with much evidence of its mining heritage. It is not an easy place to make a living.

Figure 4.9 shows that Cornwall consists mostly of sandstone rocks, but granite and metamorphic rocks form either moorlands such as Bodmin Moor or large headlands with steep cliffs, for example, Land's End and The Lizard. The granite has made Cornwall an

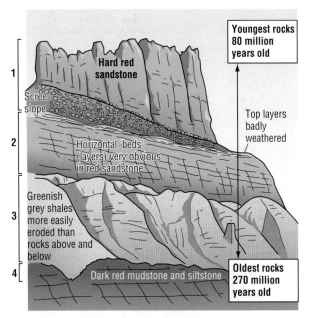

**Figure 4.6** ˙ Capitol Reef, Utah: a sedimentary 'layer cake'

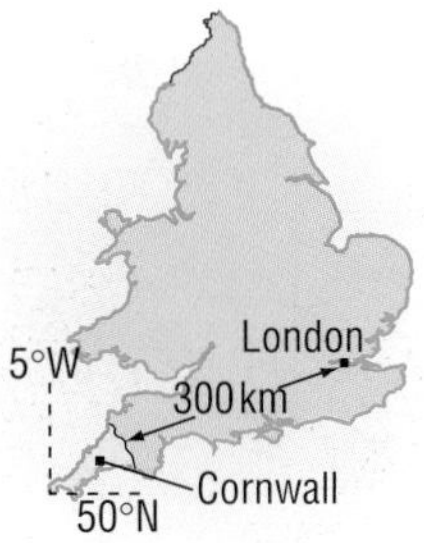

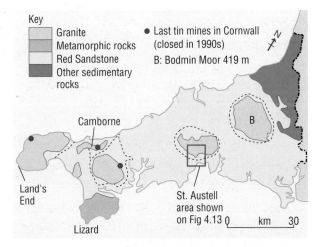

Figure 4.8    The location of Cornwall

Key
- Granite
- Metamorphic rocks
- Red Sandstone
- Other sedimentary rocks

● Last tin mines in Cornwall (closed in 1990s)

B: Bodmin Moor 419 m

Camborne

Land's End

St. Austell area shown on Fig 4.13

Lizard

Figure 4.9    Simplified geological map of Cornwall

important mining area for over 3,000 years. Figure 4.10 shows why granite areas have been mined for so long.

Tin, copper and other minerals were found in veins or **lodes** in granite. They crystallised in fissures (cracks) in the granite as cooling took place (Figure 4.10). Tin and copper were traded with Mediterranean people before the Romans came to Britain. The peak of production was in the 19th century. There were many small mines, mostly on cliff tops. Larger sources of tin and copper in the Developing World were too competitive. Many Cornish miners migrated to work in Australia, South Africa and North America. However, the last few mines only closed in the 1990s. The Cornish landscape is now dotted with derelict engine houses (Figure 4.11).

## China clay

Tin and copper mining had less impact on the landscape than quarrying of kaolin or china clay. Figure 4.10 explains how the clay, known locally as 'white gold', came to be formed. It also lists its changing uses. Transport of the dried clay was cheapest by sea and by barge on canals.

The extraction and the processing of the kaolin were both long and complicated (Figure 4.12). The kaolin was found just below the surface, in funnel-shaped areas of granite. No deep shafts were needed. Instead, wide pits or quarries were excavated and pumps were used to bring the liquidised clay (slurry) to the surface. The vast amounts of waste were piled up in conical tips beside the pits. Villages were built amongst this 'moonscape' to house the workers. Only four companies remain today, but the extraction of kaolin has produced a very distinctive landscape.

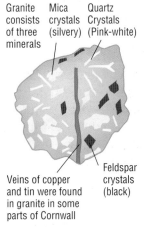

Granite consists of three minerals

Mica crystals (silvery)

Quartz Crystals (Pink-white)

Veins of copper and tin were found in granite in some parts of Cornwall

Feldspar crystals (black)

Granite is an igneous rock which cooled deep in the earth's crust. The three minerals form crystals within the granite.

The feldspar crystals weather down into kaolin or china clay. After this is processed, 90% is waste:
° coarse sand ° fine sand ° rocks

Uses of China Clay:
- 18th and 19th C: sent to the Potteries by sea and canal to be made into fine porcelain
- Present day: 12% of output used to make porcelain. 80% is used in paper-making.
- 8% is used in the manufacture of paints, plastics, cosmetics, toothpaste, medicines

Figure 4.10    Granite

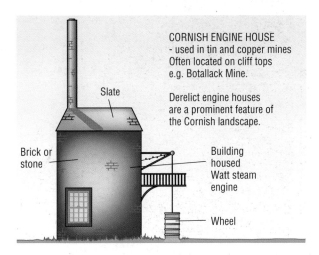

CORNISH ENGINE HOUSE
- used in tin and copper mines
Often located on cliff tops
e.g. Botallack Mine.

Derelict engine houses are a prominent feature of the Cornish landscape.

Slate

Brick or stone

Building housed Watt steam engine

Wheel

Figure 4.11    A Cornish engine house

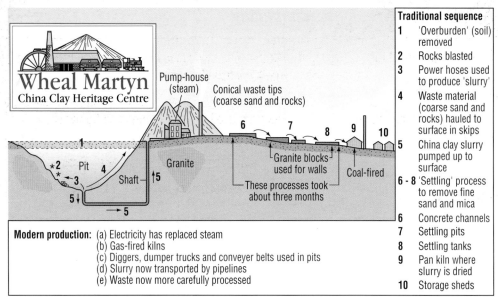

| | Traditional sequence |
|---|---|
| 1 | 'Overburden' (soil) removed |
| 2 | Rocks blasted |
| 3 | Power hoses used to produce 'slurry' |
| 4 | Waste material (coarse sand and rocks) hauled to surface in skips |
| 5 | China clay slurry pumped up to surface |
| 6 - 8 | 'Settling' process to remove fine sand and mica |
| 6 | Concrete channels |
| 7 | Settling pits |
| 8 | Settling tanks |
| 9 | Pan kiln where slurry is dried |
| 10 | Storage sheds |

**Modern production:**
(a) Electricity has replaced steam
(b) Gas-fired kilns
(c) Diggers, dumper trucks and conveyer belts used in pits
(d) Slurry now transported by pipelines
(e) Waste now more carefully processed

**Figure 4.12**  China clay production at Wheal Martyn

## The landscape of china clay mining

The impact of the mining on the St Austell area is shown in Figure 4.13. Modern methods produce less waste than before. Old tips are now covered by oak, willow and shrubs. One deep pit was chosen as the site of the Eden Project for the Millennium. This involved the building of the world's largest greenhouses to create mini-biomes such as of the Tropical Rain Forest. This, and the many museums of mining life in Cornwall, attract many tourists. They can also walk along the cliffs on the South West Coast Path, while surfers are attracted to the bays on the north coast.

**Figure 4.14**  Waste tips colonised by woodland

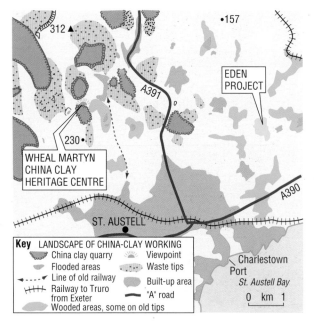

**Figure 4.13**  Landscape of china clay mining

**Figure 4.15**  The Eden Project

# A river basin

## *River words*

The area drained by a river and its **tributaries** is called a **basin**. A tributary is a stream which flows into the main river. The place where two rivers join is called a **confluence**. The place where a river starts to flow is called the **source**. Each tributary has its own source. The place where a river flows into the sea is called its **mouth**.

## *River patterns*

Look at Figure 4.16. It shows the pattern made by the River Tweed and its tributaries. Looked at from above and from the east, the pattern looks like a very twisted tree, growing from a hillside with the River Tweed forming the trunk and its tributaries forming the branches and twigs.

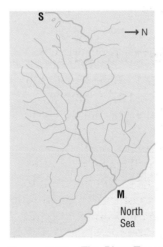

**Figure 4.16**  The River Tweed

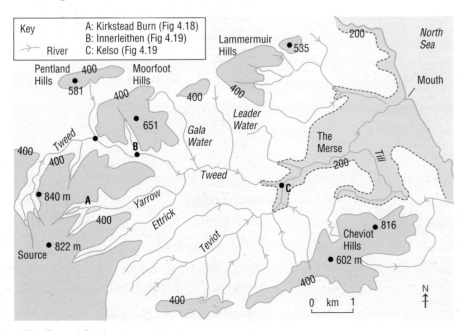

**Figure 4.17**  The Tweed Basin

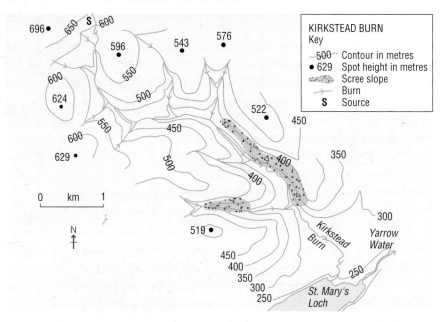

**Figure 4.18**  Kirkstead Burn

The Tweed Basin is in the eastern half of the Southern Uplands. Figure 4.17 shows the hills in which the sources of the Tweed and its tributaries are found. Notice the height of the summits.

The Kirkstead Burn is an example of a river in the higher parts of the Tweed Basin (Figure 4.18). It flows quickly and very directly. It takes the shortest route possible. It erodes the hillsides. Its valley is deep and narrow. It dumps the eroded material in St Mary's Loch.

## The work of rivers

You have already looked at the way in which rivers

★ erode the landscape

★ transport the eroded material

★ eventually deposit this material.

As a general rule,

★ most erosion takes place in the highest part of a river basin

★ most deposition takes place in the lowest part of a river basin.

As a river flows down from its source to its mouth the width and depth of its bed increase. The width and depth of its valley also increase.

Thus, near its source it is possible to step across a river bed. The valley floor is narrow. The river bed may occupy almost all the floor. The valley sides are steep and close together. The Blackhopebyres Burn is a good example of this. A section has been drawn through this burn in Figure 4.19. This burn flows very rapidly westwards to join the Glentress Water. This river has a lower, wider valley, but it is still quite narrow. Both rivers have a cross-section which looks like the letter 'V'. The Glentress Water flows into the Leithen Water. This runs south into the broad valley of the River Tweed at Innerleithen. Notice that here the Tweed Valley has high, steep sides, but has a wide, flat valley floor. It is much lower than the valleys of its tributaries. The Tweed here is transporting a heavy load of eroded material from all its tributaries. It deposits some of this material when it floods.

Near its mouth, just below Kelso (Figure 4.19) the Tweed Valley is very wide and very low. The river has high, steep banks. The bed is very broad and deep. There are low islands rising from the bed made of silt and gravel, eroded higher up the river, and transported downstream. The land above the river channel is not flat. It consists of a series of low, oval hills, called **drumlins**, deposited by ice sheets.

All rivers are different from one another. The photographs (Figures 4.20–4.22) show three

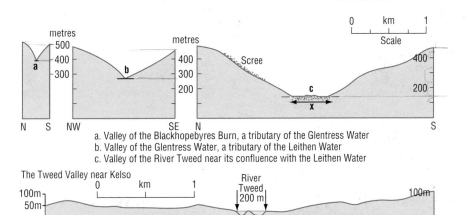

a. Valley of the Blackhopebyres Burn, a tributary of the Glentress Water
b. Valley of the Glentress Water, a tributary of the Leithen Water
c. Valley of the River Tweed near its confluence with the Leithen Water

**Figure 4.19** Contrasting valley shapes in the Tweed Basin

contrasting sections of the Tweed Basin. These would not necessarily be found in other river basins. However, there may be features which are common to many rivers such as waterfalls, deltas and meanders (see pages 56–57).

**Figure 4.21** Middle Tweed near Peebles

**Figure 4.20** Upper Tweed: near the river's source

**Figure 4.22** Lower Tweed: near the Eildon Hills

## ASSIGNMENTS

1  Chose the correct tail to match each head:
   **Heads**: a river basin; a tributary; a confluence
   **Tails**: is a stream which flows into a larger river; is the area drained by a river; is where a river joins another.

2  Study Figure 4.16. (i) What do the letters M and S indicate? (ii) Which of the following words best describes the pattern formed by the Tweed and its tributaries: straight; parallel; branching; radial?

3  Study Figure 4.18, the map of the Kirkland Burn.
   i)  Estimate the height of its source and mouth.

   ii)  Measure the straight-line distance in km between the source and the mouth.

4  Study Figure 4.19.
   i)  From the vertical scale, find the height of the valley floor of a) the Blackhopebyres Burn b) the Glentress Water c) the Tweed near Innerleithen d) the Tweed near Kelso.
   ii)  From the horizontal scale, measure the width of the valley near Innerleithen.

5  Which valley shape is most like the letter 'V'?

# Rivers falling, winding and dumping

Rivers have some distinctive features along their courses. There could be

★ waterfalls and rapids

★ deltas

★ meanders.

The presence of these features depends on

★ the types of rock over which streams flow

★ the gradient of the streams – the steepness of the slopes down which the streams flow

★ the amount of eroded material streams are carrying.

## Waterfalls and rapids

Not all rivers have waterfalls or rapids on their courses. Waterfalls are short stretches of a river where it falls vertically. Rapids are stretches where a river twists and tumbles at a steep angle over very hard rocks. They may be so resistant to erosion that there is no real stream bed. Rapids are '**white water**' stretches which are attractive to rafters and canoeists.

Waterfalls occur either where very hard rocks have resisted erosion (Figure 4.23) or where the river falls down steep valley sides which have been sheared away by glaciers during the Ice Age.

One of the best examples of the second type is the Grey Mare's Tail in the Southern Uplands (Figure 4.24). This is one of the highest waterfalls in Scotland. Waterfalls and rapids can be powerful enough to generate hydro-electric power, for example, at the Falls of Clyde.

## Meanders

Where a river is flowing quickly over a steep slope, its course is straight. Anywhere on a river's course where the valley floor is flat, the river will wind about. These winding stretches are called **meanders**. In a meander area, the river takes the least direct route. Figure 4.26 shows meanders on a tributary of the River Forth. The River Balvag flows for 4 km round its meanders to cover a distance of only 2 km (X–Y).

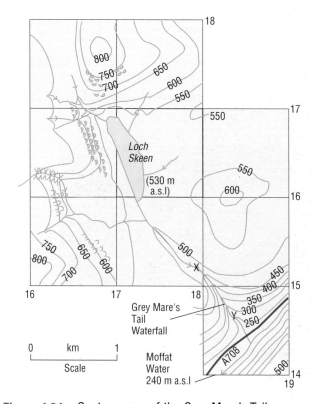

**Figure 4.24** Contour map of the Grey Mare's Tail

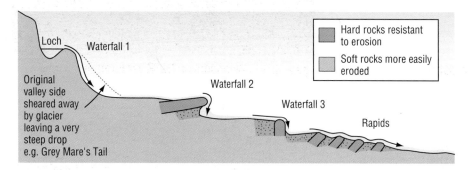

**Figure 4.23** Waterfalls and rapids

The meanders on the River Forth on the peat moss just above Stirling are shown on Figure 4.27. Below Stirling, the meanders become even more exaggerated (Figure 4.28).

In the past, meanders

★ made journeys by river slower

★ made more bridges necessary but

★ helped defend settlements.

## Deltas

As we have found out, rivers are always eroding the landscape. They transport this eroded material downstream until they can no longer do so. Rocks, the heaviest materials, are dumped first. Silt, the finest material, is carried furthest, perhaps to the river mouth.

The dumped material forms deltas where the gradient slackens, for example, at the foot of a very steep slope or where a river enters a loch (Figure 4.29). Seen from above, a delta may have a triangular shape or a branching shape. Figure 4.29 shows examples of each type from Strathyre where the River Balvag flows between Loch Voil and Loch Lubnaig. Any silt left after Loch Lubnaig will be carried down to the River Forth via the River Teith. The Forth has no delta at its mouth, and enters the sea by a **firth** or **estuary**.

Deltas in Scotland are

★ very small by world standards

★ found in the middle of river courses rather than at the river mouth.

Deltas are initially very wet areas, liable to flood but very fertile after drainage, and often densely populated as in Asia.

Some of the world's largest deltas are shown on Figure 4.30. The delta built up by the Rivers Ganga and Brahmaputra is as large as all of Scotland.

**Figure 4.25** Grey Mare's Tail

**Figure 4.26** The meandering River Balvag

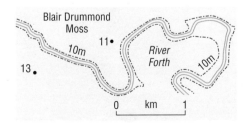

**Figure 4.27** The meandering River Forth

**Figure 4.28** Meanders on the River Forth below Stirling

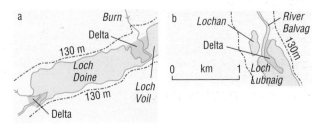

**Figure 4.29** Types of deltas

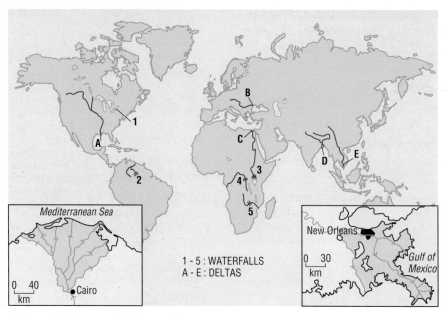

**Figure 4.30** Waterfalls and deltas around the world

## ASSIGNMENTS

1 Match each head with the correct tail:
**Heads**: A meander is a…; A delta is a…;
A waterfall is a…
**Tails**: flat area built up by a river dumping eroded material; stretch of a river where it flows slowly in great loops; near vertical drop in a river's course.

2 Explain why waterfalls occur (i) where hard alternate with soft rocks (ii) in glaciated areas.

3 Study Figure 4.24. What is the height of the waterfall? (Find the difference in height between X and Y).

4 Study Figure 4.30. With the aid of an atlas, name the
   a) Waterfalls 1–5
   b) Deltas A–E.

# Glaciers and the landscape

There have been a succession of ice ages in the last two million years. The last ice-age ended 10,000 years ago. Figure 4.32 shows the extent of the ice-sheets over Europe. A very large ice sheet spread over what is now the North Sea from Scandinavia to merge with an ice sheet covering the British Isles. This ice sheet reached as far south as the estuaries of the Thames and the Severn. Sea levels were so much lower then that there was a land bridge between Britain and Europe.

## Ice in the Alps

Figure 4.32 shows that when the ice sheets covered the north of Europe, the Alps were a source of vast valley glaciers which spread out in all directions over the surrounding plateaus and plains. There are still large glaciers in the highest areas of the Alps (Figure 4.31),

**Figure 4.31** Mer de Glace

although they are shrinking in size. Below the glaciers, the deep valleys show clear evidence of having been glaciated. (Figure 4.33).

## How glaciers erode

Ice moves downslope under the influence of gravity. Pressure near the source of a glacier builds up, and this forces the glacier down the valley. The base of the glacier is lubricated by a thin sheet of water. The glacier is a river of ice, slowly deepening and widening the valley in which it flows. A glacier erodes the landscape by

★ bulldozing soil and stones to expose the solid rock (the bedrock) below

★ removing large chunks of rock which have already been loosened by freezing and thawing (see Figure 4.1)

★ using these rocks like teeth in a giant file to gouge deep grooves in the bedrock.

## Before and after glaciation

Before the Alps were glaciated

★ the valleys were narrower and less deep

★ the peaks were less sharp

★ tributaries flowed evenly into the main valley

★ the slopes were less steep

★ the valleys were shaped like a letter 'V'.

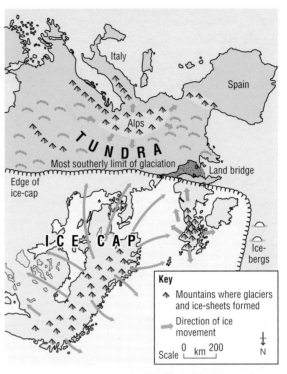

Figure 4.32    The Ice Age in Europe 20,000 years ago

Figure 4.33    The U-shaped Lauterbrunnen Valley

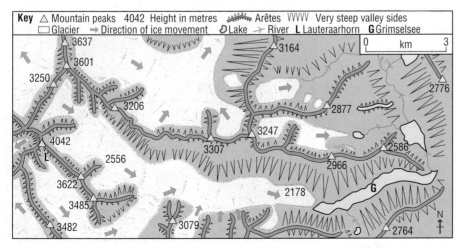

Figure 4.34    Some glaciers in the Alps today

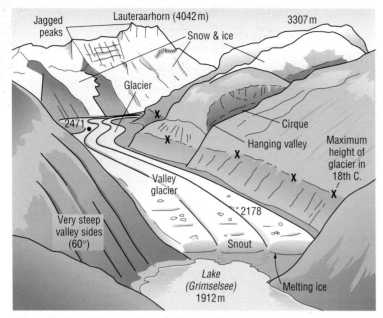

**Figure 4.35**   A present-day Alpine glacier

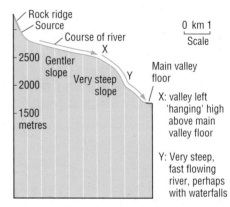

**Figure 4.36**   A hanging valley in the Alps

Figure 4.37 shows how such a landscape near Chamonix was transformed by glaciation.

## After glaciation: alpine landscapes today

In the highest parts of the Alps, there are still many long valley glaciers, where a glacier ends (the '**snout**'), there may be a long narrow lake, filling the U-shaped valley.

Many tributary valleys have been left 'hanging', after glaciers sheared off their lower sections.

There are also 'hanging' glaciers, clinging precariously to steep rock faces (Figure 4.37), which once flowed into valley glaciers.

In deep hollows called **cirques** (**corries**) above the main valley, there may be small glaciers or small lakes.

Between the cirques are steep, rocky ridges called **arêtes**. The arêtes lead up to jagged peaks.

Some peaks, such as the Matterhorn, are shaped like pyramids (Figure 4.38). These high peaks have always been above the valley glaciers. They have been shaped by frost-shattering rather than by ice.

Glaciation has produced a spectacular mountain landscape. This attracts many thousands of tourists who go to the Alps to walk, climb and ski, or merely admire the landscape.

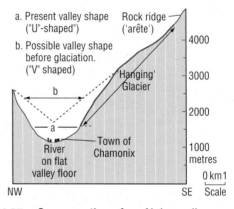

**Figure 4.37**   Cross-section of an Alpine valley near Mont Blanc

**Figure 4.38**   The peak of the Matterhorn

## ASSIGNMENTS

1 When did the last Ice Age end?

2 What was the main source of the ice sheets which affected the North of Europe?

3 Match each head with the correct tail
   **Heads**: A snout; An arete; A cirque; A U-shaped valley; A hanging valley
   **Tails**: is a deep hollow near a mountain peak; the end of a glacier; is a deep, flat floored valley shaped by ice; is a rocky ridge leading up to a mountain peak; is a valley found high above the floor of a glaciated valley.

4 Study Figure 4.34 carefully.
   a) How many valley glaciers are shown?
   b) How long is the main glacier from source to snout? How far does it drop in height?
   c) How far is the the surface of the glacier below the mountain peaks?
   d) What shape is the Grimselsee? Why is it this shape? What height is its surface above sea level? (See Figure 4.35)

5 Look carefully at Figure 4.37.
   a) What shape is the valley in which Chamonix is located?
   b) What does this tell you?
   c) Why is there a hanging glacier above the town?

# Loch Lomond National Park

The area shown in Figure 4.39 became Scotland's first National Park early in 2002.

**Landscape**: The area is similar to the Alps in that it has been glaciated, but with everything on a much smaller scale. The mountains are much lower and less rugged, and the valleys are much less deep and less steep. The many long narrow lochs are a key feature of the park, especially Loch Lomond which is 180 m deep in its narrowest area.

## Who owns the National Park?

Much of the land is owned by the Forestry Commission or privately owned in large hill sheep farms and estates.

The National Park was created by the Scottish Parliament to protect the environment and control development for the benefit of everyone. It will also maintain and develop the recreational use of the area.

## Play park or working park?

Most of the area is accessible to visitors who can enjoy many outdoor pursuits, or simply look at the landscape. Tourists can

★ walk on the hills or on the long-distance West Highland Way to Fort William

★ climb the mountains

★ fish, sail in yachts and power-boats, water ski, or canoe on the lochs and rivers

★ go pony-trekking, orienteering or mountain-biking in the forests

★ take part in motor sports on the forest tracks.

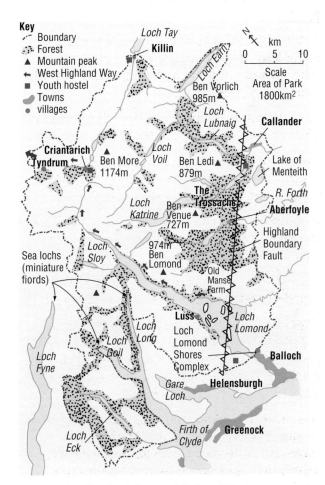

**Figure 4.39** The Loch Lomond National Park

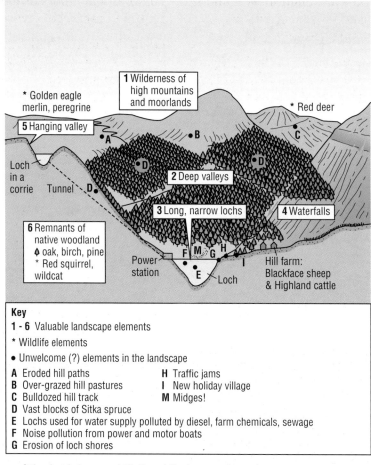

**Figure 4.40**   The landscape of the Loch Lomond National Park

Tourists are attracted to particular areas. These may be simply stopping places by a loch-side, or settlements of varying sizes. Towns and villages such as Callander, Aberfoyle and Luss, become very crowded with people stopping briefly on day outings and touring holidays. The presence of hotels, restaurants and gift shops are attractions at these 'honey-pots'. The new Shores Complex at Balloch is expected to attract many of the 7 million people who visit Loch Lomond each year. Many people depend on tourism for employment.

A major use of the land within the national park is forestry. The Queen Elizabeth Forest Park owned by the Forestry Commission covers 200 square kilometres. The Park is in scattered blocks, mostly in the Trossachs and Strathyre (Figure 4.39). In the past, the Forestry Commission was criticised for spoiling the landscape by planting large areas with Sitka spruce. In more recent times, a mixture of deciduous and coniferous trees has been planted. The Commission owns large areas of land, but employs relatively few people. It also encourages tourists to visit the forests.

**Figure 4.41**   Luss, a Loch Lomond 'honeypot'

Various leisure activities are encouraged, and it has forest cabins for self-catering holidays, for example, by Loch Lubnaig (Figure 4.45).

The level of Loch Katrine, a ribbon loch (Figure 4.39), has been raised three times to provide a supply of water for Glasgow. The area round and above the loch has been used for forestry and hill sheep farming. Tourists can sail on the loch on one of the last paddle steamers. Loch Lomond is a major source of water supply for the other large towns of Central Scotland.

Loch Sloy is a loch in a hanging valley high above Loch Lomond (Figure 4.39). It was deepened and lengthened in the mid-20th century. Water is taken through tunnels to the power station 3 km below on the shores of Loch Lomond.

Extensive hill sheep farms cover most of the National Park, some as large as 4,000 hectares. The Old Manse Farm, run by the Bannerman family, is situated on the Highland Boundary Fault at Balmaha (Figure 4.39). It has 2,000 hectares of hill grazing rising from the lochside to a height of 560 m. There is a flock of 1,100 Blackface sheep, and a herd of 30 pedigree Highland cattle. Their beef is sold directly to the public by mail order and at farmers' markets in Glasgow, Stirling and Edinburgh.

### Getting the right balance

The National Park will have to

★ cope with all the pressures on the park and

★ get the balance right between the different interests (Figure 4.40 and Figure 4.43).

**Figure 4.42** Looking north over Loch Lomond

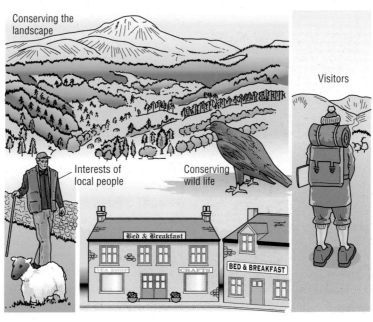

**Figure 4.43** Getting the balance right

## ASSIGNMENTS

1  Name three other lochs in the National Park.

2  a)  Describe the shape of the lochs.
   b)  What does this tell you about the valleys in which they are found?

3  What shaped this landscape in the past?

4  Name three products which the Park supplies to the rest of Scotland.

5  If you lived in the Park, what jobs might you find?

6  Give six reasons why tourists might visit the Park.

7  Why might conservationists object to further tourist developments in the Park?

8  A mining company has been searching for gold near Tyndrum for many years. Should they be allowed to continue their work in the National Park?

9  List the possible views of local people on the Park.

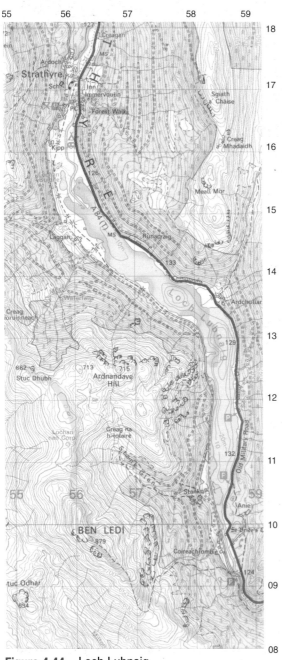

**Figure 4.44**   Loch Lubnaig

*Source*: Ordnance Survey sheet 57 (Langranger)

## TO TAKE YOU FURTHER

# Loch Lomond National Park

## *Map and photograph interpretation*

Study the 1:50000 map extract of part of the Loch Lomond National Park opposite.

1  Using the scale (2 cm = 1 km), measure the (i) visible length and (ii) the width of Loch Lubnaig.

2  Choose the words from the list which best describes the shape of the loch:
   long; broad; rectangular; irregular; narrow; round

3  a)  Is the loch more than (i) 10 m (ii) 20 m or (iii) 30 m deep?
   b)  Give the grid reference of the square which shows the deepest part of the loch.
   c)  From the spot height, give the height of the land by the side of the loch in square 5714.

4  Measure the width of the floor of the river valley above the loch (5515, 5615) and below the loch (5809, 5808).

5  Look again at 5515/5615 and 5809/5808. In which of these areas is the river i) eroding ii) depositing?

6  Name two river features which are shown in squares 5515 and 5615.

7  a)  Name the highest point shown on the map.
   b)  Is it approximately 550 m, 650 m or 750 m above the loch?

*continued* ➤

**TO TAKE YOU FURTHER** continued

**8** Looking at the photo (Figure 4.45) as well as the map.

a) What appears to be the main use of this part of the national park?

b) What evidence can you see of tourism?

**9** What evidence is there that this area was glaciated? Give examples with grid references.

**Figure 4.45**    View of Ben Ledi from Loch Lubnaig

**Figure 4.46**    A waterfall in Stank Glen

# Shaping the coast

The 11,000 km-long coastline of the British Isles is very varied in shape. The line of the coast may be straight or irregular. The land immediately behind the coastline may be low, hilly or mountainous.

The nature of the coastline depends on

★ the type of rock from which it is formed

★ the balance between erosion and deposition.

## Rock types

Harder rocks form higher coastlines; softer rocks form lower coastlines. For example:

★ limestone and chalk form **cliffs** but

★ **bays** are found where clay reaches the coast.

Cliffs often form areas of high land jutting out into the sea. These are called **headlands**.

Granite and sandstone also form sea cliffs. Even in these tougher rocks, there are weaker areas.

These are eroded to form narrow bays called **coves** between headlands.

## Erosion, transportation and deposition

The coastline is eroded by the pounding of waves. Erosion is greater during storms, especially in winter. Cliff coasts show evidence of erosion by the presence of

★ caves

★ arches

★ stacks. (Figures 4.47 and 4.49)

Eroded material is transported by the currents, and deposited further along the coast. Where there is a bend in the coast, a **spit** may form. This may be made of sand or **shingle** (smooth, round pebbles), deposited to form a low ridge above sea level. Winds blowing on-shore may pile up sand to form **sand-dunes**.

A shallow, salt-water lake called a **lagoon** may form behind a spit. This lagoon may become a **salt marsh**.

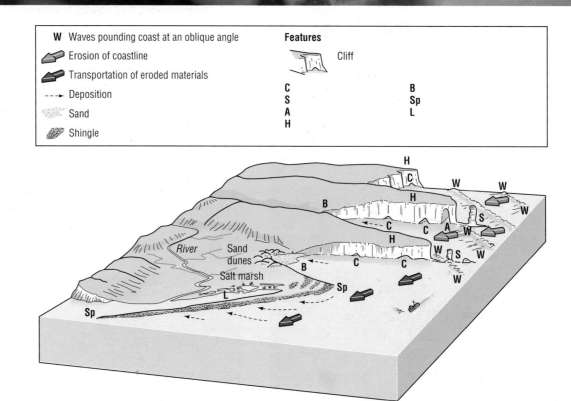

| | |
|---|---|
| **W** Waves pounding coast at an oblique angle | **Features** |
| Erosion of coastline | Cliff |
| Transportation of eroded materials | |
| - - - ► Deposition | C        B |
| Sand | S        Sp |
| Shingle | A        L |
| | H |

**Figure 4.47**    Shaping the coastline

**Figure 4.48**    Durdle Door Arch on the Jurassic Coast

## Different beaches

The coastline may have a beach formed by deposition which is either sandy or pebbly. Erosion may form a beach which is very rocky with many pools between ridges.

Figure 4.50 shows different types of coast found round Britain. Most of them are examples of drowned coasts. They show how far the sea has penetrated inland.

The 'Jurassic Coast' is a coastline of crumbling cliffs which are very famous for their fossils. The coast has now been made a World Heritage Site.

**Visit www.charmouth.org for more details.**

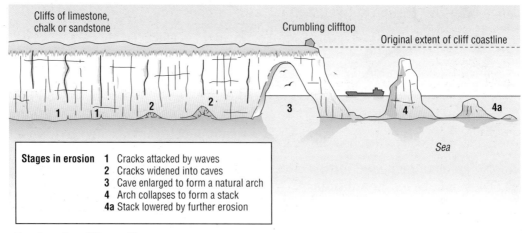

| Stages in erosion | | |
|---|---|---|
| | **1** | Cracks attacked by waves |
| | **2** | Cracks widened into caves |
| | **3** | Cave enlarged to form a natural arch |
| | **4** | Arch collapses to form a stack |
| | **4a** | Stack lowered by further erosion |

**Figure 4.49**    Erosion of a cliff coastline

## ASSIGNMENTS

Study Figure 4.47.

1 What type of rock might be forming the cliffs?

2 Complete the key to Figure 4.47. Name the features shown by their initial letters. You will find all the names in the text.

3 Which of these features are formed by
a) erosion
b) deposition?
Which features are shown in the photographs?

4 Study the coastal types A–G shown on Figure 4.50. Notice the spot heights given.
a) Which coasts are low and flat? Which coasts are hilly? Which coast is mountainous?
b) Which coasts appear to have been drowned?
c) Which coastline is most indented?
d) Which coastline has the longest inlet?
e) With the aid of an atlas, name the main inlets and any seaports shown in coasts A, C, E, F and G.

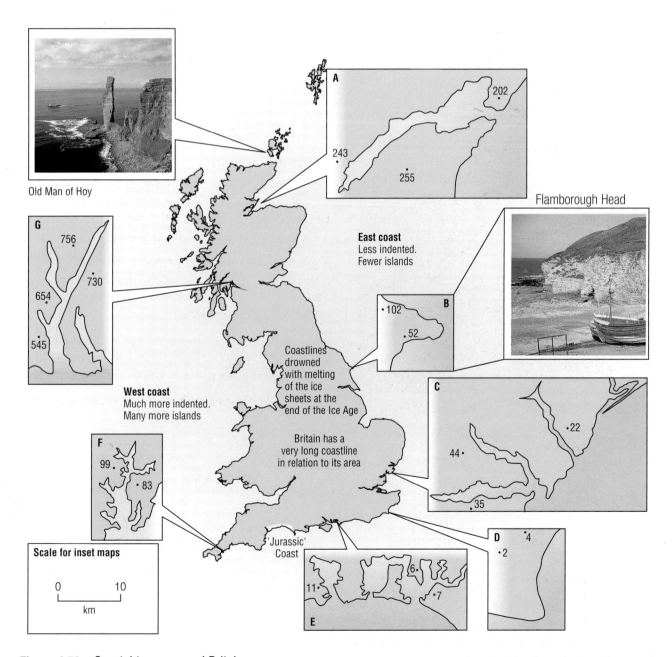

**Figure 4.50    Coastal types around Britain**

# Coastline at risk?

Figure 4.53 shows Romney Marsh on the Kent coast. Immediately to the north are the white chalk cliffs at Folkestone and Dover. Figure 4.54 shows on a larger scale the headland called Dungeness at the end of the Marsh.

**Visit www.rmcp.co.uk to find out more about the Marsh.**

Romney Marsh is a good example of a coastline formed by deposition. 2,000 years ago in Roman times, this was a bay. The old cliff coastline can be seen along the edge of the Marsh. The bay was gradually filled by materials, especially shingle, deposited by the sea, and by the rivers. 1,000 years ago, a sea wall was built. Drainage of the marsh which had formed inland was begun. Since then. further deposition has taken place. This has left old ports such as Romney well inland.

Today, Romney Marsh has been completely drained. Its rich grassland is famous for rearing the Romney Marsh breed of sheep. The Marsh and its coastline attract many visitors. There are many different and conflicting uses of the coastline.

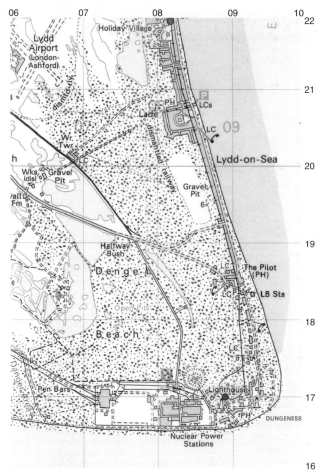

**Figure 4.54    1:50000 map extract of Dungeness**

*Source*: Ordnance Survey sheet 189 (Landranger)

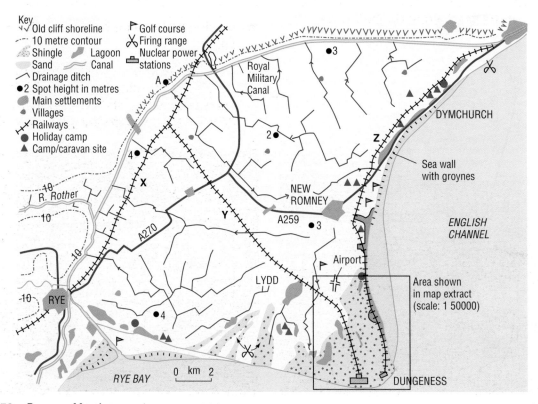

**Figure 4.53    Romney Marsh**

## ASSIGNMENTS

Study Figures 4.53 and 4.54.

1   How far is it from point A to Dungeness?

2   How high is this area above sea level?

3   Is the land flat or sloping?

4   What protects it from being flooded?

5   What two kinds of beach are there?

6   List at least three reasons why this coastline
   a)   might attract visitors
   b)   might repel visitors.

7   Why might cyclists and ornithologists be attracted to Romney Marsh?

8   Look at the 1:50000 extract (0821 to 0917). Are the coastal settlements round or linear? Explain the shape.

9   There are three different railways shown (X, Y & Z). Which do you think might carry
   a)   mainly tourists
   b)   commuters to London
   c)   only goods traffic?

10   Why do you think Dungeness was chosen as the site for two nuclear power stations (0816)? Do you think that this is an appropriate use of this coastline? Is Dungeness the only example? Write a paragraph to put forward your views.

# Pressures on the coastline

Look at Figure 4.55 which shows two of the pressures on our coastline. One is man-made – the long rows of holiday chalets above the beach. Attempts are now made to control such building as well as the setting up of caravan parks along the British coastline The other is on the beach itself where a groyne has been built. Groynes help to slow down the removal by the sea of the sand along the beach.

## Our crumbling coast

As we have seen, even the toughest rocks forming our coastline are eventually worn away. Large sections of cliff coasts frequently slump into the sea. Erosion is greatest at the base of cliffs, and undercutting eventually results in the cliff collapsing. Farmland and buildings can be lost in this way (Figure 4.56).

Attempts can be made to slow down

★   erosion by building barriers at the base of cliffs

★   transportation of of eroded material along the shore by building groynes. These are barriers made of wood or metal at 90 degrees to the shore-line (Figure 4.57).

**Figure 4.55**   Pressures on the coastline

**Figure 4.56**   Landslide on chalk cliffs near Dover

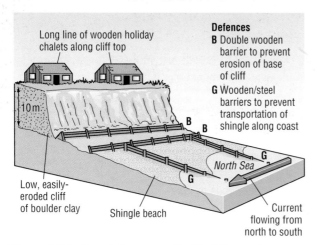

**Defences**

**B** Double wooden barrier to prevent erosion of base of cliff

**G** Wooden/steel barriers to prevent transportation of shingle along coast

Long line of wooden holiday chalets along cliff top

10m

Low, easily-eroded cliff of boulder clay

Shingle beach

North Sea

Current flowing from north to south

**Figure 4.57** Sea defences on the Norfolk coast

Beaches have also been damaged by people. In some cases, sand or shingle was dug up and carried away for use in gardens or golf courses. Some beaches, such as at Dungeness (Figure 4.54) are so fragile that visitors are asked not to drive or ride over the shingle ridges. Sand dune areas can also be eroded by too much human traffic. Coastal marshes are now mostly protected to stop the drainage of wetlands important for wildlife and rare plants.

## Blue-flag beaches

Beaches in Britain are now inspected regularly to see if they meet EC standards of cleanliness. Too many beaches and the waters off-shore are polluted by

★ rubbish dumped or washed up on the beach, especially plastics

★ industrial and domestic waste, for example, sewage sludge, fertilisers, other chemicals and in the worst cases, oil spillages.

## Industrial development

Coastal areas attract industrial development because

★ there may be a good natural harbour for large ships such as Milford Haven

★ there may be a large area of low flat land (mudflats) which is available cheaply for building such as at Grangemouth

★ there is plenty of water available for cooling purposes, for example, for power stations as at Dungeness.

★ transport by sea is the cheapest for bulk transport of oil, gas, coal, building materials.

Mines and quarries such as the proposed superquarry at Lingarabay on Harris

★ change the shape of the coastline

★ pollute the beaches as in North-East England, long after coal mining has ceased.

## Military uses

Where there is deep water off-shore, and the area is isolated, there may be a defence base and in some cases, a firing range, for example, on the Solway Firth.

Figure 4.57 summarises these pressures on the British coastline. The extract below gives an example of objections to such developments.

### River Idyll Could Be A Container Port

Protesters are battling to stop the development of a huge container port on the East Anglian coast which was the setting for two Arthur Ransome books. Hutchison Ports plans to fill in Bathside Bay on the northern fringes of Harwich to build a port the size of 100 football pitches … Environmentalists are calling for a public enquiry because..the mudflats are a rich feeding area for the wading birds and wildfowl that winter in the Stour and and Orwell estuaries. Both are sites of Special Scientific Interest…

E. Welsh: *The Times* 02 Jan 2002

There are also strong opinions about developments which have taken place, for example, on Romney Marsh

Old fishermen's cottages and shacks now put to a multitude of uses, the huge nuclear power stations destined to become useless concrete monuments of the 20th C, and the lines of pylons which march across the flat landscape, all tend to detract…

*Shell Book of the British Coastline*

## A future threat to the coastline

This last extract illustrates the effect of global warming in the Antarctic.

### Going Down? – Global Warming

An Antarctic ice shelf larger than the Western Isles has astonished British scientists by collapsing in just a month. The 3300 square kilometre Larsen B disintegrated into icebergs and fragments amid temperatures that rose on an Antarctic peninsula faster than anywhere on earth…

*A. Dalton The Scotsman 20 March 2002*

Scientists fear that if global warming continues at its present rate

★ much of the polar ice will melt

★ sea levels will rise

★ large areas of land less than 10 m above sea level will be drowned (Figure 4.59).

## ASSIGNMENTS

**1** Try to obtain copies of the ten special coastline stamps issued by the Post Office in March 2002. Postcards were also available. Find out from an atlas the locations of the places shown.

**2** What is a groyne? Why is it built?

**3** Give three reasons why coastlines are so attractive to tourists. What type of developments might attract even more people?

**4** Give three reasons why coastal locations are so favoured by industrial developers.

**5** Give four reasons why conservationists are against all developments on coastlines.

**6** If you were living in a coastal village, what might your reaction be to a proposed new terminal or power station?

**7** Which coastline shown on Figure 4.50 is the site for the port development named in the first extract?

**8** If sea level were to rise by 10 m, which of the coastlines shown in Figure 4.50 would be in danger?

**Figure 4.59** Part of Romney Marsh just above sea-level

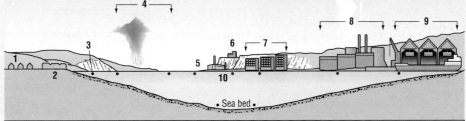

**Key**

**1** Large areas covered by chalets, caravan & campsites, holiday centres
**2** Large-scale leisure/interpretation centre e.g. Land's End
**3** Coastal quarry
**4** Ministry of Defence firing range e.g. Solway Firth
**5** Former coal mine and power station e.g. Longannet
**6** Potash mine or former tin/copper mine
**7** Nuclear power station e.g. Torness
**8** Oil/gas terminal or refinery e.g. Grangemouth
**9** New container terminal
**10** Beaches and coastal waters polluted by:
• sewage • oil • chemicals
• dangerous metals • coal dust
• radio-active waste
• seepage from old mine workings • plastics

**Figure 4.58** Coastlines under pressure

## Structure of the earth

### *In the beginning*

According to geologists, the earth (Figure 5.1) is some 4,550 million years old. It seems to have formed from a giant cloud of gases and dust that was spinning round the sun. Gradually it grew hotter and eventually turned into a ball of liquid rock and metals. Over time, the lighter materials floated to the surface and cooled into a hard crust of rock

### *A journey to the centre of the earth*

No one (so far) has actually travelled to the centre of the earth. What we do know about the inside of the earth comes from studying shock or **seismic** waves caused by earthquakes. Geologists draw a sort of X-ray picture of the different layers of the earth. The layers show the earth's structure (Figure 5.2). From surface to centre, there are **three** main layers:

★ **the crust** is the earth's hard and rocky surface and is by far the thinnest layer.

Under the oceans it is around 6 km thick, while under the continents it is up to 90 km thick.

★ **the mantle** is the thickest layer (around 2,900 km) and consists of semi-molten rocks, rather like a soft plasticine. Temperatures are very high (see Figure 5.2).

★ **the core** is at the very centre and is easily the hottest, reaching temperatures of 5,500°C. The diagram shows that there is a molten outer core and a solid inner core. The inner core is a solid ball, mainly of iron. It does not melt because of the great pressure from all the other layers, pressing down upon it.

In some ways, therefore, the earth's structure is like a giant, ripe peach. The peach skin represents the crust; the juicy flesh represents the mantle; and the stone is like the core.

## The world's plates

The earth's crust is not a huge solid piece of rock. It is like a cracked egg shell. Each piece of crust is called a **plate**. There are seven enormous plates and twelve smaller ones.

**Figure 5.1**   The earth from space

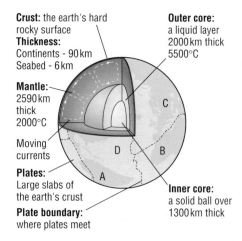

**Crust:** the earth's hard rocky surface
**Thickness:**
Continents - 90 km
Seabed - 6 km

**Mantle:**
2590 km thick
2000°C

**Moving currents**

**Plates:**
Large slabs of the earth's crust

**Plate boundary:**
where plates meet

**Outer core:**
a liquid layer
2000 km thick
5500°C

**Inner core:**
a solid ball over
1300 km thick

**Figure 5.2**   The earth's structure

Where the plate edges meet is called a **plate boundary**. Figure 5.6 (page 74) shows the main plate boundaries. It is at plate boundaries that most earthquakes and volcanic eruptions take place, and where the highest mountains are found.

## Why plates move

These plates move around very slowly – just a few mm each year (fingernail growth rate!). Continents also move around because they are 'passengers' on the plates.

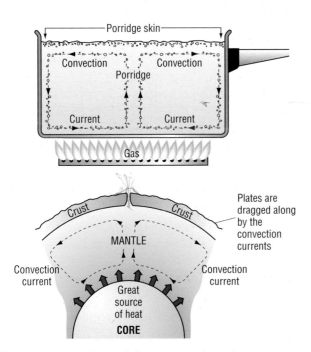

**Figure 5.3**  Porridge and plates: convection currents

Ideas about plate movement change. It is thought that plates are moved along by powerful **convection currents** in the mantle. They are powered by great heat from the core, caused by radioactive decay. If you look at Figure 5.3, you can think of the crust as being rather like the skin that forms on top of a saucepan of porridge if it is allowed to cool. When the porridge is reheated, the skin breaks up and the convection currents move pieces of skin to the sides of the pan.

## Drifting continents

Figure 5.4 shows the earth some 200 million years ago. All the continents were joined together in a 'super continent' called **Pangea**. Two ways of proving this are:

★ the north-east coast of South America seems to fit into the west coast of Africa – just like giant jigsaw pieces.

★ rocks and fossils of a similar age and type are found in these two continents (Figure 5.5).

It is believed that around 150 million years ago the continents started to drift apart. They only moved a few mm every year, but, multiply 5 mm by 150,000,000 years and see how many km you get! Plate movement, therefore, explains continental drift.

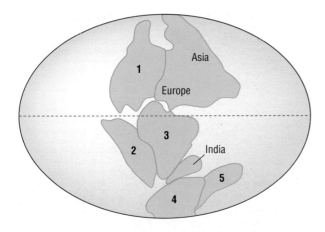

**Figure 5.4**  Pangea 'super continent' 200 million years ago

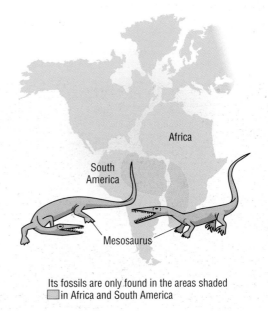

Its fossils are only found in the areas shaded in Africa and South America

**Figure 5.5**  Evidence for continental drift

## ASSIGNMENTS

**1** Copy and complete the following sentences using the words highlighted below.

The thin layer of hard rock around the earth is the _____ .

The earth's crust is divided into huge slabs called _____ .

The layer of semi-molten rock between the core and the crust is the _____ .

Where plates meet is called a plate _____ .

Volcanic _____ and _____ can take place close to plate boundaries.

**plates, crust, eruptions, mantle, earthquakes, boundary**

**2** Look at Figure 5.2. Name the three continents A–C, and ocean D.

**3** Look at Figure 5.4 and Figure 5.5.
  a) What was Pangea and how was it affected by continental drift?
  b) Name the areas 1 to 5 that eventually became separate continents.
  c) Give two pieces of evidence for continental drift.

**4** Look at Figure 5.2. Copy and complete this table

| Layer | State | Temp °C | Thickness (km) |
|---|---|---|---|
| Crust | | Up to 1,200 | |
| | | | 2,990 |
| Outer core | molten | 5,500 | |
| Inner core | solid | 5,500 | |

**5** Write a short explanation of why plates move.

# Plates, volcanoes and earthquakes

Thanks to the convection currents in the mantle, the earth's plates are moving very slowly. They do not move constantly, but, at plate boundaries, they move in three ways.

## Parting plates

At point X on Figure 5.8, the two oceanic plates are moving away from each other. At the boundary between the plates, red-hot molten rock from the mantle is oozing up, and hardening into new crust when it touches the cold water of the ocean. Much of this new land is building up as underwater mountain ranges.

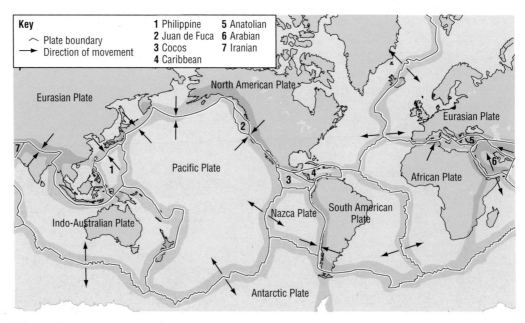

**Figure 5.6** Plates and plate movement

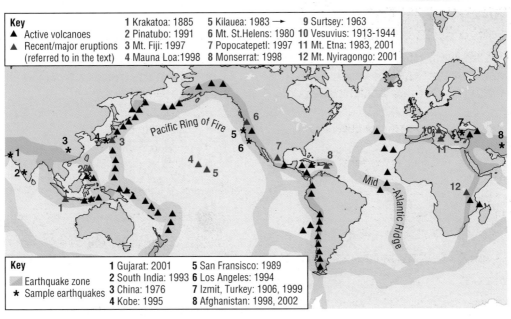

**Figure 5.7** Volcanoes and earthquakes

Perhaps the best example is the Mid-Atlantic Ridge (Figure 5.7). Sometimes, some of its peaks rise above the ocean surface to form volcanic islands such as Surtsey, near Iceland.

## Colliding plates

One result of parting plates is that the seabed is spreading. For example, the floor of the Atlantic Ocean is spreading at about 3 cm a year. Europe and North America are drifting apart. Surely the earth should get bigger because of the extra rock?

Look again at Figure 5.8, especially at point Y on the diagram. The spreading oceanic plates are forced to descend as they collide with the continental plates. The heavier oceanic plate is forced downwards into the mantle where it melts into magma. So any extra rock is balanced out by the rock which melts. **Magma** is the name given to molten rock in the mantle.

Two important geological events happen where these plates collide.

★ the molten rock or magma rises up towards the surface, erupting to form **volcanoes**

★ there is an enormous force as one plate rubs against the other. Sometimes the plates become jammed and pressure builds up over a few years.

Suddenly, the plates pull apart. This releases a huge amount of energy, causing the ground to shake – an **earthquake**.

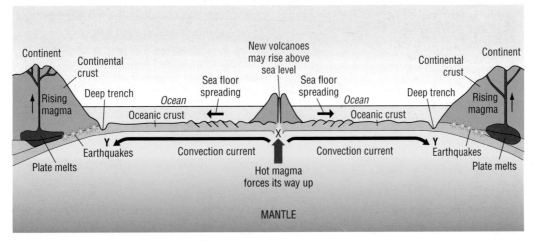

**Figure 5.8** A simplified diagram of parting and colliding plates

## *Sliding plates*

The photograph shows the San Andreas Fault. It runs through California, near San Francisco and is famous for its earthquakes in 1906 and 1989. Earthquakes happen here because the huge Pacific Plate slides past the North American Plate. When the plates stick and later slip apart, the strain on the land sends out massive shockwaves.

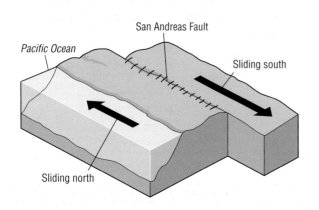

**Figure 5.9** San Andreas Fault as a diagram and photo

## TO TAKE YOU FURTHER

# Continental and oceanic plates

One of the most important factors influencing the nature of earthquakes and the effect of volcanic eruptions at plate boundaries concerns the nature of the crust forming the plates. Basically there are two types of crust:

◆ **continental crust** is the lighter, older and thicker of the two. Because it is lighter, continental crust is unable to sink into the mantle below, so it is never destroyed. As a result, it is very old, geologically speaking – often 3,500 million years in places.

◆ **oceanic crust** forms the ocean floors. It is the heavier, younger (only 200 million years), and thinner of the two types. Compared to the granite of the continental crust, the basalt of the oceanic crust can sink down into the mantle. There it is melted and destroyed because of the high temperatures and pressure.

### ASSIGNMENTS *TO TAKE YOU FURTHER*

**1**  a)  Name 3 plates with continents on them.
   b)  Name two plates without continents on them.
   c)  Name the plate on which Britain is located.
   d)  Which two plates meet near San Francisco?
   e)  Which three plates are likely to affect Japan?
   f)  Which two plates divide New Zealand?

**2**  Copy and complete the following sentences using the words highlighted below:
   ◆  The plates meeting in Iceland are _____ .
   ◆  The Nazca Plate and the South American Plate are _____ .
   ◆  The Pacific Plate and North American Plate are _____ _____ each other near San Francisco.

   **sliding past, colliding, parting**

*continued* ➤

**TO TAKE YOU FURTHER** continued

3  Look at Figures 5.6 and 5.7. Complete the following sentences, selecting the correct highlighted words.
   ◆  Earthquakes and volcanoes tend to occur in **narrow belts/all over the world**.
   ◆  These belts coincide with the **middle/edge** of a plate.
   ◆  One very important belt of volcanoes and earthquake activity is called the 'Ring of Fire' and lies around the rim of the **Atlantic/Pacific Ocean**.

4  Explain how new crust is formed where plates are parting.

5  Explain what happens to oceanic crust when it collides with continental crust.

6  Describe how volcanoes and earthquakes can happen when oceanic and continental crusts collide.

**TO TAKE YOU FURTHER**

# Fold mountains

In some places, two continental plates are colliding. Because they are made of lighter material and will not sink into the mantle, they slowly and steadily push, buckle and fold up any layers of sedimentary rocks lying between them. One example is the Indian Plate, which 45 million years ago, drove northwards into the Eurasian Plate, pushing up the dramatic folds of the Himalayas – the world's highest mountain range. This pressure continues and is responsible for:

◆  the Himalayas continuing to gain height (5mm/year)

◆  the earthquakes which affect South Asia, for example, Gujarat in 2001 (see page 89).

**ASSIGNMENTS** *TO TAKE YOU FURTHER*

1  Draw up a table to bring out the main differences between continental and oceanic crust

2  a)  With the help of an atlas, show the following fold mountains on a blank world map: Himalayas, Andes, Alps, Atlas and Rockies. Add a title and key.
   b)  Explain how fold mountains are formed, referring to the Himalayas.

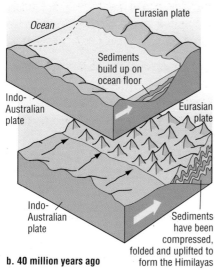

**Figure 5.10**  Formation of the Himalayas as a diagram and photo

# Volcanoes and predicting eruptions

## An unexpected eruption

Eruption of Galeras – a dormant volcano in the Andes of SW Colombia (14 Jan 1993).

> *'The volcano began to shake, and I turned to run … I had made only a few metres when the air was rent by a sound like a thunderclap or a sonic boom. Immediately afterwards, I heard a deafening cra-a-a-ck, the sound of the earth's crust snapping…I flew down the slope and then the rock hit me. It was as if someone had taken a swing at my head with a baseball bat … a bone protruded from my lower left leg … another rock had nearly severed my right foot at the ankle…'*
>
> Stanley Williams

Stanley Williams was one of a group of geologists working in the volcano, in the mistaken belief that it was safe, when it erupted. He was felled by a rock that tore a hole in his head, exposing his brain. Another barrage broke both legs. He suffered two cracked vertebrae, a smashed jaw, and severe burns from the fire, which consumed his backpack and clothes. He survived, but nine of the geologists died instantly, their bodies smashed by falling rocks.

## Types of volcanoes

Galeras is one of some 1,500 volcanoes in the world. It was thought to be **dormant**, or sleeping. As the extract suggests, it quickly became **active**. Some of the worst ever eruptions have come from volcanoes believed to be dormant. Over 30,000 were killed in 1991 when Mount Pinatubo in the Phillipines erupted. It had been dormant for 600 years. Many volcanoes are **extinct**, or dead. Arthur's Seat in central Edinburgh is a long extinct volcano.

## A composite volcano such as Galeras

Volcanoes are formed by molten material from the mantle. It is called **magma** and is forced through an opening in the earth's crust called a **vent**. When the magma comes out of the ground, it is called **lava**.

One of the main types of volcanoes is called a **composite** volcano (Figure 5.11) and has the following main features:

★ it is usually **cone-shaped**

★ it is formed from **layers of lava and ash**

★ at the summit of the main vent there is a bowl-shaped pit called a **crater**.

## A composite volcano erupts

When composite volcanoes erupt they can be very violent. Figure 5.11 shows that the volcano erupts when magma, under enormous pressure, is forced up the vent from the chamber. Usually, magma is expelled through the main crater:

★ firstly, as steam, gas, dust, ash and lava bombs. Ash and dust are formed when earlier solidified rocks are shattered with explosive force into tiny pieces. **Lava bombs** (some as big as houses) are formed from blobs of lava that cool down in flight. Some have been tossed up as high as 10 km.

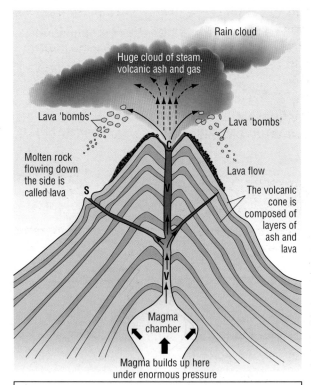

**Figure 5.11**　A composite volcano

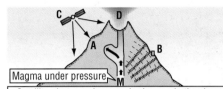

Volcanic ash may be punched higher and further into the atmosphere. For example, two weeks after Mount Pinataubo erupted in 1991, its ash had circled the earth.

★ secondly, as a covering layer of slow-moving lava. Over the years, the layers of ash and lava build up to form a typical composite volcano.

## A famous eruption

Millions of years ago, the earth was certainly more volcanic than today. Yet there are still around 600 active volcanoes in the world. Their eruptions can be both awesome and destructive. Whole landscapes can be altered, even obliterated; climate can be affected; and lives drastically changed.

Perhaps the best known example is Krakatoa (see Figure 5.7 for its location). It was a small island between Java and Sumatra. Today it is a lot smaller! When it blew off its top in 1883, the energy of the explosion was 5,000 times as great as the Hiroshima atomic bomb. Vast amounts of material were ejected, resulting in the world's loudest ever eruption. Sound waves from the explosion were heard in Australia, almost 2,000 km away. Fine volcanic dust spread through the atmosphere and lowered the earth's temperature by several degrees for the following year. Worse still: the eruption triggered a 40 metre high wave called a **tsunami**. It smashed into hundreds of coastal

settlements up to 80 km away. Most of the 40,000 victims of Krakatoa were drowned by the tsunami.

## Predicting eruptions

Volcanoes kill, but, nowadays, scientists use different ways of forecasting eruptions. Some of the methods are shown in Figure 5.12.

- Satellite photography records changes in the shape and temperature of the volcano
- Large swelling on the side of the volcano
- Tremors as deep as 55km can be detected by seismometers
- Instruments can detect gas emissions

**Figure 5.12** Predicting explosive eruptions

**Figure 5.13** Popocatepetl ('Smoking Mountain')

## ASSIGNMENTS

1 Match the following beginnings with the correct endings (highlighted below):
A volcano that regularly erupts is _____.
A volcano that is not expected to erupt again is

_____.

A volcano which has not erupted for several thousand years but might erupt again is_____.

**extinct, dormant, active**

2 Look at Figure 5.11 and read about the cone erupting.
Describe what happens when a volcano erupts by putting the following stages into a sensible order.

- gas, steam, ash and lava bombs are blown out through the crater
- lava flows down the side of the volcano
- magma builds up under great pressure in the chamber
- magma erupts through the vent

3 Look at Figure 5.11. Make a table showing the (i) different parts of the volcano and (ii) explaining how they were formed.

4 Look at Figure 5.12 Match the letters A–D with the four methods of predicting eruptions.

### Predictions at Popocatepetl

On 18 December 2000, some 30,000 people were evacuated from villages close to Popocatepetl. New monitoring techniques that listen to the 'sounds' of pressure building up in the volcano were successful in predicting Popocatepetl's biggest eruption for a thousand years.

**Figure 5.14**  A monitoring station for Kilauea

**TO TAKE YOU FURTHER**

Not all volcanoes look alike. Not all active volcanoes erupt in the same way. A lot depends on the type of lava and the different conditions under which volcanoes erupt. All the volcanic examples below are found in different states of the USA. All have a different effect on the landscape.

### Shield and dome volcanoes

Unlike composite volcanoes, which are formed from lava and ash, shield and dome volcanoes are made up from hardened lava.

◆ **Shield volcanoes** are formed from lava that is thin and runny. Figure 5.15 shows Mauna Loa, the world's largest volcano, on the island of Hawaii. Over a few million years, thousands of gentle lava flows have spread from the main vent. These flows are only a few metres thick and are formed from basalt. The diagram shows the gentle slopes of Mauna Loa which is similar to its neighbour Kilauea. The whole structure rises from the floor of the Pacific Ocean and is almost 10,000 metres high – even taller than Mount Everest!

◆ **Dome volcanoes**, however, are formed from lava so thick that it can hardly flow. It quickly cools and hardens into a steep-sided, rounded mass of rock. Frequently, the lava in the vent hardens and forms a plug. This traps gases and magma under enormous pressure until a giant explosion occurs.

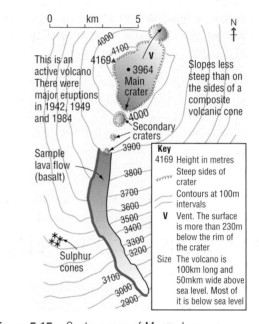

**Figure 5.15**  Contour map of Mauna Loa

**Figure 5.16**  The eruption of Mount St Helens

*continued* ➤

## TO TAKE YOU FURTHER continued

One of the best examples is Mount St Helens. For several months, its northern side had been swelling. On 18 May 1980, a large earthquake triggered an enormous landslide. This released gas and steam under enormous pressure which blasted sideways an enormous chunk of the mountain top (Figure 5.16).

### Calderas

Figure 5.17 shows Crater Lake, Oregon. Some 8 km in diameter, the lake occupies a caldera. Calderas are steep-sided, basin-shaped depressions. They are much larger than craters. Crater Lake caldera formed when a volcanic cone called Mount Mazama collapsed. After Mazama erupted, the volcano collapsed through the roof of its emptied magma chamber. Since then, a later eruption has formed a small cone called Wizard Island. It rises from the floor of the caldera some 260 metres above the surface of the lake. Some 670 metres deep, and very deep blue, it was gradually filled by rain and melting snow.

### ASSIGNMENTS TO TAKE YOU FURTHER

1 Draw a table to show the main differences between shield and dome volcanoes.

2 a) Draw a labelled sketch of Crater Lake caldera to show: Wizard Island; the steep sides of the caldera; Crater lake in the caldera.

   b) Write a short, illustrated account explaining how Crater Lake was formed.

**Figure 5.17**   Wizard Island on Crater Lake, Oregon

# Lava on the move: Mount Nyiragongo, 2002

**Figure 5.18**   Lava flowing in Goma

## "NYIRAGONGO VOLCANO DISASTER" DEMOCRATIC REPUBLIC OF CONGO

"A river of lava 800 metres wide had bulldozed through Goma town centre, oozing into sidestreets and pouring into the lake on the far side. A fog of hot air and sulphurous steam hung over the burning ruins. Creaking and groaning, the lava slowed and cooled into a wall of black rock, three metres deep in places."

www.volcanolive.com
20 Jan 2002

## Location of Nyiragongo

Nyiragongo is one of Africa's most active volcanoes. 3465 metres high, it lies in the Democratic Republic of the Congo, very close to the neighbouring country of Rwanda. Figure 5.19 also shows the town of Goma. It lies 18 km south of the summit of Nyiragongo and is built on the shore of Lake Kivu.

In January 2002 Goma, had a population of over 500,000. Many of these were refugees who had fled the civil wars that afflicted this part of central Africa in the 1990s.

## Nyiragongo erupts (again)

At 11 am, on Thursday, January 17th, 2002, Nyiragongo erupted, pouring out a swift-flowing stream of lava (Figure 5.18). Goma lay directly in its path of destruction. Within 24 hours:

★ up to 500,000 people had fled, mainly to Gisenyi from Goma and the surrounding area

★ 14 villages, and 50% of Goma had been destroyed by the advancing wall of lava, up to 3 metres high in places

★ 45 people had been killed. More, many of them looters, died later as heat from the lava set off explosions at fuel stores, petrol and power stations

★ only two out of four hospitals were left standing, water treatment plants were destroyed and electricity supplies were cut

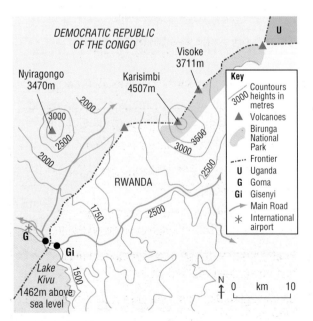

**Figure 5.19** Mount Nyiragongo and Goma

Only when the lava flowed into Lake Kivu did it stop, clouds of steam billowing up from the waters as the lava cooled.

## Return to Goma

By Sunday, the 20th, people began to return home to a devastated Goma.

> *"they retraced their steps, carrying on their heads their household possessions. Women balanced huge bundles of sticks and clothes. Men bore battered and bursting suitcases. Children carried chickens. One old chap even balanced a bicycle on his shoulders."*
>
> **The Independent 21 Jan 02**

Returning to Goma involved various risks:

★ people had to cross the thin, brittle crust on top of the lava, still as hot as 1000°C

★ poisonous sulphurous fumes were given off by the lava

★ water supplies were contaminated and people were drinking from Lake Kivu

★ earth tremors suggested that further eruptions were a possibility.

Yet people were willing to take these risks rather than stay in refugee camps in Rwanda. The camps reminded them of the civil wars which had affected Central Africa.

> *"There is no food, no water, no sanitation. We are here like animals. If we are to die, it is better to die in Congo, not Rwanda."*
> Richard Mwambo *The Independent* 21 Jan 02

## Aid to Goma

As a result of civil war, aid organisations were already in the area. Agencies such as *Save the Children* rushed essential supplies to Goma. These included:

★ tents, plastic sheeting, bedding and blankets

★ water purification equipment to prevent the problem of cholera

★ food and medical supplies.

Goma's residents began to reconstruct the town. Teams of people smashed the hardened lava into small pieces (Figure 5.20), and bulldozed them into rough roads. However, it will take years to rebuild the town. Some geologists suggest that it should not be rebuilt at all because of the threat of yet another eruption.

## Nyiragongo and the African Rift valley

Another eruption, with huge risks for people, is highly likely. This active composite volcano:

★ has erupted 20 times since 1884

★ holds the record for the fastest-ever lava flow. In 1977 up to 300 people and a herd of elephants were killed when lava suddenly flowed down Nyiragongo's steep side at up to 100 km per hour

★ is located on the edge of the Great Rift Valley (Figure 5.21). This valley, and its branches, stretches 5,000 km from Israel to

**Figure 5.20**   Hardened lava in Goma

Mozambique. It is a deep, steep-sided, trench with cracks called faults at its sides. It includes some of the world's most active volcanoes, including Nyiragongo. Figure 5.22 shows that the Rift Valley has formed where plates are parting.

## The African Rift valley in the future

Geologists believe that the Great Rift Valley is slowly splitting apart. In a hundred million years, a large chunk of East Africa will be pushed into the Indian Ocean (see Figure 5.21).

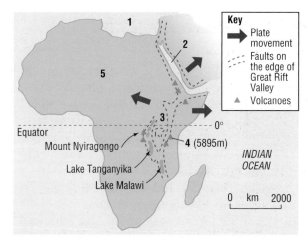

**Figure 5.21**   The Great Rift Valley and Parting Plates

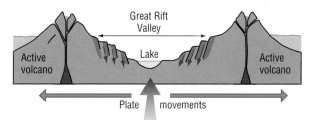

**Figure 5.22**   Cross-section through Great Rift Valley

## ASSIGNMENTS

**1**   Look at Figure 5.21. With the help of an atlas, name seas 1 and 2, lake 3, mountain 4, continent 5.

**2**   Read about the eruption of Nyiragongo. Answer the following
   a)   Where is Nyiragongo located?
   b)   When did the eruption take place?
   c)   What form did the eruption take – a massive explosion of ash and gases or a very fast flowing stream of lava?
   d)   What damage did the eruption do?
   e)   How many people were affected and in what ways?

**3**   a)   Why did people return to Goma so soon?
   b)   What risks did they face as they returned?

**4**   Explain the need for the different types of aid that were sent to the survivors.

**5**   Draw a fully labelled sketch of main physical and human features shown in the photograph (Figure 5.18).

**6**   Briefly describe the location, length and main features of the Great Rift valley.

**7**   Do you agree that Goma should not be rebuilt? Give reasons for your answer.

## TO TAKE YOU FURTHER

# People and volcanic landscapes

## *Volcanoes – dangerous assets?*

Volcanoes are usually thought of as purely destructive features of the landscape. Out of the 550 active volcanoes, one out of every six has killed people and damaged settlements by means of:

◆ explosive blasts
◆ dangerous gases
◆ rapid lava flows and
◆ ash falls.

Yet millions of people live on or close to active volcanoes such as Mount Etna, often at high population densities. In spite of the possible risk, many are willing to live close to such a potentially dangerous natural hazard. Figure 5.23 shows that there are many benefits from volcanic activity, both past and present. It shows that the soils formed from volcanic rock are very fertile. Building materials, thermal energy, dramatic scenery and world famous sites such as Pompeii and the Giant's Causeway are other beneficial results of volcanic activity.

### ASSIGNMENTS *TO TAKE YOU FURTHER*

1 Look at Figure 5.23. Match the numbers 1 to 10 with the bullet points in the key.
   ◆ volcanic rock quarried for buildings, for example, Aberdeen
   ◆ rich soil weathered from volcanic rock like Java
   ◆ geysers and hot springs such as those in Yellowstone National Park, USA
   ◆ sacred mountains such as Mount Fuji, Japan
   ◆ hot water for towns, greenhouses and geothermal energy like in Reykjavik, Iceland
   ◆ rugged mountainous scenery like Yosemite National Park

   ◆ defensive site for settlements such as Edinburgh
   ◆ defensive site for walls such like Hadrian's Wall
   ◆ sites of historic interest such as Pompeii, Italy
   ◆ famous landmarks, for example, Giant's Causeway, Northern Ireland

2 Either write a fully illustrated report on a volcanic eruption that you have researched. You should cover:
   ◆ when it happened;
   ◆ its location;
   ◆ the features of the eruption;
   ◆ the cause of the eruption;
   ◆ the damage and the effect on people.

   Or write a fully illustrated report on People using Volcanic Landscapes. (It should cover: the different ways in which people have used volcanic features.) Your report should have an introduction and a conclusion. You should use simple maps and diagrams that you have drawn yourself. Use a variety of sources, for example, textbooks, travel books, maps, photographs as well as the internet. Do not copy or download large chunks of text or maps and claim that they are your own work.

**Figure 5.24**   Outdoor swimming pool in Reykjavik

**Figure 5.23**   Using volcanic landscapes

# Our trembling earth

## 1906: an earthquake strikes

The 1906 San Francisco earthquake (Figure 5.25) struck the city at 5.13 a.m, with "a rumble and a roar". It lasted 65 seconds and was the deadliest to ever strike the USA. Two-thirds of the city was destroyed. Most of the damaged buildings were concentrated in the reclaimed waterfront area, built of landfill. The landfill material shook vigorously. Houses collapsed and streets buckled – "It was as if the waves of the ocean were coming towards me". Then fires broke out, including one started by a woman cooking bacon and eggs on a faulty stove. That fire burnt down most of the city's Central Business District. These fires could not be put out because there were burst waterpipes and so blocks of houses were dynamited to make firebreaks. Eventually, the fires died out. Some 700 people had perished in the earthquake and over 300 000 were left homeless.

Since 1906, the people of San Francisco keep asking questions:

★ When will the next quake strike?

★ What damage will it cause?

★ How many will be killed now that the city is much bigger?

## What is an earthquake?

An earthquake is a trembling or shaking of the ground. Every year, the earth is affected by over a million earthquakes. Most of these vibrations are too weak to be felt. When they are severe, however, earthquakes can have the deadliest impact of all natural disasters.

## What causes earthquakes?

Earthquakes can occur almost anywhere, but most occur in narrow bands where plates meet. The largest concentration is around the 'Pacific Rim of Fire', especially in Japan and California (Figure 5.26).

Sometimes the plates stick together. Pressure builds up. Eventually, and suddenly, the plates jerk apart. This sudden movement release enormous amounts of energy in the form of **shock** or **seismic waves** which trigger off earthquakes on the earth's surface.

Figure 5.27 shows two important earthquake features:

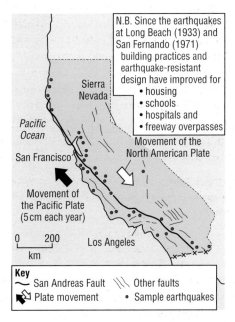

**Figure 5.26**    California: faults and sample earthquakes

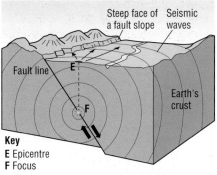

**Figure 5.27**    Focus and epicentre of an earthquake

**Figure 5.25**    San Francisco earthquake (1906)

★ the **focus** – this is the place in the earth's crust where the earthquake starts. Most focuses are less than 100 km from the surface.

★ the **epicentre** – this is the place on the earth's surface directly above the focus. From here the shock waves spread out over the earth's surface rather like ripples on a pond when a stone is thrown.

## Recording and measuring earthquakes

The seismic waves produced by strong earthquakes can travel through the earth's core and reach the other side of the world in 20 minutes. These waves are detected using very sensitive instruments called **seismometers**. The size of the waves is recorded on a **seismograph** (Figure 5.28). The size of the waves indicates the strength of the earthquake.

Two scales are used to describe the strength of an earthquake:

★ the **Mercalli scale** measures the amount of damage that is caused

★ the **Richter scale** measures the amount of energy that has been released. On this scale (Figure 5.29), scale 6 is 10 times as powerful as scale 5, and scale 7 is 10 times more powerful than scale 6, and so on.

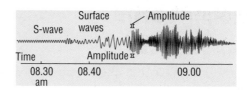

**Figure 5.28** Seismogram of Gujarat earthquake (26 Jan 2001)

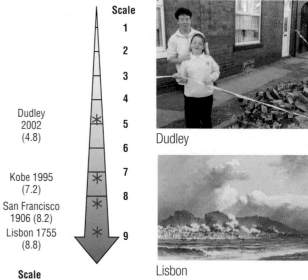

**Scale**
1 Only detectable by instruments
2-3 Hardly felt, even at the epicentre
3-4 Minor tremor, but little damage
4-5 Felt over a wide area, and small-scale structual damage
6-7 Quite destructive. Poorly constructed buildings collapse
7-8 Major earthquake: extensive damage
8-9 Mega earthquake. Cracks in ground open up

**Figure 5.29** The Richter scale and sample earthquakes

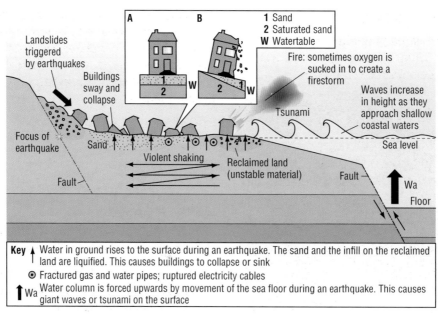

**Figure 5.30** The impact of earthquakes in the 'Pacific Rim'

## The impact of earthquakes

The effects of an earthquake depend on various factors:

★ the strength of the earthquake

★ the depth of the focus. Usually, a shallow focus causes more damage on the earth's surface

★ the number of people living near the epicentre

★ when it strikes – at night or during the day, for example, rush hour in a crowded city

★ the strength and design of the buildings

★ whether it happens in a rich or a poor country.

Figure 5.30 shows the possible effects of an earthquake in the 'Pacific Rim'.

## ASSIGNMENTS

1 Copy and complete the following sentences using the words highlighted below:
An _____ is a violent shaking of the earth's crust.
Earthquakes are concentrated in _____ where _____ meet.
Earthquakes start in the earth's crust at the _____ and the place on the surface directly above is the _____ .
A _____ is a huge wave caused by an undersea earthquake.
**plates; tsunami; earthquake; belts; epicentre; focus**

2 What does the Richter scale measure? Give some examples.

3 a) Under the heading answer the following questions.
**1906 San Francisco 'Quake**.
b) Where and when did the earthquake happen?
c) Why did it happen?
d) What were the effects of the earthquake?

4 Why do some earthquakes cause more damage than others?

## TO TAKE YOU FURTHER

# Reducing the earthquake threat

### Predicting earthquakes

Although the earliest earthquake predictor was developed by the Chinese as early as 132 AD (Figure 5.31) successful forecasts are rare.

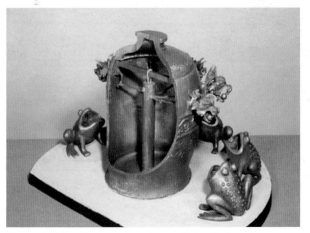

**Figure 5.31** Early earthquake predictor (Chinese)

The Chinese did successfully predict the 1975 Haicheng earthquake (7.3 on the Richter scale). Some 300 people were killed but thousands of lives were saved. However, the following year 300,000 perished in Tangshan (7.8 on the Richter scale).

Prediction methods include:

◆ lasers which are used to detect small earth movements near fault lines

◆ seismograms which show early tremors or foreshocks

◆ analysis of water levels in wells (rocks may become more porous because of stresses)

◆ studying animal behaviour, for example, snakes come to the surface and fish in ponds become agitated.

*continued* ➤

**TO TAKE YOU FURTHER** *continued*

## Preparing for earthquakes

In spite of these attempts, earthquakes cannot be consistently predicted. Perhaps the best answer is to minimise the impact of an earthquake. Figure 5.33 shows some of the methods that are used to prepare for earthquakes in places such as Japan and California. These include:

- constructing earthquake-proof buildings such as reinforced concrete structures, designed to sway and twist without falling down (Figure 5.32)

- deep foundations sunk into solid bedrock with rubber shock-absorbers absorbing the seismic waves

- heavy weights on the top of high-rise buildings providing a counter-movement to any shaking of the structure

- shutters shutting down over windows so that people are not showered with glass

- pedestrians evacuating buildings and assembling in open areas

- holding practice evacuation drills, for example, on 1 September in Tokyo (the anniversary of the Great Kanto earthquake 1923)

- special instruments called **accelerometers** shutting down the Tokaido railway if an earthquake is detected.

### ASSIGNMENTS *TO TAKE YOU FURTHER*

1 Suggest why is it very difficult to predict earthquakes and describe the main methods of prediction that are used.

2 Read the section on 'Preparing for earthquakes' Seven preparation methods are described. Match each method with the letters A to G shown on Figure 5.33.

3 Refer to the text and to Figure 5.26. Why is California so prone to earthquakes?

4 Mini-research topics. With the assistance of reference texts, write brief notes on ONE of the following:
  A What are P, S and L waves? Which cause the most damage and why? Which earthquake waves travel the fastest?
  B What is the modified Mercalli scale? Draw a series of diagrams to illustrate the various earthquake impacts shown on this scale.

**Figure 5.32**   An earthquake-proof building

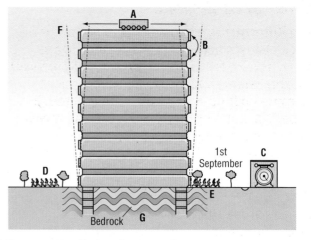

**Figure 5.33**   Earthquake prevention

# A tale of two earthquakes

**FACTFILE**

**Location**: Kobe-Osaka, Japan
**Population**: 1.4 million
**Date**: January 16th, 1995
**Time**: 5.46 am
**Richter scale**: 7.2
**Duration**: 20 seconds
**Death toll**: 6,500 killed 22,000 injured

**FACTFILE**

**Location**: Gujarat state, North-West India
**Population**: 51 million
**Date**: January 26th, 2001
**Time**: 8.50 am
**Richter scale**: 7.9
**Duration**: 2 minutes
**Death toll**: 30,000 killed 150,000 injured

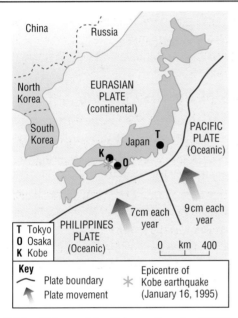

**Figure 5.34**  Plates and the Kobe earthquake (1995)

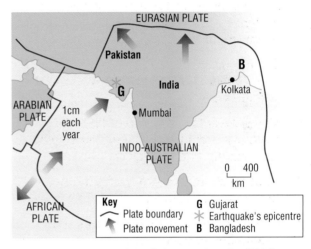

**Figure 5.36**  Plates and the Gujarat earthquake (2001)

## Cause of earthquake

The Kobe earthquake was caused by two of the three plates which meet near Japan (Figure 5.34). The Philippine plate usually slides beneath the **Eurasian plate** but it stuck. Enormous pressure built up on a **fault** running through Kobe. When it moved, powerful seismic waves spread out, causing the worst earthquake to strike Japan since Tokyo was devastated in 1923.

## A devastating earthquake

The impact of this quake was particularly severe because:

★ the **focus** was shallow, only 30 km below the earth's surface

★ the **epicentre** was close to Kobe

★ Kobe, like other Japanese cities, is a very densely populated urban area.

## Cause of earthquake

Earthquakes are not unknown in India. They occur because the Indo-Australian plate is colliding with the Eurasian plate. Figure 5.36 shows that the epicentre near the town of Bhuj is not located near the edge of plates. However, huge pressures built up in the faults in the Ran of Kutch. When one snapped, seismic waves spread out, causing India's most powerful earthquake since 1956.

## A devastating earthquake

This earthquake had a severe impact because:

★ the strong seismic pressures resulted in a quake that lasted almost a minute

★ population density is high in the settlements

★ many buildings were not built to withstand earthquakes.

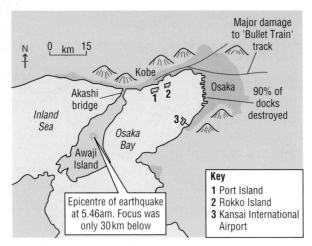

**Figure 5.35** Features of Kobe-Osaka area

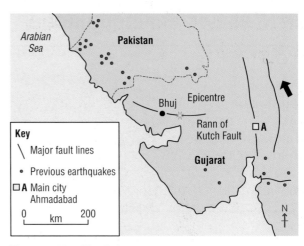

**Figure 5.37** The Gujarat area

## Effects of the earthquake

Although Japan is the world's best prepared country for earthquakes, this one was not expected. The estimated cost was $90 billion and showed that even the richest areas can be devastated by earthquakes.

**Primary effects** – the immediate impact involved:

★ the destruction of almost 200,000 buildings, killing and trapping people inside the rubble. These included older wooden houses with heavy roof tiles designed to withstand typhoons. Floors of taller buildings constructed in the 1970s 'pancaked' as the floors piled up. However, newer earthquake-proof buildings survived

★ the collapse of stretches of elevated motorway and bridges along the Tokkaido railway line (see Figure 5.38).

**Secondary effects**

★ hundreds of fires swept through the city. These spread from fractured gas pipes, damaged electricity cables and domestic gas cookers

★ thousands were made homeless. Many were afraid to return home because of powerful aftershocks

★ broken water pipes and blocked roads made it difficult for the fire and other rescue services to assist

★ initially there was a shortage of blankets, emergency food supplies and clean water.

## Effects of the earthquake

Although Gujarat state is one of the most prosperous in India, many people are poor and the authorities were not well prepared. The impact was enormous, costing some £3 billion, and damage spread across an area the size of Scotland.

**Primary effects** – the immediate impact involved:

★ the flattening of large parts of cities and villages, killing and trapping people. Many concrete high-rise apartment blocks, some only 4 years old, collapsed. In Ahmedabad some of the flats were built of sub-standard materials. In some villages, roofs loosely attached the walls collapse on to the houses. Yet, houses constructed in the traditional way survived (see Figure 5.40 below).

**Secondary effects**

★ gas and water pipelines, phone lines and power stations were knocked out

★ thousands of people were homeless. Many stayed out in the streets because they were afraid of the effect of aftershocks

★ at first there was a shortage of blankets, tents, plastic sheeting and medical supplies. Clean water supplies and water purification tablets were scarce.

# Experiencing the 1995 Kobe earthquake

**5.46 am**

It is impossible for me to ever forget the very rude wake up call in my Kobe hotel at precisely 5.46 am. The most awful sounds of steel being stressed, coupled with the banging of building panels and the crash of moveable objects, all combined to make me painfully aware that I was in the middle of a nightmare.

Trying to stand was impossible in the first moments and any attempt resulted in an opposing force sending me crashing into some piece of furniture or a wall. I could see the rolling surfaces of the room heaving and at times leaving cracks large enough to put your hand into only to find, seconds later, that they had closed again.

**6.30 am**

The hotel staff were mustering everyone in the lobby. Continual aftershocks and raw fear prevented us from venturing outside and, since flying glass can be a major cause of casualties, we huddled in the lobby.

**The next day**

In the city centre, many multi-storey buildings were leaning at crazy angles, in others the floors had collapsed on each other. The more damaged structures appeared to have been built in the sixties and seventies. More modern buildings appeared to have survived.

In the suburbs there was mass destruction of homes, mostly wooden houses. Fire had taken its awful toll on those trapped in the wreckage of family homes.

Survivors had set up camp in the nearest car park with what meagre belongings they were able to retrieve. Camp consisted of a blanket on the ground, huddled around a fire made from the shattered ruins. Piped water was generally non-existent but I noticed several hand-operated pumps bringing water from old wells. Some shopkeepers were setting up stalls on the pavements , selling foodstuffs. It was interesting and heartening to notice the complete lack of looting.

Written by an Australian businessman

# Experiencing the 2001 Gujarat earthquake

We spent Saturday night in Bhuj in our car – there was no electricity in the town, no running water, no telephones, no relief work in progress, and we were lucky to cadge a plate of rice and potato for supper from a roadside soup kitchen. In the morning we drove to Bacchau, a town of 25,000 people full of concrete buildings, nearly all of which have been crippled or smashed.

We walked up to the Sida Bachal apartments: four storeys now, it was six storeys on Friday morning. At 8.46 am on Friday the ground and first floors simply disappeared … A platoon of the Indian Army's Engineers had arrived … Yesterday they brought three people out. "We're bringing two more out now." … And here they came. The young woman came first, dressed in a sari, her hair stiff with dust, her face, too, caked with it, and the expression on her face frozen with shock, pain or terror … Her husband followed, ashen with dust…

The army's sappers have set to work briskly and effectively. But it has to be said that this is too little, too late and too ill-organised because the disaster is of an awesome, formidable scale…

Every where in Bacchau the clinging sweet smell of rotting flesh is rising mixed with the acrid fumes and black smoke of fires, as corpses pulled out of the wreckage, are burned on the street with paraffin for fuel.

The Independent 29 Jan 01

**Figure 5.38**  Collapsed railway on Tokkaido line

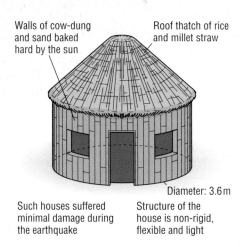

Walls of cow-dung and sand baked hard by the sun

Roof thatch of rice and millet straw

Diameter: 3.6 m

Such houses suffered minimal damage during the earthquake

Structure of the house is non-rigid, flexible and light

**Figure 5.40**  A traditional Kutchi house

**Figure 5.39**  Emergency teams in Kobe

**Figure 5.41**  Collapsed buildings in Ahmadabad

## ASSIGNMENTS

Attempt question 1 **or** question 2.

**1**  For either Kobe or Gujarat or a case study you have researched, write a fully illustrated report about the earthquake and its effects. You should cover: its location; when it happened; its strength and which plate movements were responsible; the effects of the earthquake on the place and the people; the need for aid and any difficulties in receiving aid.

**2**  Choose two earthquakes, one in a rich country and one in a poor country.
a)  Outline the main features of the two earthquakes.
b)  Compare the effects of the earthquakes and explain the differences between them.

Your report should have a brief introduction and conclusion. Draw your own maps and diagrams. Use a variety of sources, for example, textbooks, travel books, maps, photographs as well as the internet.

Do not copy or download large chunks of text or maps and claim that they are your own work.

# Chapter 6 Farming and Conservation

## Distribution of different types of farming

Farming involves growing crops and raising animals. The map in Figure 6.1 shows that: much of the British Isles is used for farming and that farming differs from one area to another. Over many years, farmers in different parts of the British Isles have developed their own type of farming. These include:

★ **Arable farming** which means that most of the land is ploughed and crops such as wheat, barley, potatoes are grown. The map shows that it is found mainly in the east. Generally, the land is low-lying, soils are fertile and summers are dry ,warm and sunny. Usually, farms and fields are large, and farmers use a lot of machinery.

★ **Hill farming** involves raising mainly sheep and some beef cattle on the rough pasture (coarse grasses and heather) found in mountains and hills. The land is often too steep for machinery, soils are thin and poor, and the cold, wet climate makes it difficult to grow crops.

★ **Stock farming** mainly involves the rearing and fattening of mainly beef cattle such as Aberdeen Angus, and sheep.

However, farming can be a very risky business. Crops can fail because of poor weather conditions, a disease striking a crop, or a sudden drop in prices for farm products. So most farmers choose:

★ **Mixed farming** – farmers earn their money by selling both crops and livestock. Figure 6.1 shows that many farms mix arable with dairy farming.

★ **Dairy farming** involves growing permanent grass, and grazing dairy herds such as Friesians and Jerseys for milk production. It is mainly found in western lowland areas

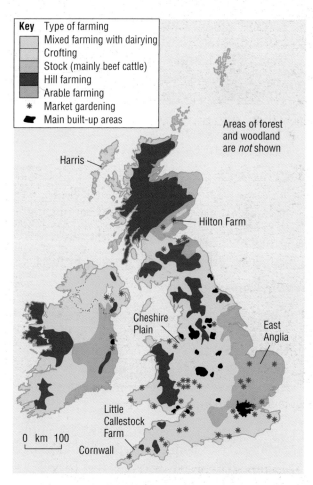

**Key**  Type of farming
Mixed farming with dairying
Crofting
Stock (mainly beef cattle)
Hill farming
Arable farming
∗  Market gardening
Main built-up areas

Areas of forest and woodland are *not* shown

Harris

Hilton Farm

Cheshire Plain

East Anglia

Little Callestock Farm

Cornwall

0  km  100

**Figure 6.1**   British Isles: simplified map of farming

**Figure 6.2**   Mixed farming landscape

where the high rainfall encourages grass to grow. Some dairying areas such as the Cheshire Plain and Ayrshire are close to large cities such as Liverpool, Manchester and Glasgow. These provide a market for milk and milk products.

Finally, two types of small farming systems are:

★ **Market gardening** – growing fruit vegetables and flowers, usually on small areas of land, and sometimes in glasshouses. The map shows that market gardening is often found close to large cities, for example, London, or in areas with a favourable climate such as south-west England with its very mild winters.

★ **Crofting** is part-time farming found in the remoter western areas of the UK and Ireland. Crofts are small, a few animals are kept, and crops are grown as fodder.

### A guide to some crops and livestock

**Arable** crops include

★ **Cereals** such as wheat, which grows best in dry (<750 mm of rain per year) and warm conditions (>15°C in summer), barley, oil seed rape and oats. Oats survive in wetter areas (>1000 mm a year), and where it is cooler.

★ **Root crops** such as turnips, swedes and potatoes, and **fodder crops** which are used as animal feed, for example, hay (dried grass) and silage (grass allowed to ferment in airtight conditions).

**Extensive farming**, however, means lower yields. In Britain this is typical of hill farms which are usually large but have steeper slopes and poorer soils (Figure 6.3).

**Livestock** includes pigs, poultry and beef cattle such as Aberdeen Angus and Hereford cows, kept for their quality meat. Dairy cattle such as Friesian and Jersey cows are kept for their milk.

**Sheep** such as Blackface and Cheviot breeds survive in upland areas with heavy rainfall (>1500 mm a year), low temperatures and snow.

# Intensive and extensive farming

Compared to farms in Canada, the USA and Australia, farms in Britain are generally smaller. To make a decent living, farmers try to produce the maximum amount from their fields. This is known as **intensive farming**. Because farmers use intensive methods, for example, market gardeners using polythene greenhouses to grow several crops a year, and using a large labour force, they produce a **high yield** from their land.

### ASSIGNMENTS

1 Match the following types of farming with the appropriate description:
   **Hill farming** is … the production of milk from dairy cattle grazed on rich pastures.
   **Dairy farming** is … the growing of crops such as wheat, barley and oil seed rape.
   **Arable farming** … is the growth of fruits, vegetables and flowers.
   **Market gardening** is … the rearing of sheep and beef cattle in upland areas.

2 a) What is **mixed farming**?
   b) What are the advantages of running a mixed farm?

*continued* ➤

**Figure 6.3**  Sheep farming landscape

## ASSIGNMENTS continued

**3** Attempt either this question or question 5.
Look at the map showing the distribution of types
of farming. Complete this paragraph choosing
words from the list below.
In Britain, most mixed farming with _____
is found in the _____ lowlands such as the
Cheshire Plain where there is a lot of permanent
_____. Mixed farming also extends into the
_____. The _____ lowland areas
such as East Anglia have a warm, dry climate and
are suited to _____ farming.
_____ is found in the North-West

Highlands, the Western Isles and western Ireland.
Hill farming is found in uplands such as the
_____ and the _____ mountains.

**crofting; western; dairying; pasture; arable;
eastern; Midlands; Caha; Pennines**

**4** Explain the difference between intensive and
extensive farming.

**5** With the help of climate and relief maps in an atlas,
describe and explain as fully as possible where the
main types of farming are found in the British Isles.

## TO TAKE YOU FURTHER

# Sketching based on a photograph

Photographs of farming scenes can give a great
deal of information. It is useful to draw an
**annotated sketch** (a sketch with notes
attached) to bring out the most important
features of the landscape. Figure 6.5 shows the
main stages involved.

**Figure 6.4**  Mixed farming

**Stage 1:** Draw a frame roughly the same size
as the photograph. Very lightly
sketch in a simple grid.

**Stage 2:** Draw the relief features. remember
relief is the shape of the land. So
outline the highest ground, usually in
the background and lowland,
perhaps with a river in the
foreground.

**Step 3:** Now show smaller features such as:
field boundaries, a shelter belt of
trees a farmhouse/ farm buildings,
any livestock, a farm road etc.

**Step 4:** Label these main features. You
should use arrows to pick out the
features. You can write labels at the
edge of the frame or on the sketch,

**Step 5:** Finish the sketch by adding thinner
lines or shading to show slopes.

## ASSIGNMENTS TO TAKE YOU FURTHER

**1** Figure 6.5 shows a simple sketch based on
Figure 6.4.

Draw a sketch based upon either Figure 6.2
showing a mixed farmscape or Figure 6.3 showing
a hill sheep farmscape.

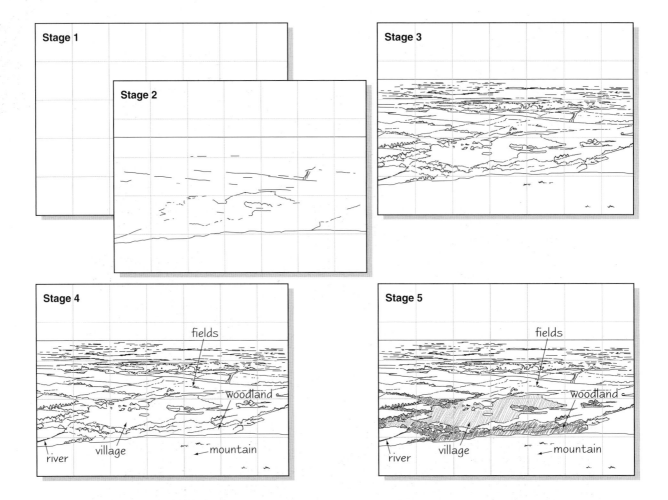

**Figure 6.5**  Sketching a farming landscape

# Making decisions on the farm

## The farmer as a decision maker

From earliest times, farmers have had to make decisions about the crops they want to grow, the machinery they use and the animals they keep. Some factors which might influence a farmer and his family are shown in Figure 6.6. These are:

★ **physical factors** – these are to do with the natural environment. They include the relief (the shape and steepness) of the land, the soil, and the climate

★ **human factors** – these are to do with the influence of people. They include the price of crops or machinery, and rules and regulations laid down by governments.

## The European Union and farmers' decisions

Farmer have their own tried and tested ways of doing things on their farm. But often they have no choice over the decisions they make. For example, they have no control over the weather. Nor do they have much influence over governments. In the EU (European Union), many farmers' decisions have been dictated by rules and regulations made in Brussels. For example:

★ the **CAP** – in 1962, a **Common Agricultural Policy** was agreed. This tried to protect farmers' incomes and to grow as much food as possible. Farmers were too successful, however, and too much food was grown. 'Food mountains' (of wheat, butter and beef) and 'food lakes' (of wine, milk and olive oil) were produced. The CAP is far too expensive, so the EU is now paying farmers to switch to other land uses.

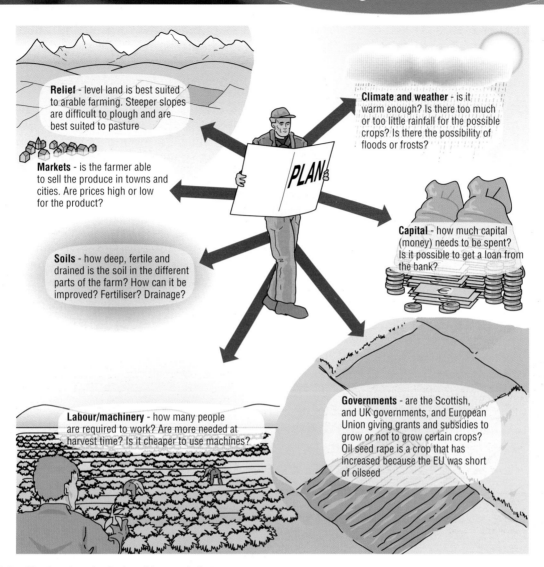

**Relief** - level land is best suited to arable farming. Steeper slopes are difficult to plough and are best suited to pasture

**Climate and weather** - is it warm enough? Is there too much or too little rainfall for the possible crops? Is there the possibility of floods or frosts?

**Markets** - is the farmer able to sell the produce in towns and cities. Are prices high or low for the product?

**Capital** - how much capital (money) needs to be spent? Is it possible to get a loan from the bank?

**Soils** - how deep, fertile and drained is the soil in the different parts of the farm? How can it be improved? Fertiliser? Drainage?

**Labour/machinery** - how many people are required to work? Are more needed at harvest time? Is it cheaper to use machines?

**Governments** - are the Scottish, and UK governments, and European Union giving grants and subsidies to grow or not to grow certain crops? Oil seed rape is a crop that has increased because the EU was short of oilseed

**Figure 6.6**  'Anyfarm' – physical and human influences

★ **Set-Aside scheme** – the EU pays farmers to stop growing crops on part of their arable land. Farmers can choose to: leave land fallow, usually under grass; plant trees – more money is paid for deciduous trees than for coniferous trees; change the land to a non-farming use such as caravan park, golf course, farm shops and farm museums.

These changes are seen as cheaper than storing huge surpluses of food.

## Crises in farming and making decisions

Since the 1990s, decisions have been forced on many farmers because of different crises.

★ **falling incomes** – farmers are not earning so much because the price of many products has fallen such as lamb, beef, pork,

milk etc. This is one of the reasons why farmers are selling their products through Farmers' Markets (see page 101).

**Figure 6.7**  Non-farming use of land: a golf course

★ **BSE** – another reason for loss of money was the ban on British beef exports because of BSE (mad cow disease). On a dairy farm near Telford, one family decided:

*'We had just bought 20 pedigree heifers from Holland when the BSE crisis broke. We paid over £1000 per animal and a week later they were worth less than £400. It was the nail in the coffin … I had been successfully breeding and selling birds as a hobby... We now have 100 or so breeding parrots and can sell hand-reared youngsters for between £200 and £1200'.*

★ **Foot and Mouth disease** – in 2001, over 2000 farms had stock (cattle, sheep and pigs) slaughtered because of Britain's largest ever outbreak of Foot and Mouth disease. Foot and Mouth does not kill the animals but the government policy was to slaughter both infected animals, and neighbouring healthy stock. So, a further 7,000 farms had healthy stock slaughtered to prevent the disease spreading. Farmers in Cumbria were badly affected.

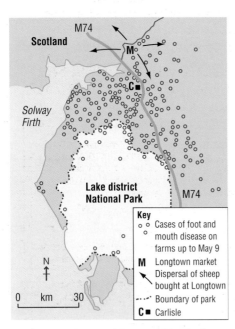

**Figure 6.8** Cases of Foot and Mouth disease in Cumbria (2001)

★ Figure 6.8 shows the concentration of Foot and Mouth cases in the north. Farmers in this area lost flocks and herds built up over many years.

★ Few farms were affected in the Lake District National Park, however, because of strict rules on the movement of animals and people. However, the tourist industry was badly affected. Walking and climbing were restricted as footpaths were closed. Many hill farmers in the National Park lost a great deal of money, especially those who had diversified into tourism, for example, campsites and by running bed and breakfast guest houses.

All farmers were compensated for the loss of their livestock. Many farmers have re-stocked, but some made the final decision: to give up farming completely.

### ASSIGNMENTS

1 Look at the diagram of influences at 'Anyfarm'. List the main physical factors and list the main human factors influencing farmers.

2 a) What EU policy caused 'food mountains and food lakes'? Give examples of the food involved.
 b) What is 'set-aside'?
 c) Which is the best alternative use of arable land – leave it fallow – plant trees or switch to non-farming use? Explain your choice.

3 Look at Figures 6.2 and 6.3 on pages 93–94. They show a hill farm and a mixed farming farmscape. What factors have influenced the farmer's land use decision in each case?

4 Write a short account about the main problems affecting British farmers in recent years.

**TO TAKE YOU FURTHER**

# Family farming in Poland

## Farming in Poland

It has been suggested that in the future there will be even fewer farmers in the UK. There will be more farmers, however, in the EU as a whole. Membership of the EU will increase from 15 to 25 countries by 2004. Poland will be one of these new countries. Figure 6.9 shows some of these new countries, and the location of the Masters farm 50 km east of the historic Polish city of Krakow.

Unlike most 'developed' countries, over 25% of the workforce in Poland still works in farming. Most Polish farms are small, usually less than 8 hectares. The Masters' farm is even smaller, just 3 hectares. Yet it provides work and food for Mr and Mrs Masters and their three children (Figure 6.10).

**Figure 6.9**   Location of the Masters' farm

**Figure 6.10**   The Masters family –

## How the Masters' farm works

Whether large or small, farms are run as a business. The Masters are hoping that, when Poland joins the EU, there will be extra money from grants and subsidies from Brussels.

Figure 6.10 shows the way the Masters' farm works as a business. Like any other farm, the business can be divided into three parts:

◆ input – this is what is put into the farm by the farmer's family (labour, machinery, fertiliser etc.) and nature (soil, rainfall, warmth etc.)

◆ processes – this is the actual work on the farm, for example, growing crops and rearing animals

◆ output – what the farm produces.

The Masters mainly farm for themselves, selling a little meat, cheese and grain. Extra money is made from offering bed and breakfast accommodation to tourists. Mr Masters has joined an organisation which offers organic farm holidays to visitors from Western Europe.

Perhaps, after 2004, the Masters will be better off and able to afford a car and a refrigerator.

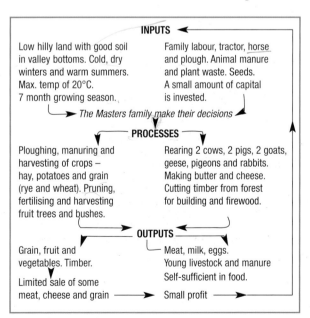

**Figure 6.11**   A Polish organic farm: systems summary

*continued* ➤

**TO TAKE YOU FURTHER** *continued* ➤

### ASSIGNMENTS *TO TAKE YOU FURTHER*

1 With the help of an atlas, name the countries identified by their first letter on the map (Figure 6.9).

2 Write a short description of the Masters' farm. You should cover: location, size, inputs, processes and outputs.

3 Will the Masters benefit from Poland's membership of the EU? Give reasons for your answer.

# Changes at Hilton Farm, Perthshire

## *From arable to mixed*

Two generations of the Johnston family run Hilton Farm which lies 3 km south of Perth (Figure 6.13), near the village of Bridge of Earn. Hilton farm covers an area of 130 hectares. Figure 6.13 shows that its fields face south. They drop from Friarton Hill, about 100 metres high, down to less than 5 metres beside the River Earn. The map also shows that the farm is divided into six blocks by important railway links and the M90 by-pass. This is a nuisance because time is wasted travelling from one part of the farm to another. The farm, however, is centrally located in Scotland and very close to excellent road links (Figure 6.13).

The farm has been in the family for over 70 years. In the early 1990s, like many farms in the area, Hilton was run as an arable farm. Now it is a mixed farm. Crops, such as barley, wheat and turnips, are still grown and cover a lot of the land. However, today, the rearing of wild boar is the main source of income for the Johnstons. Why did they change?

★ the prices of crops such as barley have been falling – farmers, like other business people, have to make a profit

★ in 1993, about 16 hectares of land were flooded (Figure 6.13) – there is always a risk that this could happen again

★ like many other farmers, the Johnstons recognise that farmers need to diversify. **Diversification** means increasing the number of ways in which farmers can make a living. The Johnstons diversified by introducing wild boar.

## *Wild boar*

Figure 6.14 shows some of the wild boar at Hilton farm, one of around 66 farms in the UK which raise this breed of pig. In spite of the name, the wild boar here are no longer 'wild',

**Figure 6.12**  A bypass overlooking Hilton Farm, Perthshire

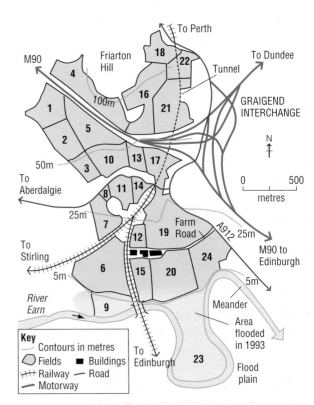

**Figure 6.13**  Hilton Farm: general map

**Figure 6.14**   Wild boar in a field at Hilton Farm

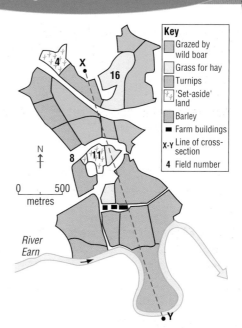

**Figure 6.15**   Land use on Hilton Farm

but all modern farm breeds of pigs are descended from wild boars. They are still wild in the Coto de Doñana. In 1995, the Johnstons started with 10 piglets. Today, there are around 360 wild boar on the farm. They are fed on wheat-based pellets, and are kept outdoors on the steeper, poorer land, where they are able to shelter in arks. Occasionally, they are taken to upland forested estates for up to 6 months, where they break up and fertilise the ground. This helps forests to regenerate.

The decision to rear wild boar has been a success. People buy their meat because it is different, and not intensively reared indoors. The Johnstons are directly involved in the sale of the boar at the farmers' Saturday markets in Perth (Figure 6.16), Stirling and Edinburgh. These markets allow farmers, fish farmers and related producers to sell directly to the public. By avoiding large supermarkets, farmers hope to improve their profits. Butchers and restaurants as far away as Liverpool use their wild boar produce.

## Land use at Hilton Farm

Like other farmers, the Johnstons decide how best to use their different fields (Figure 6.15). Various physical and human factors affect their decisions about the animals and crops.

★ **Wild boar** are raised on the higher, steeper fields. The cross-section shows that harder igneous rock lies under these fields. The soil is stonier and these fields are better drained. As a result, the wild boar cause a lot less damage as they dig and burrow.

★ **Wheat and barley** are grown on the lower, flatter land nearer the river. Possible flood danger is balanced by the high crop yields from the fertile soil (see Figure 6.17).

**Figure 6.16**   Farmers' market in Perth

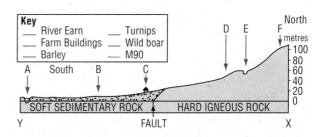

**Figure 6.17**   Cross-section of land use at Hilton Farm

★ **Turnip** fields are rented to other farmers to sell to shops and to feed their sheep. As turnips need less attention, the fields chosen are further from the farm buildings.

★ **Grass, cut for fodder**, however, requires more attention. Mainly it is grown close to the farm. One field (16) is further away but it has a storage shed.

★ **Set-aside** (see page 97). Part of one field (4) was chosen as it was the furthest away from the farm Two other fields (8/11) were chosen as a favour to a neighbour whose daughter wanted to keep horses close to their house.

## ASSIGNMENTS

1 Copy the following, selecting the correct highlighted choice:
Hilton farm is located just **south/north** of Perth. It is a **mixed/arable** farm, whose income comes mainly from **wild boar/barley**.

2 a) What is the meaning of diversification?
  b) Why did the Johnstons switch from arable to mixed farming?

3 a) What are wild boar? Where are they reared on the farm?
  b) Suggest why rearing wild boar has been a good move for the Johnstons.

4 Look at Figures 6.15 and 6.17. Copy and complete the cross-section. You should match the letters A–G with the list provided.

5 Explain how the following have affected land use at Hilton farm: slope and soil; distance from the farm buildings, and EU policies.

6 Describe and explain the changes in land use along the line of cross-section.

7 What is a farmers' market, and how do they help farmers make a living?

# Going organic: changes at Little Callestock Farm, Cornwall

The photograph (Figure 6.18) shows Little Callestock farm in Cornwall. It is located between Newquay and Truro, Cornwall's main city (Figure 6.19). Like many Cornish farms, Little Callestock is a **dairy farm**. Since 1995, the farm has been owned by Nick and Liz Down who have made important changes on the 59 hectare farm.

## Changing dairy breeds

A herd of about 55 Jersey cows is raised on the farm. Originally Friesians were kept. Friesians and Jerseys are both popular dairy breeds. Compared to beef cattle, dairy breeds need more drinking water and richer pastures. These allow them to convert more of their food into milk rather than meat. The main reason for the switch was the fact that the rich, creamy milk from the Jerseys could be sold for a higher price. Originally the milk was made into high quality yoghurt. Today, it is blended with other organically produced milk and sold in Tescos, the supermarket chain.

**Figure 6.18** Little Callestock Farm

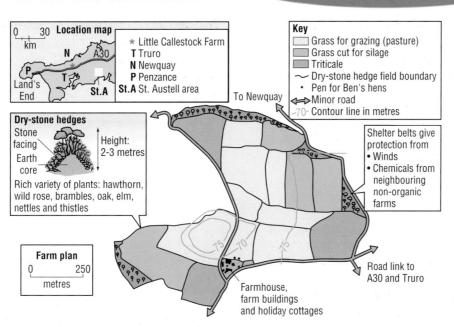

Figure 6.19   Little Callestock Farm: farm plan

## Changing to organic farming

Mr and Mrs Down decided to go organic in 1999. Organic farming means making no use of man-made chemicals to produce crops and raise cattle. Why did they switch?

Initially, it was for economic reasons. Farming is a business, and farmers have to make a living. There was an increasing demand for organic food products, including organic milk. Along with their customers and other organic farmers, the Downs were concerned about the overuse of chemicals on the environment and on the quality of our food.

Figure 6.19 shows three ways the fields are used at Lower Callestock.

★ for **grazing** – Cornwall's mild damp climate encourages all year-round grass growth so the Jersey herd can be kept outdoors almost all year (see Figure 6.21)

★ for **silage** – this is animal feed (or fodder) made from the cut grass and clover – it is then stored in airtight conditions and allowed to ferment so that it can be used as additional winter fodder

★ for **arable** – triticale, which has recently been introduced, is a cereal, a cross between wheat and rye, and is sold as organic fodder.

Figure 6.20   Grass for silage at Little Callestock Farm

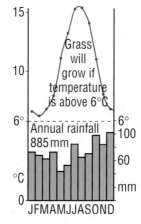

Figure 6.21   Climate graph for Newquay

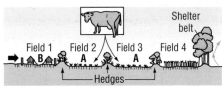

**Crop rotation** ∿ Grass and clover
〰 Triticale

Triticale will only be grown in Field 4 for one year.
The following year, clover will be grown in Field 4;
triticale will be grown in either Field 2 or 3.
Clover: bacteria in roots take the nitrogen from the air
and enrich the well-drained, fertile soil.
**Natural Fertilisers**(A) Cattle dung as cows are moved
from field to field (B) Chicken manure: poultry pens
are also moved regularly
**Other fertilisers brought in** ➡
Seaweed, river sand, natural phosphates & potash

**Figure 6.22**  Keeping the soil fertile

Whatever the land is used for, soil quality is maintained by organic techniques. Some of these are shown in Figure 6.22.

## Ben's Hens

Nick and Liz's son, Ben, is 13 and runs his own little business. He raises free-range hens, selling the eggs to holiday-makers on the farm. An important feature of organic farming is its concern for animal welfare. Ben's hens are kept in two open-air pens, each with a hen house for safety and shelter. Unlike hens kept in huge sheds or battery units, Ben's hens have the freedom to scratch around in the grass, and produce fewer, dearer but far tastier eggs.

**Figure 6.23**  Cows waiting to be milked at Little Callestock

## Changing farm buildings

Like many other farmers, the Downs have had to diversify. Cornwall is a very popular tourist destination. It is also an area of high unemployment. Nick and Liz, assisted by European Union grants, have converted older farm buildings into self-catering apartments (Figure 6.24). These have been very successful, attracting visitors throughout the year.

**Figure 6.24**  Farm buildings converted into flats atπ Little Callestock

### ASSIGNMENTS

1  Copy the following, selecting the correct highlighted choice:
   Little Callestock is a **mixed/dairy** farm. It is located some **8/15** km north-west of **Truro/Penzance**.

2  Study Figure 6.18. Draw a simple sketch showing and naming these features: young Jersey cattle, rich pastures, drystone hedges, farm steading and woodland.

3  a)  Draw a graph to show the following land use figure for Little Callestock: Grazing 52%; Silage 20%; Triticale 28%.
   b)  What features of Cornwall's rainfall and temperature encourage dairy farming?

4  a)  What is organic farming?
   b)  Why did the Downs switch to organic farming methods?

5  What methods do they use to keep the soil fertile?

6  Research and debate: What are the arguments for/against organic farming and free range rearing of poultry?

# Changing crofting landscapes

## What is crofting?

**Crofting** is a special type of farming found only in Scotland. Figure 6.25 shows that it is mainly located on the north-west coast of Scotland, the Western Isles, and Shetland.

Compared to many farms, a typical croft is:

★ **very small** – usually there are only about 2 hectares of arable land

★ **worked part-time** – because crofts are so small, almost all crofters depend on another full-time job to make a living – a crofter might also be a postman, teacher, fish-farmer, work for the local council or countryside ranger

★ **a way of life** – in the crofts of the Western Isles, the Gaelic language is at its strongest; sadly Gaelic has declined, but it can still be heard as the daily language in the crofting areas.

In Lewis and Harris, some crofters still weave tweed, while in Shetland knitwear is produced. Other crofters run their own business from home using computers and the internet. They are examples of tele-workers.

## How did crofting begin?

Crofting began in the late 18th century with the **Highland Clearances**. These involved landowners forcing people from their land to make way for sheep farms. As a result, many families migrated to countries such as Canada, or to work in the shipyards and factories of central Scotland. Other families moved to very small plots of land on the coast of the Highlands. These small plots were called crofts. Crofts were deliberately kept small so that the crofters had to take on other work for their landowners.

Figure 6.26 shows a crofting landscape on the east coast of Harris in the Western Isles. In the early 19th century, crofters moved here from the fertile land on the west coast of Harris. There was little room for farming and land was very rocky. The crofters made their own tiny fields called 'lazy beds'. Soil was piled up and fertilised by seaweed.

To make a living, some took up fishing. Others produced **kelp**. Kelp is seaweed which was gathered and burnt to give a fertiliser. Kelp-making declined when it became cheaper to import fertiliser.

## Features of crofting today

Today there are some 11,500 crofters. Figures 6.26–6.29 show some of the ways in which these crofters live and farm with their families.

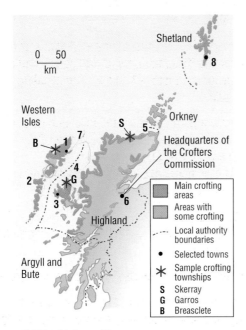

**Figure 6.25** Main crofting areas

**Figure 6.26** Crofting landscape (east Harris)

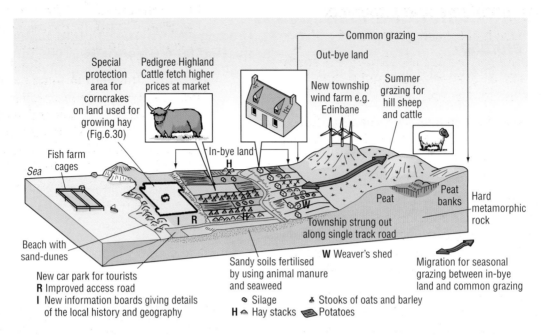

**Figure 6.27** A modern crofting landscape

Figure 6.27 shows:

★ The group of croft houses and their croft land. Such a group of crofts is called a **township**. In this case (but not always) the houses are strung out in a line along the road. This is called a **linear settlement**. There may be a general store/post office, a primary school, several churches and a village hall. Use is made of travelling vans, including a mobile library service. High transport and fuel costs mean that prices are higher in the islands compared to mainland areas.

★ The small area of **in-bye land**. This is the name given to the arable land. The fields are usually long and narrow, and may grow oats, potatoes and grass. Grass is cut for hay and silage.

★ The area of common **grazing**. This land is shared by all the township crofters. On this moorland area of rough grass and heather, crofters graze their sheep and cows (see Figure 6.28). Traditionally, lamb and beef are the main farming product from the croft. They are sold to the farmers of lowland Scotland for fattening. The diagram also shows that the common grazings are used to cut **peat** for fuel. Usually cut in late spring, the peats are left to dry in the wind until autumn. Then they are taken home to form the winter peat stack.

**Figure 6.28** Gathering sheep, Scarista

**Figure 6.29** Carlabagh/Carloway township in Lewis

## Crofting: problems and prospects

Crofters have had to face problems of:

★ high transport costs make it very expensive to take livestock to market and to buy feedstuffs for the animals

★ low prices for livestock as a result of BSE and the outbreak of Foot and Mouth disease in 2001. However, many people recognise that crofting has good prospects

★ many young people believe crofting offers a better way of life compared to the city – there is a Crofts' Entrants' Scheme which gives money to help would-be crofters and in 2001 there was a waiting list of 540

★ crofting is an environmentally friendly way of farming. This can be seen in new schemes at various townships such as Skerray, Breasclete and Garros (see Figure 6.25). These encourage:

◆ planting native woodland such as birch, hazel and rowan

◆ the re-introduction of traditional crops and crop rotation in the in-bye land. This enriches the soil and the stubble from the cut crops provides food for the large variety of birds in these areas

◆ leaving uncultivated edges of fields to encourage wild plants

◆ the re-introduction of the corncrake (see Figure 6.30). Once this bird was widespread throughout Britain. However, its numbers declined because of modern farming methods. Now grants are given to crofters who delay the cutting of hay and silage as long as possible Crofters also mow the grass from the middle of the field outwards to the edges. In this way the taller grass protects the young corncrake chicks from seagulls.

The corncrake has been protected since 1981. Once widespread, it is now only found in N.W. Scotland in the summer. It migrates to South Africa for the winter Crofters can be paid to
• delay mowing of hay till late summer
• change mowing patterns e.g. cut the hay from the centre outwards
• leave 'islands' or strips of uncut hay to shelter corncrakes (**B** and **C**)
• maintain strips of natural grass, reeds, nettles, iris, on field margins (A)

**Figure 6.30**   Saving the Corncrake

### ASSIGNMENTS

1  With the help of an atlas, name the following features on Figure 6.25: islands 1, 2 and 3; stretches of sea 4 and 5; city 6 and towns 7 and 8.

2  Copy the following sentences, selecting the correct highlighted words.
   ◆ Crofts are mainly found in the **Southern Uplands/Highlands**, Western Isles and Shetland.
   ◆ A typical croft is **large/small** and is usually worked **part/full time**.
   ◆ Crops grown on a croft are mainly **oilseed rape and wheat/hay, oats and potatoes**.
   ◆ Crops are grown on the **common grazing/inbye land**.
   ◆ In summer, sheep and cattle are kept on the **common grazing/inbye land**.

3  Why is crofting mainly a part time job? Name other jobs which crofters may have.

4  Write a short paragraph explaining the ways in which crofting is an environmentally friendly way of farming.

5  Look at the O.S. extract in Figure 6.31. It shows the area around the township of Carlabagh (Carloway) in Lewis.
   a)  Is this mainly a linear or a dispersed settlement pattern? Give evidence from the map.
   b)  Give map evidence that this area has been settled for a long time.
   c)  What services can you make out on the map? Give a six-figure reference for each example.

*continued* ➤

**6** Look at Figure 6.29 – A crofting landscape on Harris.

a) Draw an annotated sketch to bring out the features that seem to be 'typical' of a crofting landscape.

b) Write a short account explaining how such a crofting landscape developed from the late 18th century onwards.

**The Scottish Crofting Foundation has developed a website to encourage interest in crofting as a way of life: www.crofting.org.**

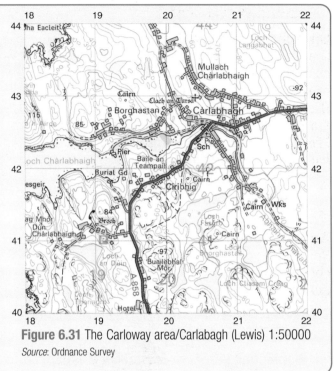

**Figure 6.31** The Carloway area/Carlabagh (Lewis) 1:50000

*Source*: Ordnance Survey

# Farming in South-east Spain

## *Traditional farming in Almeria*

In the countries around the Mediterranean Sea, farming is a mixture of old and new. Figure 6.32 shows a very traditional picture of olive trees growing near the mountain village of Felix (Figure 6.33). With a population of 600, Felix is located in the province of Almeria in south-east Spain (Figure 6.37).

Little has changed for farmers around Felix:

★ they keep sheep and some goats, grazing them on the usually poor quality grass

★ they use little in the way of machinery – wheat is still harvested using sickles

**Figure 6.32** Olive trees

**Figure 6.33** The Felix area (Spain) 1:50000

★ they harvest almonds and olives from trees grown on terraces, cut long ago from the steep mountain sides.

Olives have long played an important part in the Mediterranean diet. They are eaten, often as part of salads, paellas and pizzas, and are crushed for cooking oil. The olive is perhaps the most typical Mediterranean crop. It has features that allow it to adapt to the **Mediterranean climate** (see Figure 6.35) with its two distinct seasons:

★ Hot, dry summers

★ Warm, wet winters

**An extra point**: The south-east corner of Spain around Almeria is the driest part of the country. Sometimes its climate is described as desert. It has less than 250 mm of rainfall each year. This area certainly has been dry enough to use it in filming the famous 'spaghetti western' films. The sets are still used as a tourist attraction.

## Modern farming in Alicante

The road from Felix descends to the coastal plain of Alicante. In the past thirty years the farming landscape of this coastal area has been transformed. Figs 6.36 and 6.37 show some of the features of what is called the '**Costa del Polythene**'. What was once an area of dry scrub land has been changed into a vast sea of polythene tunnels covering 25,000 hectares. Inside these, millions of tonnes of peppers, tomatoes, cucumbers, aubergines, strawberries and flowers are produced. Some of these crops are grown not just once but up to three times a year. Most of them are sold in the supermarkets of northern Europe, often in winter time. when they are normally out of season.  Why is this area now the 'winter salad bowl' of Europe?

★ **climate** – the already high temperatures are even higher under the polythene tents; this allows the plants to grow at a faster rate

★ **modern irrigation techniques** – underground water is pumped up to storage tanks; it is then drip-fed through plastic pipes to the plants

★ **improved transport** – fleets of refrigerated lorries quickly speed the out of season vegetables and fruit along new motorways such as the E 15 (see Figures 6.37 and 6.38).

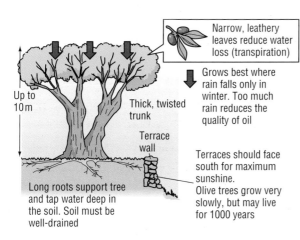

Figure 6.34    Growing olive trees

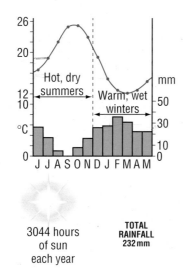

**Figure 6.35**    Climate graph for Almeria

**Figure 6.36**    'Costa del Polythene'

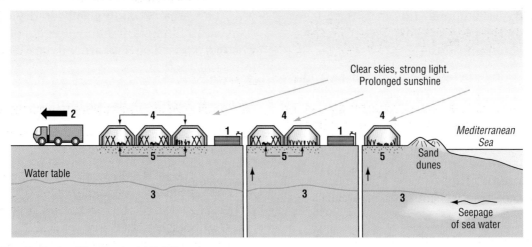

**Figure 6.37**  Features of the 'Costa del Polythene'

## Problems of the 'Costa del Polythene'

The water resources are rapidly being used up. Water is already pumped up from a depth of around 100 metres. Nearer the coast, salt water now is seeping into these deep rocks from the sea.

Many workers in the hot, humid polythene tunnels are from Morocco. Many are illegal immigrants who have to put up with poor housing conditions and racial prejudice.

Around expanding towns like El Ejido, and resorts such as Roqueta de Mar, there is a lot of competition between farmers and builders for land.

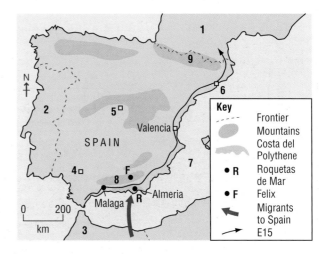

**Figure 6.38**  Map of Spain

### ASSIGNMENTS

1  Figure 6.38. With the help of your atlas, name the following: Countries 1–3; cities 4–6, sea 7; and mountain ranges 8–9.

2  a)  Look at the climate graph for Almeria. What is (i) the temperature in January and July? (ii) the rainfall in December and June?
   b)  In six words, what are the main features of Mediterranean climate?
   c)  Which features of Mediterranean climate make growing crops (i) easy and (ii) difficult?

3  a)  Name three things grown in the area around Felix. What animals are reared?
   b)  Why are terraces important for upland farmers?

4  a)  What is the 'Costa del Polythene'?
   b)  List some of the products grown there.
   c)  Where are these products mainly sold?

5  Copy and complete the diagram (Figure 6.37) by matching the numbers with the following: refrigerated lorries; polythene tunnels; water storage tanks; ground water supplies; 2/3 crops per year.

6  Look at Figure 6.34. Explain how the olive tree is adapted to the Mediterranean climate.

7  In what ways is traditional farming at Felix different to farming on the 'Costa del Polythene'?

8  Has the development of the 'Costa del Polythene' been worthwhile? Give reasons for your answer.

**TO TAKE YOU FURTHER**

# Map work

Look at the two 1:50 000 map extracts: the area around Felix (page 108) and the area around Roquetas de Mar.

**1** How high is the village of Felix?

**2** What is the highest point on the map?

**3** Explain the zig-zag nature of the road leading to the village.

**4** Are the terraces on north or south facing slopes?

**5** What is the main land use in the following grid squares in Figure 6.39: 3568; 3270; 3570? Select from: salt pans; urban; polythene tunnels.

**6** Which main motorway passes through the area?

**7** Using tracing paper, draw a simplified land use map of this area. You should show:

main roads; built up area; salt pans; areas of polythene tunnels; the Mediterranean Sea; areas of rough grazing; some spot heights. Add labels to show possible areas of land use conflict.
Write a brief note describing land use in the area.

**Figue 6.39** The Roquetas de Mar area (Spain) 1:50 000

111

# Land use conflict: the Coto de Doñana National Park

## *Developments in Spain*

In the past fifty years Spain has changed. It was then one of the poorer countries in Western Europe with over 50% of Spaniards working in farming. Today only 5% are employed in farming. Fewer farmers now grow more farm produce, thanks to more machinery, more fertilisers, and new irrigation schemes and new methods.

Most people are employed in services, including the tourist industry. Money from tourism has created more jobs, helping to make Spain a wealthier country,

However, these changes have been at a cost. Increased farming output and the growth of tourism means an ever increasing demand for water. Water is required for everything, from drip irrigation systems to swimming pools. As a result, in many parts of Spain, there is now conflict over water and land resources. A particular conflict can be seen in the Coto de Doñana National Park, at the mouth of the River Guadalquivir (Figure 6.41). This is about 300 km west of the Costa del Polythene (see page 109).

## *Coto de Doñana: a wetland*

The Coto de Doñana is basically the delta (see page 57) of the River Guadalquivir. Figure 6.41 shows that the Guadalquivir flows some 700 km to the Atlantic from the upland areas of

Andalucia. Where the river meets the sea, high sand dunes have formed. Behind them, **marshland** (called 'marismas' in Spanish) has developed. These marshlands are, in fact, not only Spain's largest wildlife reserve but one of the world's main **wetlands**. The Doñana is important because it is home to a rich mixture of:

★ **plant life** such as cork-oak, stone pine, marsh plants, rosemary, lavender and heather

★ **animal life** such as lynx, deer, mongoose wild cats and wild boar

★ **bird life**, especially huge flocks of migrating wildfowl who arrive in wintertime, as well as flamingos, herons, spoonbills, red kites and the very rare Spanish Imperial Eagle.

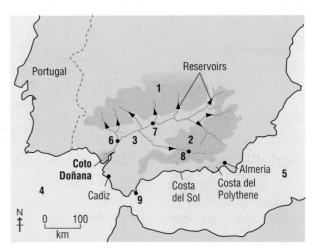

**Figure 6.41**　Location of the Coto de Doñana National Park

**Figure 6.40**　Coto de Doñana

**Figure 6.42**　A lynx

**Figure 6.43**   Visitors to the Coto de Doñana National Park

## Description of the Coto de Doñana

'... I thought I was looking out over the Atlantic –
until I saw the position of the sun ... I was
looking north over the vast 'marismas' which
reached halfway to Seville, and made this the
largest wildlife reserve in Europe ... Over half
Europe's bird species live or breed in the Doñana,
or visit the region during their migration flights.'
from *Spain's Secret Wilderness*
by Mike Tomkiss.

## *A wetland under pressure*

A wetland is an area of waterlogged land. The
Doñana is especially wet in the winter and
spring (see graph). Even in the scorching
summer heat, the water table normally
supports shallow lakes.

For years the area was unspoilt with its rich
plant, animal and birdlife. Local people
grazed their horses and cattle. There were
no roads, and the Doñana was protected
because it was a royal hunting reserve. In 1969
it became a National Park but since then it has
been affected by different pressures (Figure
6.44). These include:

★ **agriculture** – farmers use chemical
fertilisers and pesticides which drain into
the Guadalquivir

★ **industry and mines** – waste also comes
from some of Seville's factories. In 1998, a
mining dam burst and released millions of
litres of toxic waste into a tributary river,
killing nesting birds and fish in the area
around the park

★ **tourism** – local business people want to
develop new holiday resorts. These create
jobs, and this is very important in
Andalucia, the poorest area in Spain.
However, a typical tourist uses 275 litres of
water every day.

New wells have been sunk for groundwater. As
water is pumped up, the water table is
lowered, and sea water is drawn in. This could
damage the vegetation, and affect the animal
and bird life.

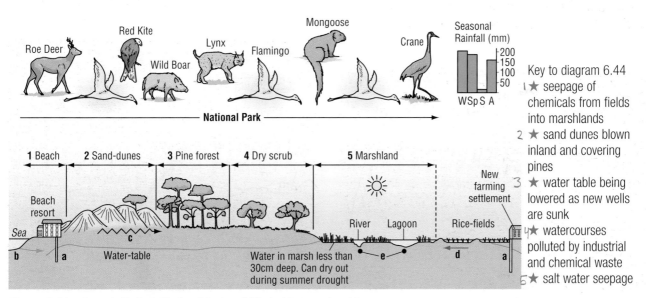

**Figure 6.44**   Coto de Doñana National Park: wildlife habitats and problems

113

Figure 6.45   A Spanish Imperial Eagle

Figure 6.46   Pollution in the Guadalquivir River

## ASSIGNMENTS

1   With the help of an atlas, name the following features in Figure 6.41: mountains 1 and 2; river 3; sea areas 4 and 5; towns 6, 7 and 8; and rock 9.

2   Copy the following sentences, selecting the correct highlighted choice:
   ◆   The Coto de Doñana **National Park/Game Reserve** is located in **south-west/north-east** Spain.
   ◆   It is in **Catalonia/Andalucia**, the **poorest/richest** area in the country.
   ◆   The park is the **source/delta** of the river **Ebro/Guadalquivir**.
   ◆   The Doñana National Park is a world famous **wetland/upland**.

3   a)   What is a wetland?
     b)   Give three different reasons why the Doñana National Park is important. You should name actual examples of plants, animals and birds as part of your answer.

4   Look at Figure 6.44. Match the letters a–e with the 5 items in the key.

5   Two possible ways of helping to solve pressures on the Doñana National Park are: more organic farming, and developing ecotourism (see page 167). Discuss these two possible solutions (and any others) and write a brief report on your findings.

## TO TAKE YOU FURTHER

### Development issues: quotes

'Inevitably, it seems the park is under threat from development and several lynx have been killed by traffic on the road to the beach resort at Matalascañas'   (1)

'Matalascañas, a fast growing beach resort is unlikely to excite; with five large hotel complexes, a grim shopping centre and tasteless beach front developments along a featureless promenade, it looks as if it's just been thrown together (as indeed it has), and it would be difficult to imagine a more complete lack of character'   (1)

'The proposals for a huge new tourist centre – to be known as the Costa Doñana – on the fringes of the park have been shelved, but worryingly two smaller tourist developments just to the north of Sanlucar and near Mazagon on the park's

continued ➤

**TO TAKE YOU FURTHER** continued

*western flank have been given the go-ahead, vividly demonstrating that the pressure for development remains. Bitter demonstrations organised by locals who saw the prospects of much-needed jobs in the Costa Doñana development – accompanied by mysterious outbreaks of vandalism against park property – have abated into an uneasy truce'* (1)

*'A more permanent threat to the Doñana's ecosystem is the new ricefields north of El Rocio, whose run-off waters sluice pesticides into the marismas'* (2)

Sources:
(1) *The Rough Guide to Andalucia* by G. Garvey and M. Ellington
(2) **www.andalucia.com**

### ASSIGNMENTS *TO TAKE YOU FURTHER*

**1** Either
Show the habitats and pressures upon them in the Doñana National Park. With the help of Figure 6.44. Write an account about the problems facing the Park.
Or
Write an acccount of the various features likely to be seen by tourists on a safari-style minibus trip around the park. Figure 6.47 and various photos will help.

**2** Read the various extracts on these pages, and the earlier material on the Doñana National Park. Imagine that there is to be a public meeting to discuss: a proposed new resort expansion at Matalascañas, and further rice field expansion near El Rocio. Write a report on the viewpoints of: a local property developer; a Doñana National Park ranger; a local unemployed person with a young family, and a farmer.

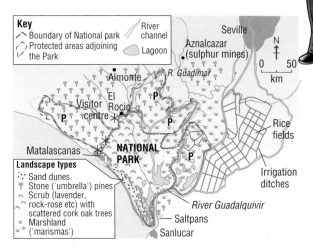

**Figure 6.47**   Land use in the Cote de Doñana National Park

**Figure 6.48**   Matalascañas tourist resort (Spain)

**Figure 6.49**   Rice fields in El Rocio (Spain)

# Settlement

A settlement is a place where people live and/or work. Settlements may be permanent, temporary or seasonal.

A **temporary** settlement may be set up and taken down in a matter of days by nomads such as those in the Sahara Desert. A **seasonal** settlement is where a **permanent** building is used on a temporary basis such as a holiday home or a shelter used by shepherds in summer. For the rest of the year, the settlement will not be used (Figure 7.1).

## Settlement features in the UK

Apart from building materials and design, settlements may differ from one another in

★ their sites (Figure 7.14)

★ the number of buildings

★ the arrangement or pattern of the buildings as seen from above

★ their population

★ the services provided

★ their function or functions.

In some inhabited areas, there may be only a scattering of isolated buildings, for example, farmhouses, a windmill or a water mill.

**Figure 7.1** A holiday home

When farms needed many workers, there was often a row of farm cottages as part of the farm steading. There might also be a few houses grouped beside a water mill. This became a 'milltown', a name later shortened to 'milton'. There were also small groups of houses, detached from farms, known as **hamlets**. They did not have services such as a school or church.

These services were usually available in villages. (Figure 7.8). The church, the school, and services such as the inn and shops, served both the village and surrounding hamlets and farms.

Through time, villages grew into towns perhaps because they had an important church, castle, market, industry or were situated on an important routeway by land or sea.

## Settlement size

In many parts of the world, especially the Less Developed Countries, most people still live in villages. However, an increasing percentage of the world's population lives in **urban** areas, that is in

★ **towns** like Hamilton

★ **cities** like Inverness

★ **conurbations** such as Manchester and its adjacent towns (see pages 127–8)

★ **metropolitan areas** or 'mega' cities, such as Los Angeles (see pages 136–8) and Mumbai.

As urban areas develop

★ they become progressively larger, both in population and land area

★ the buildings become higher and more densely packed in the centre of the built-up area

★ they become more varied in their functions, and their importance increases

★ the range of services they provide becomes much larger (Figure 7.8).

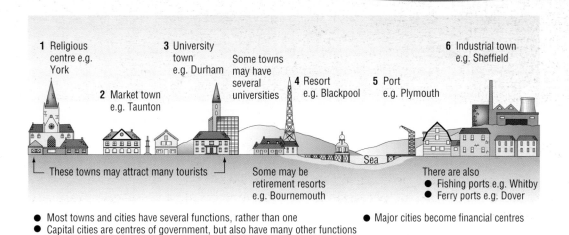

1 Religious centre e.g. York

2 Market town e.g. Taunton

3 University town e.g. Durham

Some towns may have several universities

4 Resort e.g. Blackpool

5 Port e.g. Plymouth

6 Industrial town e.g. Sheffield

These towns may attract many tourists

Some may be retirement resorts e.g. Bournemouth

Sea

There are also
● Fishing ports e.g. Whitby
● Ferry ports e.g. Dover

● Most towns and cities have several functions, rather than one
● Capital cities are centres of government, but also have many other functions

● Major cities become financial centres

**Figure 7.2**   Town types

**Urbanisation** is the process of

★ more and more people living in towns and cities

★ a great increase in the number of cities, especially the largest ones (Figure 7.55).

## Settlement functions

As settlements evolve, they may become important for a particular **function** or role. This is because of

★ the nature of the area they serve

★ the ease of access by land and/or sea

★ past history

★ the availability of raw materials

★ sources of power

★ changing population needs

★ the actions of individuals.

Settlements serving a large agricultural area became market towns, for example, Haddington, where farmers and merchants came to sell their products. Many towns such as Hawick, began or grew rapidly during the Industrial Revolution. Ports developed to serve such industrial centres. Improved communications and increased leisure time

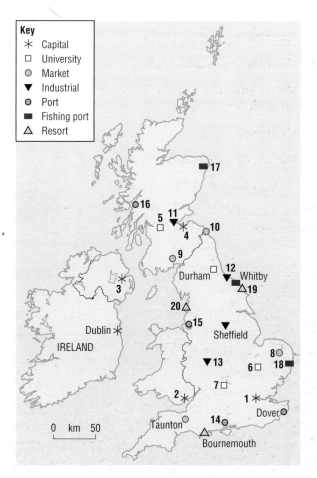

**Key**
\* Capital
□ University
● Market
▼ Industrial
● Port
■ Fishing port
△ Resort

**Figure 7.4**   Town types in the British Isles

**Figure 7.3**   Berwick-on-Tweed, a market town

brought about the growth of **resorts**. Later in the mid-20th century, new towns were planned and built as new industrial centres. Later still, new settlements such as Dalgety Bay in Fife, evolved as **dormitory towns**, from which many people commute daily to work in large cities like Edinburgh.

In the 20th century, some coastal towns, for example, Bournemouth, became retirement resorts beause of the attractions of the climate. Historic towns and cities with other major functions have become tourist attractions such as London and Edinburgh.

**Figure 7.5**   A town with different functions

Few towns, except perhaps resorts, have only one function. Most settlements may have several (Figure 7.5). Some functions decline and disappear; sometimes a new function evolves.

**Figure 7.6**   The new Scottish Parliament building under construction in Edinburgh

| | ✳ | ■ | ● | ▼ | ▲ | ● | ■ |
|---|---|---|---|---|---|---|---|
| Edinburgh | | ✔ | | ✔ | ✔ | | |
| Aberdeen | | ✔ | | ✔ | | | |
| Glasgow | | | | | | | |
| Dundee | | ✔ | | | | | |
| Kelso | | | ✔ | ✔ | | | |
| St. Andrews | | ✔ | | | ✔ | | |
| Perth | | | ✔ | ✔ | | ✔ | |
| Paisley | | ✔ | | ✔ | | | |
| East Kilbride | | | | ✔ | | | |
| Glenrothes | | | | ✔ | | | |

**Figure 7.7**   Towns with several functions

### ASSIGNMENTS

1   Explain the difference between seasonal and temporary settlements. Give an example of each.

2   Arrange in a table the following types of settlements in order of size and importance: *town; conurbation; village; metropolitan area; hamlet; city*. Give an example of each.

3   With the aid of an atlas, name the settlements shown on Figure 7.4: capitals 1–4; university towns 5–7; market towns 8–10; industrial towns 11–13; ports 14–16; fishing ports 17–18 and resorts 19–20.

4   Look again at Figure 7.2. Identify the functions a–d which are shown for one town in Figure 7.5.

5   Copy and complete the table (Figure 7.7). Tick the boxes to show the functions of the named settlements. (Several have been done for you). What does this confirm?

# Settlement and services

Some small settlements may consist only of houses. They are simply where people live. The inhabitants probably **commute** (travel) to work, and must travel to the nearest village if they wish to

★ attend school

★ shop

★ go to church

★ go for a drink or a meal.

Schools, shops, churches, and pubs are examples of **services** which may be be found in settlements.

Today, many villages have fewer services than they once had as shops and schools close down. Villages in the past probably had several shops – a butcher, a baker, a grocer – as well as a post office. Villages then were more isolated and had to be self-supporting. Now they might just have a general store combined with a post office. Even these stores are now in danger of closing.

Why does this happen?

It may be because the population is

★ declining

★ more mobile.

More people have cars and can travel to towns with a greater range of services. Village shops thus lose trade and may not be able to afford to stay open.

**Figure 7.9**  The post office/general store in Fowlis Wester (Perthshire)

However, people in villages and the countryside have always had to travel to the nearest town to

★ go to secondary school

★ visit a doctor's surgery

★ go to hospital

★ consult a bank manager

★ buy furniture

★ see a film.

In turn, people in towns do not have all the services they need. They (and the villagers) must travel to larger towns or cities to

★ go to college or university

★ go to a specialist hospital

★ buy designer clothes.

This travelling gives them access to a more important range of services.

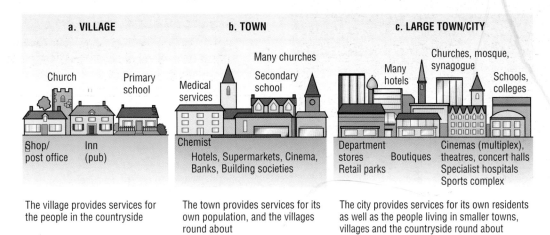

**a. VILLAGE**

Church

Primary school

Shop/ post office

Inn (pub)

The village provides services for the people in the countryside

**b. TOWN**

Many churches

Secondary school

Medical services

Chemist

Hotels, Supermarkets, Cinema, Banks, Building societies

The town provides services for its own population, and the villages round about

**c. LARGE TOWN/CITY**

Churches, mosque, synagogue

Many hotels

Schools, colleges

Department stores
Retail parks

Boutiques

Cinemas (multiplex), theatres, concert halls
Specialist hospitals
Sports complex

The city provides services for its own residents as well as the people living in smaller towns, villages and the countryside round about

**Figure 7.8**  Settlement services

**Figure 7.10** A supermarket on a town's outskirts

Figure 7.8 summarises a general distribution of services. It shows that there is a direct connection between the size of a settlement (both in area and population) and the number and range of services.

Usually, people living in villages and small towns have better lifestyles and more pleasant environments, but people living in cities have better education services, health care, shopping and recreation facilities (Figures 7.10 and 7.11).

Since there are more job opportunities and higher wages, people are able to make the most of the excellent services to be found in cities. People are therefore drawn into the cities from the countryside, villages and small towns. They are drawn to cities and regions such as South-East England where they think they will have a better lifestyle.

**Figure 7.11** An out of town retail park

## Where people live in the UK

As in many countries, the population of the United Kingdom is unevenly distributed (Figure 7.12). This distribution is controlled by

★ the height and relief of the land

★ the climate

★ the attractions of towns and cities.

The vast majority of the population lives in towns, with one person in every twelve living in London, the only megacity in the UK.

## 'Maybe it's because I'm a Londoner...'

Why has London grown to such a vast size?

★ It is the capital

★ It has many other functions which provide a great variety of jobs

★ It has an exceptional range of services (Figure 7.13).

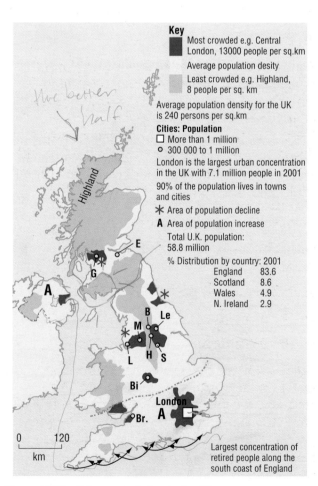

**Figure 7.12** Where people live in the UK

**Figure 7.13** London's West End

As a result, it has always drawn in large numbers of people from all other parts of the UK, including Scotland. There are some disadvantages to living in London

★ the expense such as buying or renting a house

★ the noise and the bustle

★ traffic jams and overcrowded trains

★ the high crime rates.

As a result, there is also an outward flow of people (much smaller than the inward flow) who choose to live in small towns and in the countryside within daily commuting distance of London or to move far outwith commuting distance (except by air) of London to live and work, for example, in Edinburgh or the Scottish Highlands. Working from home using IT (*teleworking*) has helped to make this possible, even in the most remote areas.

Outwith London, in general, population is growing in

★ Northern Ireland

★ South Wales

★ Southern England.

Northern Ireland has the most youthful and fastest-growing population in the UK. In contrast, coastal areas of Southern England have the highest concentrations of elderly people. Many retired people have moved to resorts along the south coast ('*Costa Geriatrica*').

## ASSIGNMENTS

1  a) Would you find all the services which are found in villages and towns in a city?
   b) Why does a city have so many services? Explain your answers.

2  Explain what is meant by
   a) commuting
   b) population mobility.

3  a) List the services which you think should be most accessible to everyone.
   b) List the services which people might be prepared to travel furthest to use.

4  Study Figure 7.12.
   a) Does the population of the UK live mostly in rural or urban areas?
   b) With the aid of an atlas, name the large cities identified by initial letters.
   c) Are most of these cities in (i) Southern England (ii) Northern England (iii) Central Scotland?

6  Giving figures, name the
   a) most crowded
   b) least crowded parts of the UK.

7  Draw a graph to show the % distribution of population in the UK by country. What does your graph show?

# Settlement sites

All settlements originated at favourable **sites**. (Figure 7.14). Water supply, and shelter from bad weather and floods were key factors. Water was perhaps the most important.

Some settlements (**dry-point sites**) avoided flood danger by choosing higher ground above a river's flood-plain or a low hill rising above marshy ground.

Other settlements (**wet-point sites**) sought waterside locations where a river could be

★ crossed in shallow water by a **ford**

★ crossed by a **bridge**

★ used for transport

★ used for fishing

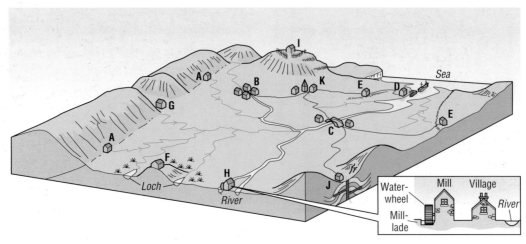

**Figure 7.14** Examples of some settlement sites

★ used for water power, as well as being a source of drinking water.

Settlements also grew

★ at **confluence** points where two rivers flowed together

★ where **springs** came to the surface at the foot of waterless hills

★ at river mouths where **ports** evolved.

Many settlements (on **defensive** sites) began as strongholds on hill tops; others grew where rocks and minerals could be quarried or mined. Through time, some settlements may have occupied different sites in a small area (Figure 7.15). Some settlements (**route centres**) have grown where important **routeways** meet.

## Sample villages

**FORD** (Figure 7.15)
**Situation**: In the Scottish Highlands, at the southern end of Loch Awe.

**Site**: The name suggests why the village grew at this point. However, the diagram shows that the first people here either lived on top of hills or on the loch (Figure 7.16) because defence was most important. Much later, the ford became a crossing place for cattle drovers, and the settlement became a resting place on their journey. Since then, the village has grown along the two roads which meet at the bridge. The village has remained small, with people working in forestry, farming and tourism.

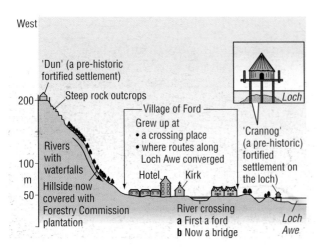

**Figure 7.15** Changing sites at Ford (a Highland village)

**Figure 7.16** A reconstructed crannog on Loch Tay

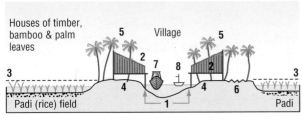

Key

1 **'Klong'** - a canel used for irrigation, fishing, and transport
2 Houses on stilts above floods
3 Highest flood level
4 Canal banks
5 Mango, banana and palm trees
6 Mushrooms
7 Water taxi used to carry mushrooms to Bangkok
8 Flat-bottomed boat: one per family

**Figure 7.17**   Khlong Thi Sip: a village in Thailand

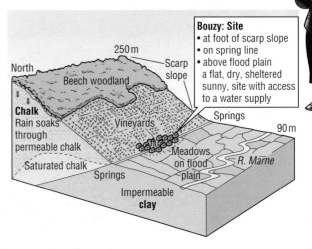

**Figure 7.18**   Site of Bouzy (France)

## KHLONG THI SIP (Figure 7.17)

**Situation**: On the flood-plain of the Chao Phraya River, a few km north of Bangkok in Thailand.

**Site**: This is a good example of a wet-point site. The area is very wet; there are few roads, and villages have to be built along canal banks. Houses are raised on stilts above flood level. The village has a long, narrow shape because of its site.

## BOUZY (Figure 7.18)

**Situation**: In the Champagne district, about 125 km N.E. of Paris.

**Site**: This village is a good example of a dry-point settlement along a spring-line. Above the site of Bouzy, there was no water available. Below the village, there was too much water on the flood plain. The site was also on the boundary between two different types of farmland: the damp meadows and the vineyards which produce the sparkling wine, champagne. The village has grown along the spring line.

## MONTALCINO (Figures 7.19–20)

**Situation**: In the Appennines in Tuscany 60 km south of Siena.

**Site**: A very restricted site on top of a hill. The site was chosen 850 years ago to give the village maximum safety from attack. It was built beside a fortress inside high walls above steep crags. Today it has a population of about 2,000. Many people travel to work in nearby towns. The village is a market centre for the farms on the steep slopes below the walls. Its school, churches, shops and restaurants serve people from a wide area round about.

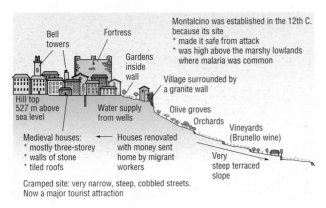

**Figure 7.19**   Montalcino: a hill-top village in Tuscany

**Figure 7.20**   Montalcino

**ASSIGNMENTS**

1 Match the settlements A–K in Figure 7.14 with the types given in the text.

2 Look at Figure 7.15. Where did the first people near the modern village of Ford live? Why did they choose these sites?

3 Which of the four sample villages are examples of
   a) wet-point
   b) dry point settlements?

4 Which of the four sample villages is **linear** (long and narrow) in shape? Explain why this is so.

5 Which of the four villages had
   a) the highest site
   b) a hill-foot site
   c) a site by a crossing-place of a river
   d) a water-supply from springs
   e) a water-supply from wells?
   f) Which is in Italy?

6 Suggest three reasons why many tourists might visit Montalcino.

7 What does
   a) the situation and
   b) the site tell you about any settlement?

# Settlements in the Tweed Valley

The five Ordnance Survey map extracts in Figure 7.21 show examples of settlements in the Lower Tweed Valley. This is an area which is moderately populated. Very few people live in the hills, but on the low ground (The Merse) there are

★ many farms spread evenly about the countryside

★ a good number of villages

★ a few small towns.

**ASSIGNMENTS**

Study Figure 7.21. Give map references with your answers to questions 2–6.

1 Study the extracts A–E, and match the following descriptions to the relevant extract.
   i) a small rectangular-shaped village (ii) a small town at a bridge point (iii) several scattered farms (iv) two adjoining villages (v) a village above a wet valley floor.

2 Study Extract A. (i) Are the farms evenly or unevenly spaced? (ii) Which farm seems to be the oldest?

3 Study Extract B. (i) How high is Morebattle above sea level? (ii) Why was it not built nearer the river? (iii) Where is there evidence of an older settlement? (iv) List three important services in the village.

4 Study Extract C. (i) What height is Gavinton? (ii) How many rows of houses are there in the village? (iii) Which services found in Morebattle are also found in Gavinton? Which one is not? (iv) Why was the Langton Burn important in the past? Give examples.

5 Study Extract D. (i) Why was Town Yetholm not built in GR8027? (ii) Which is the larger village? (iii) Why is neither village built along the river banks? (iv) Which services do the two villages share?

6 Study Extract E. (i) State three facts about the site of Kelso (ii) Give two facts about the historical importance of Kelso. (iii) Name two important services located in Kelso not found in any of the villages (iv) Give at least three bits of evidence which show that tourists visit Kelso.

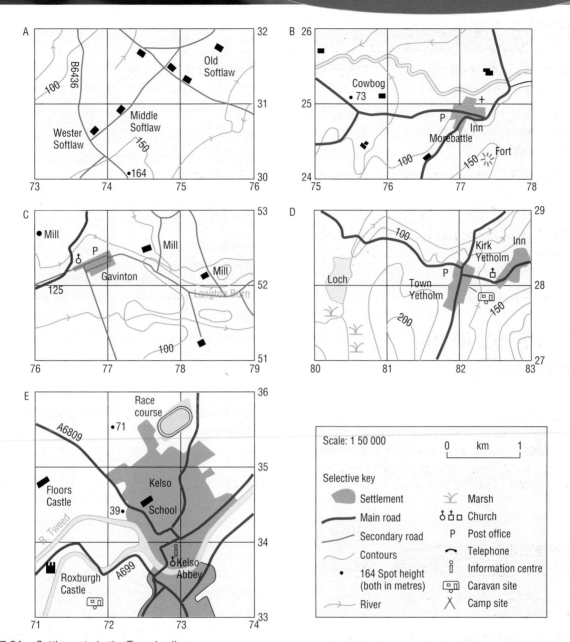

**Figure 7.21** Settlements in the Tweed valley
*Source*: Ordnance Survey sheet 74 (Landranger)

# House types in Scotland

The drawings in Figure 7.22 show some of the types of houses which are found in Scotland. There is information about the materials used and the architecture.

The materials used in building were once limited to what the local area could provide (Figure 7.23).

For example, buildings in central Aberdeen were made of granite. Buildings in central Glasgow, however, were made of sandstone.

Houses in mining villages were brick-built, using local clay and sand. Where building stone could not be quarried, cut and shaped, buildings were made of

★ angular boulders left behind by glaciers or

★ rounded boulders from beaches and river banks or

★ stones from ruined buildings.

Buildings varied in appearance across the country.

**(i) In big towns**

**a** Tenements

Chimney stacks

Slate roof

F2

F1

Tenement built late 19th C.
**F1** First floor or storey
**F2** Second floor

**b** Multi-storeyed ('high-rise') block of flats

**Materials**

Steel, concrete metal sheets ('cladding') breeze blocks

Flats built in mid 20th C. on site of demolished tenements

Stone cut into regular shape

Three or four flats on each storey

Shop at street level

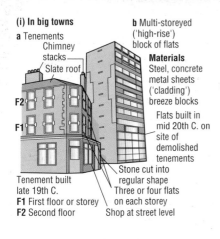

**(ii) In small towns and villages**

Crow step gable

Pantiles

A traditional 18th C. house in Eastern Scotland

Pantiled roof

Curved orange tiles of baked clay

Walls often painted (white, blue, green, pink)

Gable end

Outside staircase ('forestair')

Walls of rough stone ('rubble') protected by harling

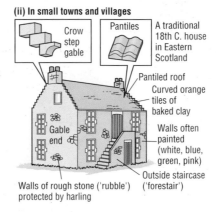

**(v) Bungalow (an example of a detached house in the Inner Suburbs)**

Steep slate roof

Stack

(Attic space)

Stack

Chimney indicates that it was built when coal fires were in use

Walls may be painted white

All rooms at ground level (one storey)

Walls of brick protected from weather by 'harling' (a mixture of pebbles and lime)

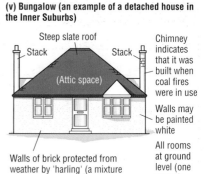

**(iii) In the countryside**

A traditional crofting house in the Outer Hebrides

Very few of these houses remain in use

Sloping roof made of turf-thatch

Oldest croft houses had no chimneys

Roof weighed down by wire and stones

Walls of rough stone, sometimes whitewashed

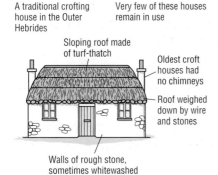

**(vi) Villas (built c.100 years ago in what was then the outer suburbs; now in inner suburbs)**

Sandstone walls

Sandstone chimney stacks

Slate roof

Attic space

Two storeys

No harling on walls

**Villa 1**

**Villa 2**

Common interior wall i.e. the two villas are semi-detached

Cream-coloured sandstone weathered to dark grey

**(iv) In the countryside**

Farm cottage (renovated as holiday home)

Orange pantiles

Wall of large blocks of pink/ orange sandstone

Original 12-paned window

Gable-end wall made of small, irregular stones

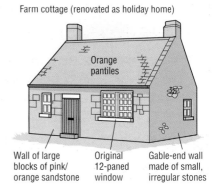

**Figure 7.22**   House types in Scotland

Granite quarry

Slate quarry

Angular boulders left by ice

Stones taken from ruined buildings

Sandstone quarry

Easily split for roofing slates

Rounded boulders left by rivers

Clay for bricks and tiles

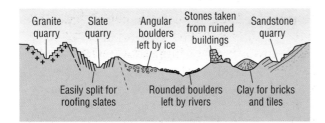

**Figure 7.23**   Some sources of building materials in Scotland

Today, the use of concrete slabs and blocks, bricks and plastic roof tiles mean that new houses look the same anywhere. Most quarries are now worked out, or are too expensive to operate.

**Figure 7.24**   House type 1

**Figure 7.25**   House type 2

## ASSIGNMENTS

Study Figure 7.22 carefully, especially the text.

1 Name three materials used to make roofs watertight, and explain how they are obtained.

2 Is the gable end of a house at the front, the side or the back?

3 Match the following terms for house types to the correct definitions:
**Types**: Terraced; detached; semi-detached
**Definitions**: two houses joined together; a row of houses joined together; a house standing alone.

4 What is 'harling'? Why is it necessary?

5 Explain what is meant by a 'storey' and a 'flat'.

6 List as many differences as you can between a tenement and a multi-storey block.

7 Which houses in Figure 7.22 were built of stones which were (i) collected rather than quarried (ii) irregular in shape, size and colour? Why was this done? What word is used to describe walls built in this way?

8 Explain what is meant by (i) forestair (ii) crow-step gable.

9 Name one distinctive feature of older houses which is not needed in new houses.

10 Study the two photographs (Figure 7.24 and Figure 7.25). Make simple sketches of both houses. Add notes to identify the type of house; the materials used for walls and roofs; the number of storeys; the colours and any distinctive features.

# Changing settlements – Manchester

Manchester (Figure 7.26) is a good example of how a city has grown and how it has changed through time.

In the city centre, there is evidence of a Roman camp and of a medieval town.

Manchester has grown, both in area and in population. The original town was situated

★ 15 km west of the Pennine Hills

★ where the River Irwell was joined by two smaller rivers before flowing into the River Mersey

★ 30 km east of the Mersey Estuary.

## Outward growth

During the 19th century, the cotton industry flourished. Manchester expanded along main roads towards other industrial towns such as Rochdale, to the north and east. Figure 7.27 shows how this took place in Kearsley, near Bolton. At first, the settlement was long and narrow, like a ribbon through open countryside. In the following 80 years, these open spaces have been mostly built over.

## Changing functions and townscape

In the 20th century, the cotton industry collapsed. The port of Manchester in Salford

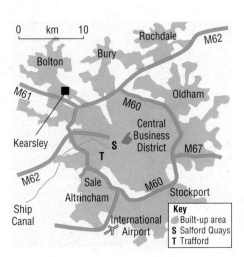

**Figure 7.26**  The Manchester conurbation

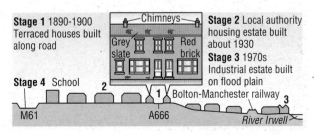

**Figure 7.27**  An example of how the conurbation grew

**Figure 7.28** Central Manchester's changing townscape

closed. Other industries (such as iron and steel, engineering) also declined. As a result, there were

★ fewer manufacturing jobs in Manchester

★ many **brownfield** sites (industrial wasteland) available for re-development

★ many buildings, especially warehouses, in the city centre which could be converted for other uses.

Twenty years ago, Manchester set about attracting new business to the city centre, for example, conferences and tourists. The Metrolink tramway system was built to ease the traffic flow. The Commonwealth Games in 2002 resulted in even more improvements in the townscape (Figure 7.29).

# Changing settlements – New Lanark

The village of New Lanark is another example of a settlement which has seen a major change in its function. This village is situated in the deep valley of the River Clyde below the site of the ancient town of Lanark (Figure 7.30). It is an example of a **planned** village. Some planned villages in Scotland were built to house farm and estate workers or fishermen and their families. New Lanark was planned as an industrial village with cotton-spinning mills and houses close together.

The site was chosen by David Dale, a Glasgow cloth merchant, on the advice of Richard Arkwright, an inventor of spinning machinery. Later, the mills and the village were managed by Robert Owen. He gained world-wide fame as

**Figure 7.29** The City of Manchester stadium

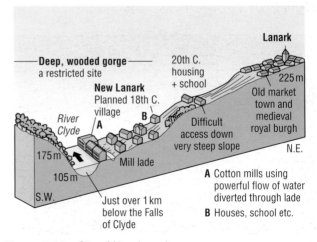

**Figure 7.30** Site of New Lanark

an enlightened employer, providing education, health and recreation facilities as well as good-quality housing in sandstone tenements for his workers.

## NEW LANARK FACT FILE

**1785–1817**: Village built in stages.
There were four mills, first using water- wheels, and then water -powered turbines a century later.
**Source of water**: The Falls of Clyde
**Products**: Cotton thread and canvas
**Workforce**: 1500 maximum
**Population**: 2500 maximum in 1820
**20th Century**: Decline in work and population
**1968**: End of production

The village was then literally crumbling away, but it was saved by the work done by the New Lanark Conservation Trust from 1974 onwards. There are no new buildings, but all the surviving original buildings have been restored. The restored village is no longer an industrial settlement. The use of the buildings (Figures 7.30–7.32) and the function of the village have

**Figure 7.33**    These mills at New Lanark are now a visitors' centre

changed. The new hotel, the youth hostel, the visitors' centre, and several small businesses provide work for about 200 people. New Lanark has become an important tourist attraction. Its importance was recognised when it became a UNESCO World Heritage Site in 2001.

**Figure 7.31**    Renovated housing in New Lanark

**Figure 7.32**    New Lanark Mills Hotel

## ASSIGNMENTS

1   Decide whether or not the following statements about Manchester are true or false
    a)   it grew up at a river confluence
    b)   it was nearer the Mersey than the Pennines
    c)   there was a Roman camp
    d)   most people once lived in brick terraced housing
    e)   it had the first industrial estate in the UK
    f)   it was a seaport
    g)   it is at the centre of a conurbation.

2   Give two reasons why it was called 'Cottonopolis'

3   Study Figure 7.30.
    a)   What restricts the site of New Lanark?
    b)   Why was the site chosen?
    c)   How did the houses differ from those in Manchester?
    d)   What did New Lanark have in common with Manchester?

4   List the ways in which Central Machester has changed in the last 50 years. How have its functions changed?

5   Explain why New Lanark is now so popular with tourists.

6   Give two reasons which might explain why New Lanark has become a World Heritage Site.

# Patterns of land use in a city

In large towns and cities, it is possible to see areas of particular land use forming a pattern. This could be in the form of a circle (Figure 7.34).

The diagram suggests that a city grows outwards in concentric circles. Figure 7.35 shows that if you travelled across a city, you would therefore pass through similar zones on either side of the city centre. These zones have different functions and look very different from one another.

## 1  The Central Business District (CBD)

The oldest part of the city is usually found in or near the CBD. Buildings are large, expensively-built and impressive (Figure 7.36).

★ This business district is the **commercial** core of the city. The CBD may contain the head offices of banks and insurance offices

★ There may be large government offices

★ There are many large or expensive shops – department stores, chain stores and boutiques

★ There are usually many hotel and restaurants, as well as cinemas, theatres and galleries

★ Many people work and shop here, but few people live here – it is not a **residential** area

★ Many people spend their recreational time here. It may also be visited by a large number of tourists.

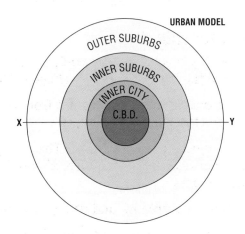

**Figure 7.34**  Urban model of land use

**Figure 7.36**  Part of Edinburgh's Central Business District (CBD)

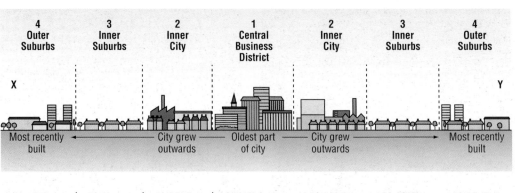

**Figure 7.35**  Pattern of land use in a city

## 2 The inner city

This is found around or next to the CBD

★ This usually has a mixture of residential and industrial uses

★ Industries developed in the 19th century along canals and railway lines running into the CBD

★ There may have been breweries, bakeries, engineering works, clothing factories etc.

★ Round them huddled densely-packed, high tenements or rows of terraced houses. People walked to work

★ There used to be many small shops, but many have now closed

★ Buildings are lower, less impressive, and more cheaply built than in the CBD. It is not an area which attracts visitors (Figure 7.37).

**Figure 7.37**    An inner city townscape

This area will have changed a great deal. All the industry may have ended. Old buildings may have been renovated or demolished. New houses have been built, but there may still be **gap sites**.

## 3 The inner suburbs

Suburbs (Figure 7.38) were residential areas which originally grew up on the edge of the Inner City. New houses were built here in the early/mid 20th century because:

★ the city's population had increased

★ people needed or wanted better housing

★ people could travel longer distances to work by tram, train or bus.

Houses were low with only one or two storeys. They were well-spaced and set in gardens. There were clusters of small shops.

Such areas may have changed very little.

## 4 The outer suburbs

This is the area which is most recent, usually developed in the late 20th century (Figure 7.39).

★ It is the outer layer, most distant from the city core (the CBD)

★ It is the most varied in its uses. There is a mixture of residential, commercial and industrial uses

★ Most buildings are low, and widely-spaced

★ Golf courses and new sports complexes provide a **recreational** use. There is much more open space

**Figure 7.38**    Inner suburbs

**Figure 7.39**    Outer suburbs

★ New roads and large car parks show that road transport is much more important than rail

★ This outer ring could continue to spread into the countryside. Further building is strictly limited to protect the **Green Belt**.

Figures 7.34 and Figure 7.35 represent a city in which the land use is arranged in concentric circles. Not all cities have this arrangement. Perth is examined later to show how far it matches this model.

**Figure 7.40**   The urban fringe

## ASSIGNMENTS

1   Match the following urban land use types with the jumbled definitions:
**Types**: Commercial; Residential; Recreational; Industrial.
**Definitions**: where people spend their leisure time; where people work in offices and shops; where people live; where people work in factories and warehouses.

2   Explain what is meant by the 'core' of a city.

3   Which of the following statements are true?
   i)   Buildings are usually tallest in the city centre
   ii)  Suburbs are areas where few people live
   iii) Most factories were once found in inner cities
   iv)  People once lived within walking distance of their work.

4   Study Figure 7.37. List the features in the photograph which are typical of the inner city.

5   Would you expect to find concentric land use zones in a city on a very hilly site? Explain your answer.

# Matching the model: Perth

## Site

Perth (Figure 7.41) is a small city which has grown up

★ on the flood plain of the River Tay

★ just below the confluence of the Tay and the River Almond

★ in a gap between two hills to the east and west

★ where the Tay could be forded at low tide and later, bridged

★ later, where sea-going ships could sail no further up-stream

★ just downstream from the royal residence at Scone.

## Growth

**3rd century**: There was a Roman fort at the confluence of the Rivers Almond and Tay.

**12th century**: 7 km downstream from this, the medieval walled city was located. There was a satellite village, Bridgend, on the other side of the Tay.

**18th and 19th centuries**: The city expanded along main roads, mainly to the west and the south. The North and South Inches were preserved as open spaces. Some expansion took place beyond Bridgend.

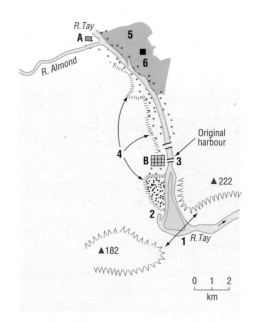

**Figure 7.41**   Site of Perth

**20th and 21st centuries**: Expansion continued, again mostly west of the Tay, into the countryside.

## Land use zones

Figure 7.42 shows a simplified map of land use zones in Perth. There is no concentric arrangement because of:

★ the barrier of the river and the danger of flooding

★ the preservation of the North and South Inches as open spaces

★ the very steep slopes of Kinnoull Hill east of the River Tay

★ building not being allowed on the Scone estate.

However, it is still possible to identify the four main zones as the **transect** Figure 7.43 shows.

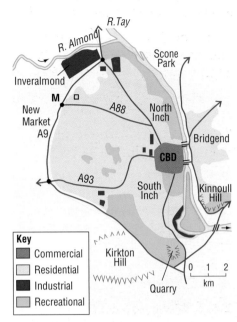

**Figure 7.42**    Perth: land use zones

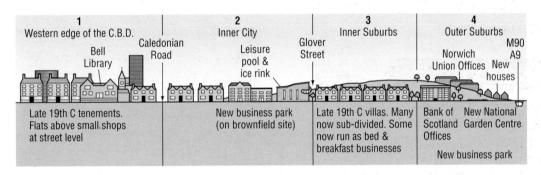

**Figure 7.43**    Land use zones in Perth along the Glasgow Road (A93)

**ASSIGNMENTS**

1  Make a copy of Figure 7.41. Give it a key identifying the features of its site labelled 1–6 on the map. Identify the two early settlements A & B.

2  Look at Figure 7.42. Which road is at present the western boundary of Perth?

3  Give two reasons why Perth has not expanded much east of the River Tay.

4  Study Figure 7.43.

(i)  Summarise the land use of the zones numbered 1–4 by using the following terms: Commercial; Residential; Industrial; Recreational. Some terms may be used more than once; some might not be used at all

(ii)  Which zone is changing most? Explain your answer.

(iii)  Suggest reasons for the location of the industrial areas shown on Figure 7.42.

# City centre versus Greenfield

## Changing locations in a city (Figure 7.44)

Within any city, land for building has become more scarce and more expensive. In general the most expensive land is found in the city centre. It could cost £5 million or more to buy one hectare. Land usually becomes available in very small blocks in the CBD and the inner city. The cost of land decreases outwards. A cheaper option would be to convert existing buildings for a different use. For example. in the inner city of Manchester, many former cotton warehouses have been adapted for use as houses, offices, clubs and restaurants (page 128).

## Brownfield v Greenfield?

If a large company wishes to expand or move to a new location, they may have the option of building on either a **brownfield** site or a **greenfield** site.

Brownfield sites may either be covered with derelict buildings or have been cleared of unused buildings. Cleared sites become gaps in the **townscape**. Such **gap sites** in cities may have been used as temporary car parks or allowed to become waste land. Planning permission has to be obtained before construction can start. It will be allowed if the design of the new building fits in with existing buildings (Figure 7.45).

Greenfield sites are open spaces, for example, gardens, playing fields and surviving areas of farmland within a city which have not been built on before. It is much more difficult to obtain permission to build on a greenfield site. In all towns and cities, land use is carefully restricted to clearly defined zones. Greenfield sites are carefully protected.

Sometimes, the developer feels that there are no suitable sites, greenfield or brownfield. Permission is then sought to build beyond the city in the **Green Belt**. This is a zone of farmland and open space (such as golf courses) round major cities. Glasgow and Edinburgh both have an official Green Belt, but Perth does not. A Green Belt is carefully protected to prevent urban sprawl.

**Figure 7.45**   Gap site development

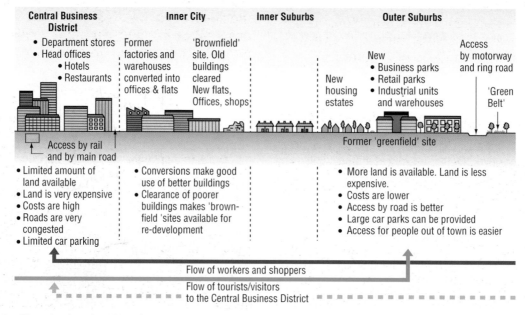

**Figure 7.44**   Changing locations in a city

## Why locate in the city centre?

Offices and stores may favour city centre locations because

★ they are easily reached by public transport

★ they are seen as important in terms of image, especially for stores.

This is despite higher costs and parking restrictions.

## Why locate on the edge of the city?

Offices and stores may favour edge-of-town locations (Figure 7.46) because

★ the new premises provide larger, custom-built accommodation in a pleasant setting.

There is much more parking space available for staff and customers, although

★ there may not be enough public transport

★ it may take too long to travel by public transport across town.

This results in more people using cars and serious traffic problems near edge-of-town developments.

## Decisions, decisions…

Some businesses usually only consider locating in the city centre, for example, luxury department stores:

★ Harvey Nichols opened in Edinburgh's CBD in 2002. They were offered a rent-free lease by the developers. This was in the hope that their presence would attract other expensive shops to the development (Figure 7.47)

**Figure 7.47** Harvey Nichols (Edinburgh)

★ Jenners has its main store on Princes Street in Edinburgh's CBD. It now has other outlets at Edinburgh Airport and at Loch Lomond Shores at the entrance to the new National Park

★ Selfridges plan to open a new store in the Merchant City in Glasgow's CBD.

Stores such as Marks and Spencer may have several locations within a large city – CBD, inner suburbs and the outer suburbs. This ensures that they attract the maximum number of customers.

The Royal Bank of Scotland, based in Edinburgh, has its head office in the CBD in a splendid New Town building (Figure 7.48) and its main customer services office in the city-edge Edinburgh Park (Figure 7.49) 9 km from the head office. It now has plans to open a new major office 2 km further out on the site of a former hospital in the Green Belt.

**Figure 7.46** A retail park outside Edinburgh

**Figure 7.48** Royal Bank of Scotland, St. Andrew's Square

**Figure 7.49**  Royal Bank of Scotland, Edinburgh Park

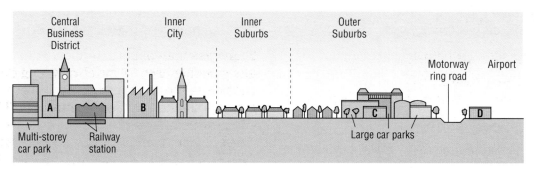

**Figure 7.50**  Cross-section of a city

# Los Angeles: 'The Big Orange'

Los Angeles is a very good example of how a small settlement can mushroom in size as its functions change in a relatively short space of time.

There are people of 40 different nationalities in the city, with the highest concentrations of Mexicans, Thais, South Koreans and Pacific Island Asians outside their own countries. The population is swollen by the influx of 24 million tourists each year. There are no fewer than 87 cities, for example, Hollywood, in the Los Angeles conurbation.

## Reasons for growth and changing functions

**1781**: Spanish religious mission established
**1821**: California becomes part of Mexico
**1847**: California taken over by the USA
**1860s**: Irrigated fruit and vegetable growing begins
**1876**: South Pacific Railroad reaches LA – export of refrigerated fruit to New York begins
**1899**: Oil production begins
**1910**: First automobiles in use
**1911**: First film made in Hollywood
**1920–1940**: Water supplies secured
**1940s**: Aviation industry established
**1960s**: Space and electronics industries established, development of the tourist industry

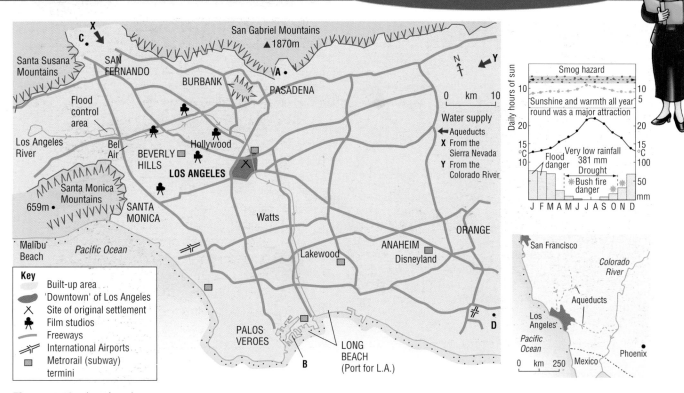

**Figure 7.51** Los Angeles

## Problems and solutions

### 1 Sheer size (Figure 7.51)

*'In Los Angeles … you can drive for three hours and still be in LA. And in that time, you can have travelled 8 or 160 km – it completely depends on the traffic.'*

Los Angeles is only part of one of the largest urbanised areas in the world. If a similar built-up area existed in Scotland, it would stretch from Oban to Hawick (NW–SE) and from Dundee to Selkirk (N–S).

Los Angeles and its adjoining cities form a sprawling urban area. Most of the buildings are low; skyscrapers are confined to '**Downtown**' areas. 'Downtown' is the American term for the Central Business District.

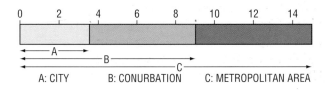

**Figure 7.52** Population of Los Angeles (millions)

### 2 Access to work

Many people have to travel very long distances each day to work. Accessibility is therefore a major problem for these **commuters**. The rate of car ownership is high, so traffic is very dense. A very complex system of '**freeways**' (motorways) has been built in the last 50 years without eliminating traffic jams (Figure 7.54). In the last ten years a mass transit system has been developed. This is a 'subway' (underground) serving the area between Hollywood and Long Beach (Figure 7.51). A recently introduced bus network serves a much larger part of the urban area.

### 3 Smog

The mass transit system has been introduced in an attempt to reduce the number of motor vehicles in use each day. Car emissions have resulted in the health hazard of '**smog**' (smoke + fog). This unpleasant haze blots out the sun which was one of the original attractions of the city. The sun should shine for 329 days per year!

### 4 Natural hazards

**Drought** – the climate of the area is semi-desert (Figure 7.51). The sunshine and warmth

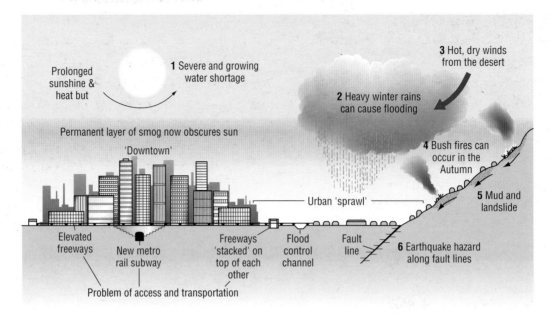

**Figure 7.53** Some problems of Los Angeles

were major factors in establishing the growing of oranges and other citrus fruits and vegetables and attracting settlers and film-makers.

However, water has had to be brought in very long aqueducts as local wells have been unable to cope. Too much water is still being wasted; water shortages are increasing. At the end of the summer drought, the scrub on the hillsides is often set ablaze. Such fires can do much damage to low-density housing.

**Winter rains** – after bush fires, steep hillsides cannot hold heavy winter rain. Lowland areas can be quickly flooded. Mudslides and landslides can destroy hillside housing.

**Earthquakes** – the site of Los Angeles is crossed by several fault lines parallel to the San Andreas Fault. Earthquakes are frequent, for example, in 1994. A giant **tsunami** (sea wave), triggered by an earthquake, could flood coastal areas.

**Population problems** – inequality. Los Angeles is one of the wealthiest cities in the world. At the same time, it has more homeless people than any other city in the USA. It has always been an attraction to poor people such as dispossessed farmers fleeing from the 'Dust Bowl' in the 1930s (see pages 181–2), Black Americans looking for work in the new industries after 1940 and a steady flow of illegal Mexican migrants.

However, some of the more recent immigrants from Asia have quickly prospered.

While the wealthiest people have high-quality housing, poorer inhabitants live in sprawling 'ticky-tacky' housing schemes. Schools find it increasingly difficult to cope with the rapidly expanding number of children of school age.

**Consequences** – vast differences in income, job opportunities and standard of living have resulted in unrest, high crime rates, and even riots.

**Figure 7.54** Traffic jam on a freeway interchange

## ASSIGNMENTS

1 Study Figure 7.51.
Using the scale, measure the distances between the points (i) A & B (ii) C & D.

2 (i) Name the port of LA. (ii) How far is it from Downtown LA? (iii) How far is it from Downtown to Disneyland?

3 (i) State three ways in which you could travel around LA. (ii) Which is the most common? (iii) Which do you think is best? Explain your choice.

4 Aqueducts are shown entering LA on Figure 7.51. (i) What are they? (ii) Why are they vital to LA?

5 From Figure 7.52, calculate the number of people who live in (i) the city of LA (ii) the LA conurbation.

6 Give at least two reasons why so many different peoples have settled in LA. Explain why so many inhabitants are discontented.

7 Write a short report, giving reasons, why (i) so many tourists visit LA (ii) you would, or would not, like to live in LA.

# Urbanisation and its consequences

Figure 7.55 shows the distribution today of the cities in the world with more than 1 million inhabitants ('millionaire' cities). It also shows that the number of millionaire cities grew very rapidly during the 20th century.

Many people in these large cities, for example, Mumbai, are poor. Many may be unemployed; some are forced to beg. The most desperate may scavenge through rubbish tips, which happens in the 'Smoky Mountains' in Manila.

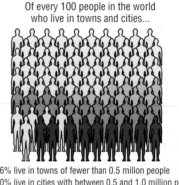

Of every 100 people in the world who live in towns and cities...

- 56% live in towns of fewer than 0.5 million people
- 10% live in cities with between 0.5 and 1.0 million people
- 20% live in cities with between 1.0 and 5.0 million people
- 5% live in cities with between 5.0 and 10.0 million people
- 9% live in cities of over 10.0 million people

**Figure 7.56** Urban population distribution

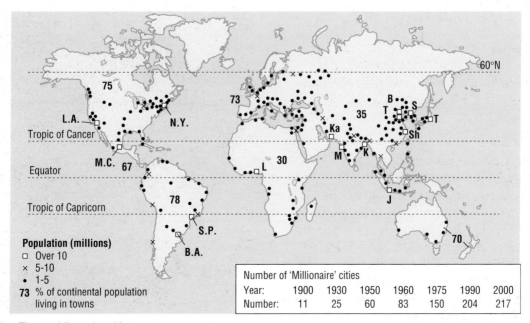

Population (millions)
□ Over 10
× 5-10
• 1-5
73 % of continental population living in towns

| Number of 'Millionaire' cities | | | | | | | |
|---|---|---|---|---|---|---|---|
| Year: | 1900 | 1930 | 1950 | 1960 | 1975 | 1990 | 2000 |
| Number: | 11 | 25 | 60 | 83 | 150 | 204 | 217 |

**Figure 7.55** The world's major cities

At the same time, there are many people who are much better off. Inequality is major problem in large cities. Successive waves of immigrants into some cities have made the population much more diverse. For example, more than 80 languages are spoken today in New York.

Many large cities have grown outwards and merged with other cities. For example, Tokyo and Yokohama have merged with four other cities round Tokyo Bay. They now form a 'mega' city of 33 million people. Much of the city is built on reclaimed land. Rapid urban growth has brought problems (Figure 7.57). Even in such a rich city, there are now unemployed people living in shanty areas.

## ASSIGNMENTS

1 (i) List the continents shown on Figure 7.55 in order of urban population, for example, Central America 67%.
  (ii) With the aid of an atlas, name the largest cities indicated by initial letters.

2 Are most of the world's major cities
  (i) in the northern or southern hemisphere
  (ii) within or outside the tropics
  (iii) in the Less Developed Countries?

3 Draw a graph to show the increase in number of millionaire cities 1900–2000. What does it reveal?

4 Write a short paragraph about the common problems of all major cities, rich or poor. Use this website for research:
  **www.nationalgeographic.com/ngm/0211**

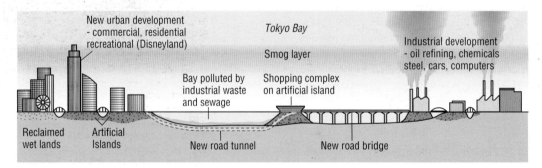

**Figure 7.57** Urban growth round Tokyo Bay

## The empty lands

The 6 billion people who inhabit the earth are not evenly distributed over its surface (Figure 8.1). This is mainly because

★ 71% of the earth's surface consists of seas and oceans

★ most of the earth's land surface is found north of the Equator.

The distribution of people can be looked at in different ways:

★ by hemispheres – many more people live north of the Equator than live south of the Equator

★ by continents – almost three-quarters of the people in the world live in two continents, Asia and Africa (Figure 8.2)

★ by countries – the country with the biggest share of the world's population is China

★ by type of habitation, in other words, urban or rural.

Another way of looking at population distribution is by **natural region**, although it less easy to obtain accurate information. We do know that the ice cap of Antarctica is virtually empty apart from a few scientific bases. On the

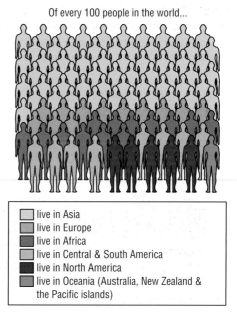

Of every 100 people in the world...

☐ live in Asia
☐ live in Europe
☐ live in Africa
☐ live in Central & South America
■ live in North America
☐ live in Oceania (Australia, New Zealand & the Pacific islands)

**Figure 8.2**   World population by continents

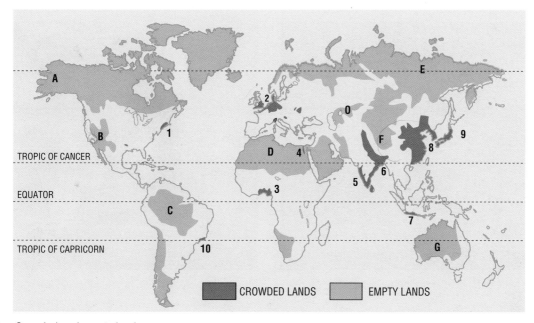

**Figure 8.1**   Crowded and empty lands

rest of the land surface of the world there are other natural regions which are inhospitable. People cannot, or do not choose to, live where it is

★ too cold

★ too hot

★ too wet

★ too high

★ too steep

★ too dry.

In some cases, a combination of these conditions makes living in a particular place difficult, if not impossible. Such an area is often called a 'negative' area. Thus the tundra, the taiga (coniferous forests), the deserts, and some of the tropical rain forests, as well as the highest mountain or plateau areas, might all be described as being 'empty'. This is compared with the 'positive' areas, which were once covered by deciduous and mixed woodland, and areas of Mediterranean or Monsoon climates which might be called 'crowded'.

Many of the areas of the world which are crowded are areas in which most people depend on intensive farming or live in large cities, for example, the North East of the USA, South East Brazil and Japan, working in offices and factories.

There are exceptions such as

★ large areas of the Tropical Rain Forest which are very crowded, for example, in West Africa and Indonesia. These are areas of **intensive** farming

★ clusters of population in the deserts at oases, or along rivers where irrigated agriculture was early established

★ the exploitation of a newly-discovered resource such as gold, oil, petroleum and the introduction of modern technology, have resulted in a great increase in the population in certain areas of the tundra, the taiga and deserts.

## Population density

Measuring whether or not a region or country is 'empty' or 'crowded' can be done by using the total population, or more significantly, the total population divided by the area. This gives the **population density** – the average number of people per square kilometre.

## Lows and highs: examples of extremes

### Low population densities (persons per square km)

2: Australia; Iceland; 3: Canada; Libya. 8: Russia. 19: Brazil. 29: USA.

### High population densities

864: Bangladesh; 600: Taiwan; 471: S. Korea

**Figure 8.3** An 'empty' area in Northern Scandanavia

**Figure 8.4** A 'crowded' area in Eastern China

## ASSIGNMENTS

1   Look at the map of the world, Figure 8.1. With the aid of your atlas, identify
    a)   the crowded lands numbered 1–10, choosing from the following list:
        Japan; Nile Valley; North-West Europe; Java; Southern Nigeria; North-Eastern USA; Bangladesh; Eastern China; South-East Brazil; India.
    b)   the empty lands lettered A–G, choosing from the following:
        Northern Siberia; Australian Desert; American Desert; Tibet; the Amazon Basin; Sahara Desert; Alaska.

2   In a table, match the empty lands A–G with the following characteristics which make them difficult places in which to live:
    Too hot; too cold; too wet; too dry; too high; too remote.

Some of the areas may have more than one characteristic.

3   Study Figure 8.2 carefully. Of the world's total population, which continent has
    a) only 5% b) only 13% c) only 1% d) only 12%?

4   60% of the world population live in just ten countries. All of them have more than 100 million people. They include Bangladesh, India, USA, Nigeria, Brazil, Pakistan, Russia, Japan and Indonesia.
    a)   Which is the 10th country?
    b)   List the ten countries in a table by continents, giving any other information you can find on page 142 about population density.

# The desert world

The Sahara, the world's greatest desert, is shown on Figure 8.5. Notice that

★   there is another area of desert in Africa

★   four other continents have deserts

★   most deserts are near the two tropics.

## Desert climate

The deserts all have

★   very low annual rainfall (under 250 mm)

★   very few days with rain

★   rainfall usually occurring in thunderstorms.

*'In July and August in the high desert, the thunderstorms come … By noon the clouds begin to form over the mountains … the clouds multiply and merge, piling up like whipped cream … building upon one another into a second mountain range … More clouds emerge from the empty sky, anvil-headed giants with glints of lightning in their depths. The sun is blazing down as intensely as ever, the air crackling with dry heat … lightning streaks like gunfire through it, volleys of thunder shake the air … The wind is rising. Overhead the clouds thicken, then crack and split with a roar like cannonfire, and the rain comes down … not softly and gently, but like heavy rain in buckets, raindrops like pellets plastering my shirt to my back, drumming on my head like hailstones. For five minutes the deluge continues … diminishing to a shower, to nothing at all. Stranger than the storms are the flash floods, bursting out of the washes and canyons, sometimes more than an hour after the rain has stopped.'*

E. Abbey *A Season in the Wilderness*

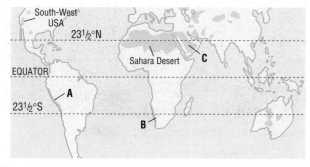

**Figure 8.5**   The World's Deserts

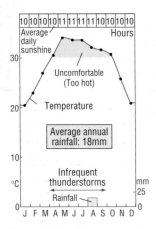

**Figure 8.6** Climate graph for Faya, Chad (18°N)

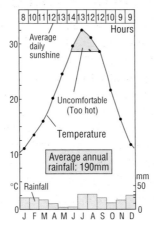

**Figure 8.7** Climate graph for Phoenix, Arizona (33°N)

The deserts all have

★ very high summer temperatures

★ long hours of sunshine

★ relatively cold winters, sometimes with frost and (on the mountains) snow.

Plants and animals must adapt to survive such arid conditions. Some tolerate the heat and drought, others wait for rain to fall.

## Desert vegetation in South-West USA

The most striking plants in the deserts of North America are the **cacti**. They are found nowhere else in the world's deserts. There are several

different types, and they can all tolerate drought by storing water in the stem. Therefore, they can expand and shrink according to the amount of water stored. Their stems are protected by a thorny armour and they have a widespread root system which helps stabilise taller cacti in strong winds.

Some desert plants (see Figure 8.8)

★ have no leaves like the cacti

★ only grow leaves after rain falls, for example, the creosote bush

★ have leaves which reflect heat from a shiny, waxy surface

★ have hairy leaves and stems to obtain moisture from the air. This is important in coastal deserts where sea fog provides most moisture.

Where water comes to the surface at a spring, clusters of palm trees may be found. Flowers such as the poppy and sunflower avoid the drought by having seeds which can lie dormant, perhaps for years, in the sand until the next rainstorm. Similarly, sandy desert areas can be briefly transformed into green pastures a few days after rain has fallen. The whole cycle from germination to seed dispersal can be over in a few weeks.

All other plants grow very slowly, for example, the saguaro produces its first branch after 75

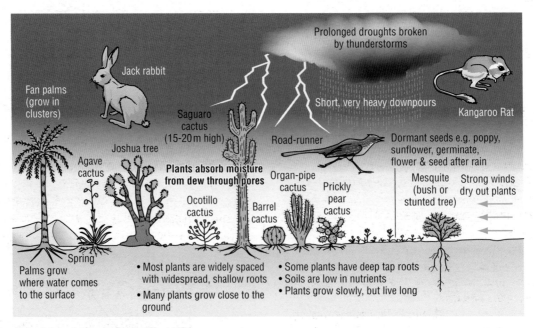

**Figure 8.8** Desert vegetation in South-West USA

years. However, the saguaro and the joshua tree may survive for many centuries, the creosote bush for over a thousand years. In the South-Western USA, some plants such as the saguaro and the joshua tree tend to be concentrated in particular areas. Many cacti, especially the saguaro, are threatened by plant collectors. Some of these areas have been protected, for example, the Joshua Tree National Park in Southern California.

### Animals in the desert

Wildlife is surprisingly rich in the deserts, especially in the USA. The great heat is overcome by avoiding it, in other words, by spending most of the daylight hours in burrows, nests or under stones. Most creatures only appear at night. Many creatures such as the kangaroo rat and the road-runner do not drink water, but obtain liquid from their dry food intake such as seeds or other animals they kill. The desert bighorn sheep, like the camel, can survive for long periods without drinking.

## ASSIGNMENTS

1 Study Figure 8.5. (i) Which is the largest desert in the world? (ii) On which continent is it found? (iii) Name the Tropic which passes through it. (iv) Name the deserts marked A and B.

2 (i) How much annual rainfall have deserts?
  (ii) What causes rain in deserts?
  (iii) What are 'flash floods'?

3 (i) Name the deserts in which Phoenix and Chad are found.
  (ii) Look at the two graphs. Which place is a) colder in winter b) warmer in summer c) sunnier in summer d) drier over the year?

4 In Phoenix, why would you pay half the price for a hotel room in July than you would pay in March?

5 Name the only continent in which you would find cacti in the deserts.

6 Why are plants in the desert widely spaced?

7 In what way do the roots of the the saguaro and the mesquite differ?

8 List in a table the ways in which (i) plants (ii) animals survive in the desert.

Find out more about the Joshua Tree National Park on website www.nps.gov

## TO TAKE YOU FURTHER

## Desert days and nights

### Day

Mid-day temperatures can be almost unbearable:

*'It was the hottest day of the hottest season. The land seemed burning. The wind blew in flame-thrower blasts. Everything was glaring hot; the saddle, the stick on my hands and the folds of my shirt. My hands and feet were swollen from the roasting; my throat felt like emery paper, my gums were choked with a paste of mucus. The wind rose and fell in gusts. When it hit us, it felt like being braised with dripping fat … The sand was too hot to stand on. Even in sandals you could feel the heat cutting through.'*

M. Asher *Impossible Journey*

Graphs cannot show the most striking feature of the desert climate, such as the great difference between day and night temperatures.

In such conditions people can quickly become dehydrated. They can lose a litre of liquid from sweat evaporating. A drink (such as a mixture of dried milk, sugar and water), a rest and shelter from the sun's rays are vital for survival (Figure 8.9).

*continued* >

**TO TAKE YOU FURTHER** *continued*

## Why is it so hot?

◆ The sun is always high in the sky

◆ The air is always dry

◆ The sky is therefore usually cloudless.

## Night

Even in the summer, the temperature can drop very quickly at night (Figure 8.9):

*'The morning dawned bleak and cold, with the desert wrapped in a mantle of mist. Visibility was down to a few metres … It was freezing that night as we curled up in our blankets … it was too cold to sleep, except in snatches. The next morning we were assailed by a biting wind, and I wrapped myself in blankets before setting off'.*

M. Asher *A Desert Dies*

### Why does it become so cold?

◆ The skies are clear

◆ There are no clouds to retain the day's heat.

The **temperature range** (the difference between the highest temperature during the day and the lowest during the night) is always very high. This is very noticeable, even when it does not become cold enough for frost. As mentioned in the extract above, mist can form. It is possible to collect moisture when this condensation takes place.

**ASSIGNMENTS** *TO TAKE YOU FURTHER*

**1** Weather forecast for Phoenix 16 August 2001
Maximum temperature: 42°C,
Minimum temperature: 29°C.
What was the temperature range?

**2** What equipment in buildings in Phoenix overcomes the great heat during the day?

**3** Why would people in Phoenix not notice the drop in temperature at night as much as travellers in the Sahara Desert?

**4** Suggest two reasons why it is very difficult to find shade from the sun's rays at noon in the Sahara.

**5** In the desert (i) would it be hotter or cooler during the day if the sky were cloudy? (ii) would a cloudy night be warmer or colder than a clear night?

**This website will give you a weather forecast for Phoenix: www.azcentral.com**

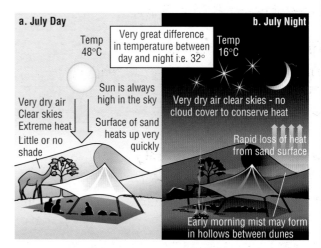

**Figure 8.9** Day and Night in the desert

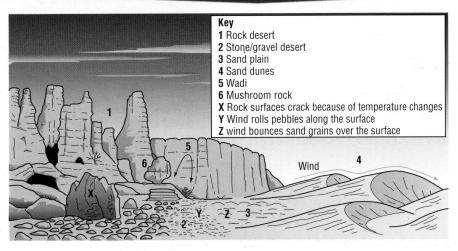

**Key**
**1** Rock desert
**2** Stone/gravel desert
**3** Sand plain
**4** Sand dunes
**5** Wadi
**6** Mushroom rock
**X** Rock surfaces crack because of temperature changes
**Y** Wind rolls pebbles along the surface
**Z** wind bounces sand grains over the surface

**Figure 8.10**   Desert landscapes

# Desert landscapes

Deserts all have an **arid** climate, but it would be wrong to think that they are all covered in sand dunes. The Sahara contains three mountain ranges rising over 3000 m above sea level. Around them there are several other types of desert (Figure 8.10).

## Blowing in the wind

The wind plays a major part in shaping the landscape of the Sahara.

★ Rocks crumble because of rapid temperature changes.

★ The rock fragments eventually become pebbles or grains of sand

★ The wind moves the pebbles and sand along the surface

★ The sand grains picked up by the wind blasts rock surfaces and wears them away. Erosion is most vigorous about 60 cm from the ground. This results in the formation of **mushroom rocks** (Figure 8.11).

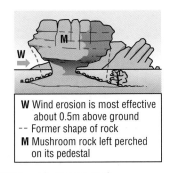

**W** Wind erosion is most effective about 0.5m above ground
-- Former shape of rock
**M** Mushroom rock left perched on its pedestal

**Figure 8.11**   Mushroom rock

## Sand

The sand produced by the erosion of the rocks eventually accumulates either in

★ sand plains with gently rippled surfaces or

★ sand dunes:  crescent-shaped dunes, called **barkhans**, giant, wave-like dunes which form **sand-seas** or long, narrow dunes, which run parallel to the wind (see Figures 8.12, 8.13 and 8.14).

**Figure 8.12**   Barkhans in the Sahara Desert

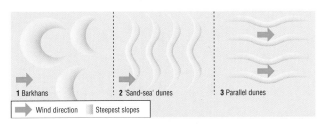

**1** Barkhans     **2** 'Sand-sea' dunes     **3** Parallel dunes

➤ Wind direction     ▬ Steepest slopes

**Figure 8.13**   Sand dunes: a 'bird's eye' view

147

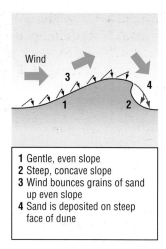

1 Gentle, even slope
2 Steep, concave slope
3 Wind bounces grains of sand up even slope
4 Sand is deposited on steep face of dune

**Figure 8.14**   Cross-section of a Barkhan

The scale of these sand dunes is awesome. Some may be 200 m high (Arthur's Seat in Edinburgh is only 50 m higher). Sometimes the troughs between them may be 60 m or more below the crests. Some of the parallel dunes are up to 300 km long. Not surprisingly, sand dunes are difficult to travel over, especially the steep faces of the barkhans. Travellers may find the sand seas most disconcerting as the following passage shows:

'The desert we walked out into the next day was utterly featureless. It was a vast, endless sand-sea, the largest in the central Sahara … The emptiness of it was suffocating. There was nothing at all to attract the eye but the metal flags spaced out every kilometre. It was like walking on a cloud … sometimes its dazzling ripples looked like water, a still ocean undulating to every horizon. In all that vastness, there was not a tree, not a rock, not a single blade of grass.'

M. Asher *Impossible Journey*

No one is exactly sure why sand dunes form. Some dunes have been stabilised by planting shrubs and trees, but most dunes are moved forward by the wind. This may be as much as 10 metres per year.

In the Sahara, there may be a great variety of desert landscapes encountered even on one day's journey:

'We were searching for the well of Tagouraret over a desert floor as flat and red as a tennis court. On one side was the familiar edge of the Baatin plateau, and on the other, the chilling hugeness of the sand sea … The surface of the earth was puckered with veins of granite. A seam of low dunes lay across our path, then a black plain, then dunes again. There was no sign of a well.'

M. Asher *Impossible Journey*

## Water in the landscape

Rivers once flowed in the Sahara. The present-day dry valleys or **wadis** are evidence of this. Some wadis are over 100 km long (Figure 8.15). There is also archeological evidence that the Sahara once had a wetter climate. There are rock paintings in the mountains showing elephants, crocodiles, and herders with goats and camels.

Wadis can be dangerous places if there is rain, and flash floods can still shape the landscape.

'We had to descend into a river bed cast between sheer rock faces about 60 m high either side of us – the whole being about 70 m wide. About a quarter of an hour into this impressive wadi, the rain suddenly started to come down as I have never seen rain. The driver became very scared … parked the vehicle on a piece of higher ground … and began to climb the rock face. I reluctantly followed him and we found an overhanging rock. Under this we sat, soaking wet and shivering cold. Suddenly a great wall of water swept down the wadi, making what had been a dry river bed into a raging torrent.'

M. Dickson *A World Elsewhere*

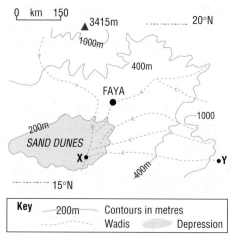

**Figure 8.15**   Desert landscape, Northern Chad

## ASSIGNMENTS

**1** Look at your atlas.
  a) Name one of the mountain ranges in the Sahara Desert. Give its height.
  b) Name the river which flows through the eastern Sahara. Where does it rise? Why does it not dry up?

**2** Name three types of desert landscape.

**3** The wind is one cause of the shaping of the desert landscape. What does it use to erode the rocks?

**4** What is a wadi? How was it formed? When was it formed?

**5** Look at Figure 8.15. How high is (i) point X (ii) Point Y? Which will be wetter, X or Y? How far is it along the wadi from Y to X?

**6** Give two bits of evidence which show that the Sahara once had a wetter climate.

**7** What is a sand sea? Why are metal flags planted in sand seas?

**8** Why might it be easier to travel through an area of parallel dunes than across an area of barkhans?

**9** Describe, in your own words, the main features of a barkhan. Explain how it is formed.

# Phoenix: a desert city

Phoenix is a very unusual city. There is no other desert city which has grown so quickly. It was only founded in 1868, on the site of an ancient Hohokam Indian settlement

**Situation**: It on the Salt River on the Colorado Plateau in the deserts of South-West USA (Figure 8.16). A major problem was its remote location.

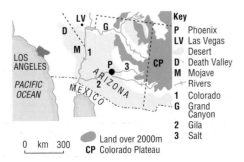

**Figure 8.16** Situation of Phoenix

**Site**: It is in a broad valley, dotted with steep hills and ridges like Camelback Mountain, with high mountains on three sides. The site provided flat land suitable for irrigation. but it could also be endangered by flash floods.

**Climate**:
*Plus points*: Winter warmth and sunshine (8–11 hours per day). Very dry air.
*Minus points*: Summer heat, thunderstorms and water shortage.

The advantages have been fully exploited. In the past, many invalids came to Phoenix in the hope that its dry air would cure them of asthma and tuberculosis. The first tourists were attracted by 'dude' ranches around Phoenix which gave them the chance to experience life in the 'Old West' (Figure 8.19).

The invention of air conditioning was the major factor in overcoming the summer heat. Wealthy retired people from the 'Snow Belt' of the USA then migrated here and settled in their own exclusive community, 'Sun City'. Improved transport links with the rest of the USA made Phoenix more accessible. This resulted in the development of mass tourism, with many millions of wealthy visitors each year. Luxury resorts and many golf courses replaced the dude ranches in 'The Valley of the Sun', which has over 4200 hours of sunshine each year.

Phoenix and its satellite towns now sprawl over a vast area of what was once a desert landscape (Figure 8.18). 'Downtown' Phoenix has a skyscraper townscape as modern as Dallas or Los Angeles. The unchecked growth of Phoenix has caused many problems:

**Figure 8.17** Lookout Mountain in Phoenix

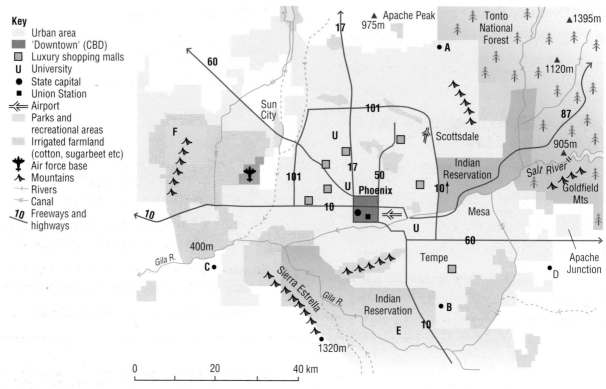

**Figure 8.18** Phoenix: a desert city

'...*Scattered around the periphery of Phoenix are cluttered eyesores of trailer courts, motels, neon signs, used car lots, giant billboards, and jerry-built housing developments...*'.

It is estimated that 19 hectares of desert around Phoenix is lost to building each day.

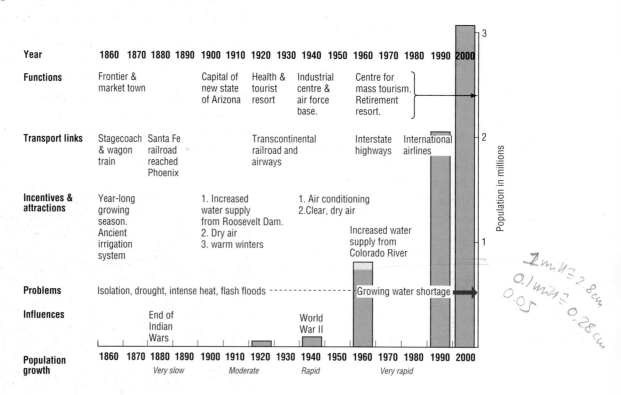

**Figure 8.19** The growth of Phoenix: '*the blob that is swallowing Arizona*'

**21st Century Problems**:

★ Too many cars; large-scale traffic jams

★ Clear desert air now badly polluted by smog

★ Increased crime rate

★ Decline in the electronics industry, for example, Motorola

★ Increasing water shortage.

## ASSIGNMENTS

**1** Study Figure 8.18. Look at the map scale (i) How far is it from (i) A to B (ii) C to D? (iii) How far, and in what direction, is Sun City from Downtown Phoenix?

**2** Find the highest and lowest points on the map.

**3** In what direction is the Salt River flowing?

**4** Look at the key. State the land use at A, C, E and F.

**5** Look at the population scale on Figure 8.19. How many people lived in Phoenix in (i) 1940 (ii) 2000?

**6** (i) Name the natural attractions which first brought people to Phoenix.
  (ii) List the present-day attractions

**7** (i) How have the functions of Phoenix changed?
  (ii) What are the reasons for the changes?

**8** Study the text carefully. Why do you think Phoenix has been called ' the blob that is eating Arizona'?

**Visit the website: www.azcentral.com**

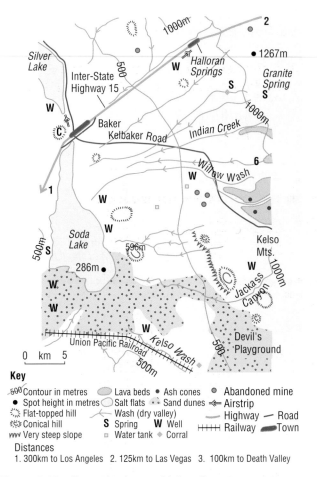

**Key**

- ⌒500 Contour in metres
- ● Spot height in metres
- ⌣ Flat-topped hill
- ⌣ Conical hill
- vvv Very steep slope
- ⬭ Lava beds
- ◯ Salt flats
- ∴ Sand dunes
- ~ Wash (dry valley)
- **S** Spring
- ▫ Water tank
- ● Ash cones
- ● Sand dunes
- ⬱ Airstrip
- ─ Highway
- **W** Well
- ⊢⊣⊢⊣ Railway
- ⬧ Corral
- ◉ Abandoned mine
- ─ Road
- ◣▬ Town

**Distances**
1. 300km to Los Angeles  2. 125km to Las Vegas  3. 100km to Death Valley

**Figure 8.20**  Desert landscape, Mojave Desert

# A desert landscape: Mojave Desert

The map in Figure 8.20 shows part of a large national park, the East Mojave National Scenic Area in Eastern California. The area shown has a desert landscape typical of South-West America. It is like Death Valley since it is exceptionally dry and in a deep depression.

The vegetation consists mainly of joshua trees, cacti and scrub (see Figure 8.8). The two small towns shown have a combined population of just over 700. They provide some services for the many tourists who wish to visit the area. A network of tracks allows tourists to explore the desert landscape.

**Figure 8.21**  Mojave Desert, dry and inhospitable

## ASSIGNMENTS

1 Give the height of the highest and lowest points in the area shown in Figure 8.20.

2 Give two bits of evidence which tell you that there were once volcanoes in this desert.

3 Which other type of rock is used in a place name?

4 What is a 'wash'? What would it be called in the Sahara? Which other features shown here would also be found in the Sahara?

5 Are the sand dunes found above or below 1000m?

6 State three ways of crossing this desert area.

7 What evidence is there of cattle ranching in this area?

8 Why is there no farming carried on in this area?

9 Name two precious minerals which might have been mined in this area.

10 What are 'salt flats'? How are they formed? Why is the term 'lake' misleading?

11 Suggest reasons why tourists visit the Mojave Desert.

12 The area shown on the map is about 1,400 sq km. Is this area a good example of the Empty Lands?

# The Tundra

The tundra is a cold desert which is mostly found north of the Arctic Circle (Figure 8.22). South of the Circle, there are areas of tundra on high mountain ranges or plateaus. The climate graph for Barrow shows the main features of the tundra climate (Figure 8.23). Tundra areas have

★ very long, very cold, dark winters with winds which make it even colder, frozen ground and permanent snow cover

★ very short, light summers with limited rainfall and waterlogged land after the thaw.

Over the course of the year, the amounts of snow and rain are so low that the tundra is classed as a desert. Yet, like the desert, the tundra is rich in plant and animal life, but only during the short summer. '*Nine months of winter, and three months of bugs*' is one person's view of the climate.

> '*With the flowers came the insects, not just flies, but bees and butterflies … Each morning we rose to the sound of rain but the pattering on the tent was in fact mosquitoes, millions of them…*'
> H. Miles and M. Salisbury
> *Kingdom of the Ice Bear*

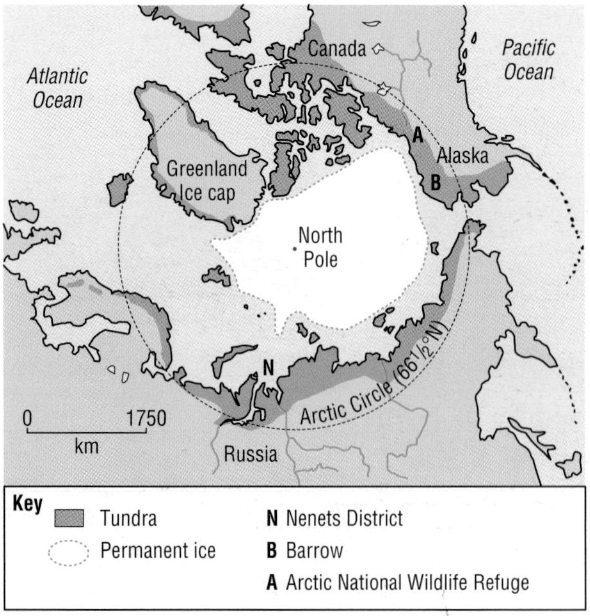

**Figure 8.22** Location of the tundra

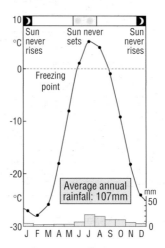

**Figure 8.23** Climate graph for Barrow (Alaska)

Conditions for plants and animals are very difficult, but people and the caribou are most affected by the hordes of insects.

The caribou migrate from their winter territory in the coniferous forest to the south. They feed on mosses, lichens and the leaves of dwarf trees and bushes of the tundra before returning southwards. They can be so affected by the bloodsucking insects and parasitic flies that they often stampede attempting to escape the flies. The insect hordes attract many migratory birds, some from the Tropics, and a few from the Antarctic. It is estimated that there are about 100 bird species on the tundra in summer. The snowy-owl, raven, ptarmigan and falcon are among the very few which remain over the winter. The tundra is home to some of the largest land mammals in the world, although there are few species, and the mammals are widely dispersed. The exception to this are the large concentrations of caribou. Animals, apart from the caribou, adapt to the extreme winter climate in different ways:

★ a few, such as bears and ground squirrels, hibernate

★ some others, such as lemmings, voles and mice remain active, but burrow below the snow and live off stored seeds

★ more animals, such as the musk ox, the arctic hare, wolves, foxes and ermine, remain on the surface. With their white coats, the arctic hare, ermine and fox are all well camouflaged. Many have tiny ears, short muzzles and legs. The musk ox stores great reserves of fat, and is protected by its windproof coat

★ insects remain dormant or survive as eggs or pupae.

## The tundra: nature's own Bonsai (Figure 8.24)

Plants adapt to the harshness of the climate by forming a low, bushy cover, less than 60 cm high, to avoid the worst of the winds. This cover includes dwarf trees, dwarf heathers, and alpine plants. Hairy stems and leaves help reduce the loss of moisture and heat. The snow acts as a warm blanket in winter. Buds form quickly and flowering takes place only a few days after the snow finally thaws. The shortness of the growing season, which may be only a matter of weeks, is partly offset by the long hours of daylight.

Vegetation also has to adapt to

★ the waterlogged soil in summer

★ the lack of soil nutrients in this thin skin of soil

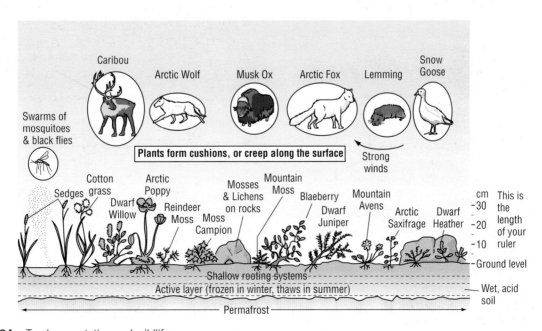

**Figure 8.24**   Tundra vegetation and wildlife

★ the underlying **permafrost** which can be found just below the surface.

This means that root systems have to be very shallow. In the most northerly areas, the permafrost, frozen soil and rock as tough as reinforced concrete, is only a few centimetres below the surface. In some areas, wedges of ice are found. Not surprisingly, plants grow very slowly and the whole environment is very fragile. It can be destroyed very easily, for example, by using heavy tracked vehicles instead of vehicles with balloon tyres. Despite the harsh environment, there are hundreds of flowering plants and, just as in the hot desert, there is a simultaneous flowering, not after rain, but after the snow melt.

## ASSIGNMENTS

1 Look at the map (Figure 8.22).
   a) Name the large island with a fringe of tundra round an ice-cap.
   b) State the latitude of the Arctic Circle.
   c) Is the tundra mostly south or north of the Circle?
   d) Where is north on this map?

2 Look at the graph (Figure 8.23).
   a) How many months does the winter last?
   b) What can make it seem very much colder in winter?
   c) State three facts about the climate of Barrow (i) in January (ii) in July.
   d) What proof is there that Barrow has a desert climate?

3 Look at Figure 8.24.
   a) Name two dwarf trees.
   b) Name two plants which flower in the short summer.
   c) Name at least one plant which produces edible berries.
   d) Name two plants which grow in swamp areas.
   e) Name two plants which provide food for caribou/ reindeer.

4 Make a table which shows how the following animals adapt in different ways to the harsh conditions on the tundra: lemmings; ground squirrels; caribou; insects; musk ox; arctic hare. Find out more from the library.

# Conflict in the Tundra

## The Nenets of Siberia

### A Traditional life in a changing landscape

The Nenets live in North-West Siberia, just beyond the Ural Mountains where the River Ob enters the Kara Sea (Figure 8.25). The climate in the area is similar to that of Barrow (Figure 8.23). There are only about 35,000 Nenets, a tiny fraction of Russia's total population. They are similar to the Sami of Northern Sweden and, in some ways, the **Inuit** of North America. About 33% of the Nenets still follow the traditional way of life. They are reindeer herders.

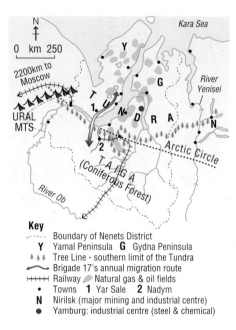

**Key**
- - - - - Boundary of Nenets District
**Y**   Yamal Peninsula  **G**  Gydna Peninsula
✦ ✦ ✦  Tree Line - southern limit of the Tundra
         Brigade 17's annual migration route
+++++   Railway ◗ Natural gas & oil fields
•        Towns  **1**  Yar Sale  **2**  Nadym
**N**   Nirilsk (major mining and industrial centre)
●        Yamburg: industrial centre (steel & chemical)

**Figure 8.25**    The Nenets of Siberia

The reindeer is the domesticated version of the wild caribou hunted by the Inuit. The Nenets migrate according to the season with their reindeer. To obtain fresh grazing in the summer, the reindeer are herded northwards onto the tundra. In order to survive the harsh winters, the Nenets and their herds return southwards to the shelter of the **taiga** (the coniferous forest) in autumn. The Nenets are therefore an example of **pastoral nomads**. Their seasonal migration is called **transhumance**.

## Nenets case study: the Serotta family

There are now many Russians in the area in which the Nenets have traditionally lived. The Russians have come because of the rich mineral deposits below the permafrost (Figure 8.25). The Yamal Peninsula has very large reserves of natural gas. There are clusters of prefabricated buildings, including workers' houses which are very different from the chums (Figure 8.27).

The Nenets people managed to resist government plans to exploit their tundra grazing lands up to a point. Their migration routes, temporary sites for settlement and summer grazing are, however, now being seriously affected by the exploitation of the gas-fields by GAZPROM, the state energy company.

The tundra in the Nenets District is now much more densely populated than ever before, with several industrial towns, as well as the gas producing centres. It is also one of the most prosperous regions in Russia because of the income from the gas and oil, but the pastoral Nenets do not necessarily share in this prosperity.

The tundra, which has been described as '*an iceberg covered by a thin, green mantle*', is unlikely to withstand the use of

★ steam-hoses to thaw out the permafrost before building begins

★ heavy tracked vehicles which tear up the mosses. lichens and dwarf plants on which the reindeer graze.

Development has benefited the state, and the incoming Russians, but the prosperity may not last – after the gas and oil are used up the tundra will suffer. A similar conservation/development conflict can be found on the other side of the Arctic Ocean in a very empty area of tundra in Alaska, the Arctic National Wildlife Refuge.

**Nenets Case Study: The Serotta Family**

The Serotta **brigade** or family group consists of 19 people. Some of the children are at boarding school in the town of Yar Sale. The brigade migrates over 400km each way between their winter shelter in Taiga and their summer grazing on the Tundra (Fig. 8.25). They have 75 larchwood sleds to carry their tents and food supplies. They do not use snowmobiles. They live in tents called 'chums', three in all, which have to be put up and dismantled daily.

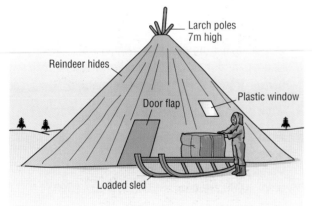

The chums have wooden planks as floors and are heated by an iron stove.
The Serotta family have a herd of 3000 reindeer. They are used for
• pulling sleds
• meat to eat and sell
• hides for clothing
• hides for tents
• bones, sinews and blood

**Figure 8.26**   Nenets case study: the Serotta family

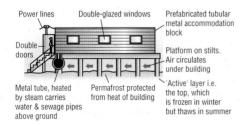

**Figure 8.27**   Workers' new housing on the Yamal Peninsula

**Figure 8.28**   A Nenets herder

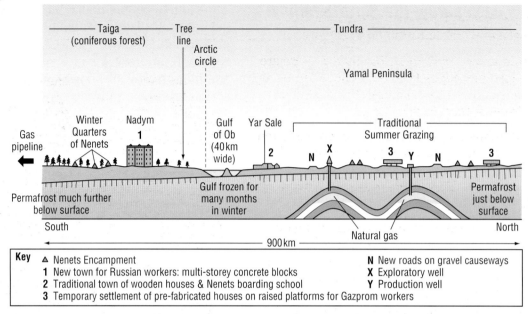

Figure 8.29   Conflicting ways of life on the Siberian Tundra

## ASSIGNMENTS

**1** Study Figure 8.25.
   a) Which important line of latitude roughly divides the Nenets District in two?
   b) What is the Taiga?
   c) What line separates it from the tundra?

**2** Explain what is meant by the following

   pastoral nomads    transhumance    brigade
              chum     GAZPROM

**3** In a table, list the different ways in which the Nenets and the GAZPROM workers insulate their houses from the cold and the permafrost.

**4** What other type of houses are found at Nadym?

**5** What are the advantages of herding reindeer, as opposed to hunting them?
Visit this website:
**www.nationalgeographic.com/ngm/9803**

## TO TAKE YOU FURTHER

# Arctic National Wildlife Refuge

*'June 26. It's 1am. The sun is almost due south, and low in the sky, but it is nowhere close to the horizon, let alone fully setting. It will not do that for another 40 days or so. I am awake at this time, not only because the sun is still up , but also because a living tide of caribou is flooding through my camp. The first caribou appeared yesterday, a few score of them, ambling slowly in a long raggedy line. Several hours later, the modest trickle had grown into a torrent some hundreds of animals across, then thousands; before long it had turned into the shuffling, wheezing, clicking caribou sea that is now washing across the coastal plain.'*

*Diary of an Arctic Year*

The Arctic National Wildlife Refuge (**ANWR**) is an area about the size of Scotland, with only a few small, scattered settlements such as Kaktovik. It is important for two conflicting reasons

◆ it has such a rich and diverse wild life, including the migrating caribou, during the short summer that it has been called the Serengeti of North America

*continued* ➤

**TO TAKE YOU FURTHER** *continued*

◆ it is known that under the tundra there are enormous deposits of oil, believed to be as rich as those found along the coast near Prudhoe Bay (Figure 8.30).

The Prudhoe Bay oilfields have been exploited since the Trans-Alaskan oil pipeline was completed in 1977, but now the output is declining. The USA needs more oil to maintain its high consumption.

There have been arguments about giving oil companies licences to explore the coastal plain near Kaktovik for 25 years. There are different viewpoints on this. Just as in the Yamal Peninsula in Siberia, there are opposing views among the native people (Figure 8.31). In ANWR, the Inupiat (Inuit) are in favour of development because they have already benefited from money from the Prudhoe Bay oilfields. This relative wealth has provided the 300 people of Kaktovik with

◆ centrally heated, wooden-frame houses

◆ a new community hall and school

◆ a clinic

◆ a swimming pool

◆ street lighting

◆ sewage ('honey-pot') collection

Kaktovik is a permanent settlement. The Inupiat hunt the the caribou when they migrate north to calve. They also still hunt the bowhead whales as they migrate past their village.

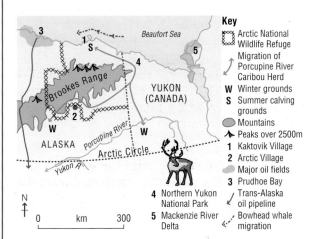

**Figure 8.30**   Arctic National Wildlife Refuge

**Inupiat View**

We are subsistence hunters. We are allowed to kill three bowhead whales each year in the fall. We have the caribou in the summer. We can live off subsistence hunting, but you cannot raise children and grandchildren without money and a job. Oil is our guarantee. Our young people need jobs, and we have to adapt to survive. We have electricity bills and house payments. It's a cash economy. We can't go backwards.

**Athapaskan Indian View**

We have no oil on our land. We live on benefits. Our village is outside the boundary of ANWR, and we are hunters. We hunt to survive. Most of our meat is caribou - we hunt them as they migrate north and south. All our other food has to be flown in - it is very expensive. We are afraid about what might happen if they start to explore for oil in ANWR. It might affect the caribou migration. If they don't come, we could starve...

**Conservationist's View**

We are standing on the world's greatest Arctic ecosystem. We say, if they can drill here, where can't they drill? If we are going to develop this, we might as well go ahead and dam the Grand Canyon. The Prudhoe Bay development has caused far more environmental damage than the government has admitted.

**View of U.S. Government**

There is no need for concern. Rest assured that we have looked at this very carefully. Any development would look after the environment. We don't think it would affect the caribou. In any case, most of the local people are in favour, and our country will need much more oil in the next few decades...

**Figure 8.31**   For and Against Development on the Arctic National Wildlife Refuge

On the other side of the Brookes Range, the 150 Gwich'in Indians who live in Arctic Village are firmly against any development. There is no oil or gas on their lands, and they depend on being able to hunt the vast Porcupine Herd as it migrates past their village (Figure 8.30). It is estimated that there are about 180,000 caribou in this herd. Hunting has had no adverse effect on the herd, but the 'footprints' of any oil development (see p. 158) might well do so. Conservationists are concerned also about the future of the musk ox, polar, black and brown bears as well as the migrant birds, including the snow geese.

If the American government goes ahead with oil production on the ANWR coastal plain, the first oil would be extracted in 2010. This would involve the construction of a pipeline, similar to the Trans-Alaskan pipeline (see Figure 8.30), to carry it southwards to the Pacific coast. The Canadian government, responsible for the national parks in the Yukon through which the Porcupine Herd migrates, is firmly against any oil production on ANWR's coastal plain.

*continued* ➤

## TO TAKE YOU FURTHER *continued*

### ASSIGNMENTS *TO TAKE YOU FURTHER*

1 What does **ANWR** mean? How large is it? Is it an example of an 'empty' or a 'crowded' land?

2 How does the Porcupine Herd get its name?

3 Describe the annual migration of this herd as shown on Figure 8.30.

4 Is the oil known to be under the coastal plain of ANWR, or in the mountain wilderness?

5 In what ways are the Inupiat living in Kaktovik better off than the Gwich'in living in Arctic Village?

6 In what ways is the life of the Nenets in Siberia a) similar to b) different from that of the Inupiat?

7 Where is the Serengeti? Why do you think conservationists compare it with ANWR?
   **To find out more about ANWR, consult these websites:**
   **www.nationalgeographic.com/ngm/0108**
   **www. arcticrefuge@fws.gov.**

## TO TAKE YOU FURTHER

# 'Footprints' in the tundra

The tundra is a very delicate **ecosystem**, particularly the active zone above the permafrost. The active layer supports the miniature plants, which may have taken centuries to grow. The period for plant growth is very short. The thaw of the active zone is very gradual, and long before it is complete, the top is frozen again.

The permafrost and the active zone together create a very distinctive landscape (Figure 8.32). The name, 'permafrost', suggests that it could not possibly be affected by new developments in the tundra, but it can be.

The building of roads, settlements, oil drilling sites and airstrips all have to be designed to prevent the heat they generate from melting

◆ the active layer in winter

◆ the permafrost all year round.

As Figure 8.27 shows, new houses can be raised above the ground. Engineers also use gravel to provide a firm base above the active layer, but quarrying the gravel scars the landscape very badly. In winter, ice roads and ice drilling pads can be used to protect the tundra from damage, but in ANWR there is a shortage of water for this purpose. Yet in summer, there may be a large number of shallow lakes on the surface of the tundra (Figure 8.32), even though the rainfall is very low.

Construction of the Trans-Alaskan pipeline in the 1970s had to take into account

◆ the problems of the intense cold

◆ the possible thawing of the permafrost

◆ caribou migration routes (Figure 8.30)

◆ the possibility of earthquakes.

The surface of the tundra was repaired as far as possible after construction.

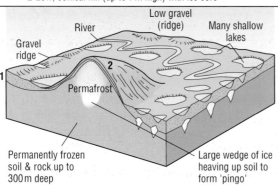

**Key** 1 'Active' top layer of soil. Frozen solid in winter; thaws out in summer to form a swampy layer 15-60 cm deep
2 Low, conical hill (up to 7 m high) with ice core

**Figure 8.32** The surface of the tundra in Summer

*continued* ➤

**TO TAKE YOU FURTHER** *continued*

Apart from construction scars and pipelines, there are other 'footprints' visible on the tundra as a result of oil and gas production:

◆ settlements

◆ roads

◆ airstrips

◆ storage yards

◆ power lines

◆ gravel pits

◆ landfill sites

◆ oil derricks and wells.

The development of new drilling techniques (Figure 8.34) could reduce the visual impact on the tundra, as well as the physical damage. Conservationists would not agree with this view.

**ASSIGNMENTS** *TO TAKE YOU FURTHER*

**1** How many months does the growing season last on the tundra? How deep is the active zone?

**2** Why does does so much water lie on the surface of the active zone in summer?

**3** Why are the gravel ridges important to oil companies on the tundra?

**4** Explain the importance of:

> refrigerated brine    liquid ammonia
> frozen slurry    directional drilling

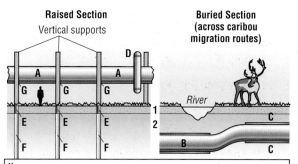

**Key**
**Pipeline**
**1** Active layer
**2** Permafrost (vertical supports may be up to 8m deep)
**A** Insulated with fibreglass to keep oil warm enough to be pumped
**B** Concrete jacket protects pipe from buckling
**C** Smaller pipes containing refrigerated brine prevent permafrost in contact with pipe from thawing
**D** Valve to prevent spillage
**Supports**
**E** Liquid ammonia inside supports keep the active zone frozen in summer
**F** Supports in permafrost surrounded by frozen slurry (sand and water)
**G** Pipeline allowed to slide on support beams as it expands and contracts

**Figure 8.33**   The Trans-Alaskan Pipeline and Permafrost

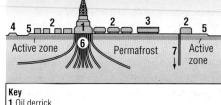

**Key**
**1** Oil derrick
**2** Storage and processing bildings
**3** Workers' dormitories
**4** Gravel access road
**5** Gravel drilling pad
**6** Directional drilling: This means that the drilling is not always vertical. the drilling pad can have several wells. Oil deposits up to 6.5km away from the pad can be trapped in this way. This reduces the impact on the tundra
**7** Used drilling mud is injected into the permafrost rather than being dumped on the surface

**Figure 8.34**   Reducing the impact of oil drilling on the tundra

# The tropical rain forest

*'It rained with sustained ferocity all night … dawn merely lightened the lines of falling water from grey-black to grey…and I could see out for no more than 10 or 12 metres… I sat up and drew a deep breath of wet, rancid air. Already covered in microscopic algae and fungus, the hammock and mosquito net and I and everyone else were beginning to smell of rancid butter…'*
R. O'Hanlon *In Trouble Again*

This extract describes conditions in the Tropical Rain Forest (TRF), a type of natural vegetation which is found close to the equator (Figure 8.35). The graph in Figure 8.36 confirms that the climate of the TRF is

★ very hot all year

★ very wet, with no real dry season.

Balikpapan is in Borneo, but the lowlands of the River Congo and the River Amazon both have a similar climate.

## Plants and animals of the TRF

The great heat and the high humidity mean that the natural vegetation is dense forest. Figure 8.37 shows some of its main features.

The animal life of the rain forest is rich and varied. It forms part of a very complex food chain. In the South American rain forest, the harpy eagle and the jaguar are the largest predators. On the forest floor, mammals are small, for example, the coati. The canopy is the most inhabited layer where snakes such as the emerald green boa, are the main predators.

### The Canopy

The canopy is a dense, continuous layer of greenery, 6 to 7 metres deep, a 'garden' full of flowers and fruit. It is grazed by a large number of birds such as macaws and toucans, and animals like monkeys and sloths, which use the

> '...Now you can climb into the canopy. Arriving there is like leaving the dim airless staircase of a tower block and emerging on to its roof. Suddenly the humid twilight is replaced by fresh air and sunshine. Around you stretches a limitless meadow of leaves, hillocked and dimpled like the surface of an enormously enlarged cauliflower. Here and there, standing 10 m or more above the rest, rises a single isolated giant tree. Emergents live in a different climate...for up here the wind blows freely through the crowns'.
>
> D. Attenborough *The Living Planet*

canopy and the lianas as an aerial walkway. Lianas hang down from the canopy; orchids, ferns and bromeliads grow from crevices in the branches. Every plant competes for space and light (Figure 8.38).

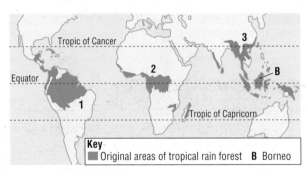

**Figure 8.35** Tropical Rain Forests (TRF)

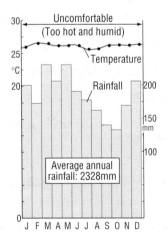

**Figure 8.36** Climate graph for Balikpapan (Borneo)

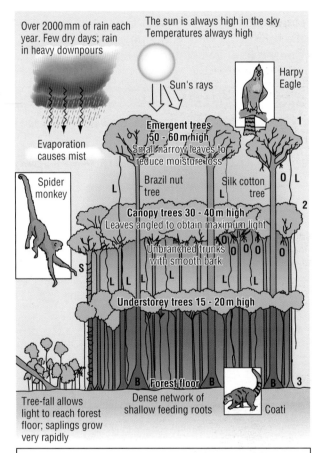

**Key 1** Hot, bright and breezy
**2** Very hot, less light, humid
**3** Hot, very gloomy; still; very humid (like a sauna)
**L** Lianas (rooted in ground; acting like guy-ropes)
**B** Supporting buttress roots
**S** Strangler figs (roots grow down to anchor in ground and feed)
**O** Orchids and bromeliads with short dangling roots

**Figure 8.37** Features of the Tropical Rain Forest

## Diversity in the forest

Most of the trees are tall, thick hardwoods, resistant to termites, and valued for their timber. The volume of timber within a given area is many times greater than that found in temperate woodland. Trees of the same type do not grow together in stands, but are scattered about. There are more species of trees and other plants, insects, reptiles, birds and mammals in the tropical rain forest than in any other of the world's natural regions.

### Importance of the Rain Forest

★ its biodiversity

★ its medicinal plants

★ air purification (trees soak up carbon dioxide and give out oxygen)

★ forests return water to the air by transpiration from the leaves

★ forests prevent soil erosion

★ its valuable timber.

### Threats to the Rain Forest

Much of the area once covered by Tropical Rain Forest (Figure 8.35) has now been cleared. This is because of uncontrolled logging, clearance for grazing or growing crops and forest fires (see page 165).

**Rain forest plants**

**In abundance**
heat and moisture
**In short supply**
Space and light
Soil nutrients

Plants must adapt to the above conditions

**Epiphytes**
These are plants e.g. orchids and bromeliads which live on canopy trees

Epiphytes root in mosses growing in crevices in the bark of canopy branches

Aerial roots collect moisture from humid air

**Drip-tip leaves**
Trees have thick, leathery leaves with long pointed tips

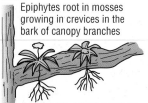

Rain          Rain

Rain

**Buttress roots**

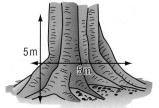

5 m

5 m

Trees have tall straight trunks with smooth bark

**Figure 8.38**    Rain forest plants

## ASSIGNMENTS

**1** Are the Tropical Rain Forests mainly located near the equator or the tropics (see Figure 8.35)?

**2** Name the continents 1–3 on which the TRF is found.

**3** Name two large rivers which flow through the TRF.

**4** Name one island which was once covered by TRF.

**5** How much rain falls each year in the TRF?

**6** Is the air in the TRF very dry or very humid?

**7** In which layer of the TRF would you find
   a)  most sunshine
   b)  least light?

**8** Name two ways in which the tallest trees are supported.

**9** Name two plants which have different ways of finding enough light and moisture to grow.

**10** Name three ways in which leaves on trees adapt to the climate of the TRF.

**To find out more consult the website www.panda.org**

# Traditional life in the Rain Forest of the Amazon Basin

**Figure 8.39**   Rerebawa

*My name is Rerebawa. I am one of the Yanomamo people. There are many of us living in the forest, scattered about, but too many to count. There are 50 people in my* **shabono**

Plantain

**Figure 8.40**   Planting with a digging stick

*(village). The forest is very good to us. There is plenty of land for our gardens. Our food plants grow quickly, and grow all year round. Our gardens only last a few years. We spend a lot of time weeding, especially in the wet season. Despite that, the clearing becomes overgrown with thorn bushes and scrub, full of snakes and rodents. It is too difficult to clear, so after three years we clear another patch of forest nearby. It is easier now that we have steel axes. We choose an area with no thorn bushes or very thick, tall trees. Our houses have to be replaced about the same time as the garden. We are indeed well-fed. We use a digging stick to plant manioc and plantains, our main crops, We can harvest our food all year round. Most of what we eat is plantain., raw, roasted or boiled. Manioc can be made into bread and beer. We also grow maize, sweet potatoes, cotton, tobacco and peach palms. We can collect honey and fruits from the forest and trap fish in pools at the end of the wet season. We hunt monkeys, deer, pigs, ant-eaters, and birds for meat with our bows and arrows. We use arrows tipped with poison, but my shotgun is better. We go trading and visiting other villages in the drier months. We keep away from the rivers, and travel on foot. We have to keep a look-out for our enemies. Not all the Yanomamo are our friends. We sometimes visit the big villages beside the mission stations where we can trade for axes, pots, nets and fishing hooks. We hope that no one will come to our land looking for gold.*

It is thought that there are about 20,000 Yanomamo Indians living in an area on the borders of Brazil and Venezuela (Figure 8.48). They are the largest group of Indians in the Amazonian Rain Forest still practising traditional agriculture. They move in village groups about the forest as they have to clear new gardens to grow their crops. They are therefore called **shifting cultivators**. They also live off the forest, hunting animals and birds and collecting edible forest products. They are therefore also **hunters and gatherers**. This is less important to them than growing crops, although the honey is very highly prized. Although they are now using manufactured implements which they obtain by trading, they are still entirely dependent on the forest for their food. They eat almost all they produce or gather. They are therefore also an example of **subsistence farmers**. The gardens they cultivate are reclaimed by the forest after only a few years. The gardens have little impact on the forest. The Yanomamo do not destroy the environment in which they live. They farm in a **sustainable** way. Even their houses are biodegradable. They use few implements – digging stick, machete and axe. Despite this low level of technology, they are highly skilled farmers (Figures 8.42 and 8.45).

**Figure 8.41**   Plantains for planting

## Threats to the survival of the Yanomamo

There have always been violent feuds between different groups of Yanomamo. This fighting has had no major effect on the population. There are, however, two major threats to their way of life.

1. Growing dependence on trading posts at mission stations.

2. Illegal small-scale gold mining on their land which can poison water supplies over a wide area.

Through contact with these outsiders, many young Yanomamo children die in epidemics.

**Figure 8.43**　View of a Yanomamo village

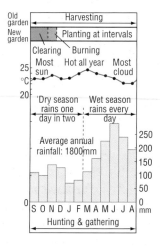

**Figure 8.42**　Yanomamo Indians: the year's work

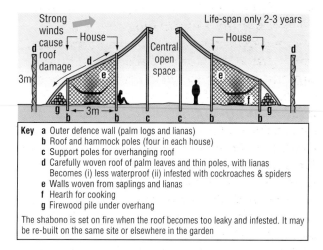

**Figure 8.44**　A Yanomamo village ('shabono')

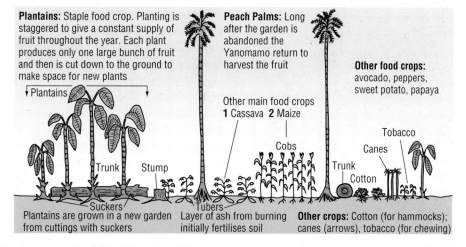

**Figure 8.45**　A Yanomamo garden ('Hikari Taka') – A Hole in the Jungle

## ASSIGNMENTS

1 Look at Figure 8.48. In which two countries are the Yanomamo lands located? How far are the Yanomamo lands from Manaus?

2 Look at Figure 8.42. Give two reasons why crops grow all year round in Yanomamo gardens.

3 Explain why the Yanomamo choose September and October to clear a patch of forest for a new garden.

4 What is a 'shabono'? Why does its roof slope so steeply? Why is a shabono in use for only a year or two?

5 Give two reasons why the gardens are abandoned after two or three years.

6 Match the following crops with the part which is harvested:
**crops**: cotton; peach palm; maize; pepper; tobacco; canes; manioc; plantain
**part**: fruit; tubers; leaf; seed-head; stalk; cob

7 Make a table to show which implements are a) made by the Yanomamo b) obtained by trade: axe; basket; clay pot; hammock; nylon fishing net; arrrows and arrowheads; machete; digging stick; aluminium pot; fish hooks.

8 Explain what is meant by: hunting and gathering; shifting cultivation; sustainable farming.

# The destruction of the Rain Forest

### Extension of the BR429: Rondonia, 1980

*Eventually, 99 km from its start, the BR429 came to an abrupt stop before a solid wall of forest. Facing it were three bulldozers. The lead bulldozer brought down the tree immediately. Groaning and whining, branches flailing as they tore from the foliage. It crashed to the ground in a confetti-like shower of leaves. The bigger trees sometimes required two bulldozers together, one pushing behind the other. But Amazonian roots are spread close to the surface … and most giants keel over with ease – their roots popping out like champagne corks. The lead bulldozer then moved on to the next tree, while the second bulldozer pushed the trunks and foliage to either side. Finally, a large tractor with V-like blades, scraped off the soil and left a smooth track wide enough for a truck. 'We are moving at about 1 km a day'.*

A. Cowell *A Decade of Destruction*

The Tropical Rain Forest has been regarded as an undeveloped region by the Brazilian government. The population of Brazil has been growing very rapidly, especially in the states near the Atlantic Ocean which contained 90% of the Brazilians. Too many of them were poor, landless people. The coastal cities were growing too rapidly. It was therefore decided to offer these people free land in the North. Roads such as the BR429 were built. These also gave access to companies developing the rich mineral resources of the area.

Figure 8.46 summarises the reasons for clearing the forest, and some of the consequences. The government's policy was '*a land without people for people without land*'. One result has been a large population increase in certain areas. In 1960, there were only about 10,000 people in the state of Rondonia. Thirty years later, the population had increased over 100 times. What became of one settler family is described here.

*Renato and Maria, descendants of German immigrants, travelled more than 2,500 km from the coast. They brought their six children to claim their free 50 hectare holding beside the BR429 in Rondonia. They erected a shelter and cleared 6 hectares of their farm with a chainsaw before burning the debris. They planted coffee, maize and rice. Malaria was a problem, and they were wary of the Indians in whose territory they had settled. Unfortunately. all their crops failed because the soil was too poor, and they abandoned their farm after only one year. Renato is now a sharecropper on a bigger farm. He pays his rent with a share of what he grows. Many of the colonists now live in shanty towns along the new highways.*

G  Gardens of surviving local Indians 'Holes in the Forest'
**1** Building new highways to develop Amazonia
**2** Clearing land along the new highways for small farms for new settlers
**3** Clear-felling large areas to extract a few hardwoods
**4** Clearing vast areas to create large cattle ranches is a major cause of deforestation
**5** Constructing H.E.P. schemes floods large areas of forest
**6** Mining gold using hydraulic hoses and mercury damages river courses
**7** Large scale open-cast mining of
**7a** bauxite and
**7b** iron ore
**7c** Iron smelters using charcoal
**7d** More forest cleared to make charcoal

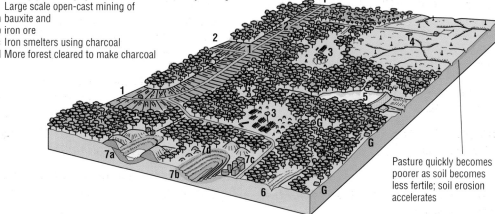

Pasture quickly becomes poorer as soil becomes less fertile; soil erosion accelerates

**Figure 8.46**  The Destruction of the Amazonian Rain Forest

## Other causes of deforestation (Figure 8.46)

There have been larger scale projects such as **plantations** of cacao, rubbber and coffee but they have not always been successful. New large areas of forest are still being clear-felled to take out rare and valuable mahogany and rosewood logs. Most of the trees felled are considered to be of no value, and the debris is often set alight. Most of the deforestation has been for cattle ranching to produce beef. The ranches were acquired by large companies or wealthy individuals. Large areas were needed, for example, a meat-packing company owned a 46,000 hectare block in Acre state in South West Brazil. It is thought however that most ranches will only last for about 10 years. Experiments to find better grass for grazing have not succeeded.

**Key**
..:¨ Outer limit of Rain Forest        River  ····· Frontier
─ New highways                    ← Migration of landless people to Amazonia
**1** Trans-Amazonian  **2** Pan-American highway  **3** BR364  **4** BR010  **5** BR429
● Cities with more than 1m people in Amazonia  **M** Manaus  **B** Belem
*Examples of new developments:* ▲ Carajas Iron Mines  Tucurui HEP scheme
**Y** Yanomamo land  **R** Rondonia  **X** Xingu National Park  ▲ Andes
*Examples of ecotourism:* **B** Bananal Island  **MNP** Manu National Park in Peru
                                                          (World heritage site)

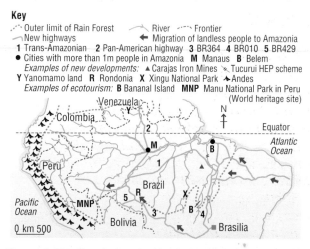

**Figure 8.48**  Developing the Amazonian Rain Forest

**Figure 8.47**  New colonists' housing in Rondonia

**Figure 8.49**  Cleared Rain Forest

Conservationists have become greatly concerned about the damage to the environment and to the native peoples. Abandoned farms and ranches are reclaimed by thorny scrub. It will be at least 100 years before there is a new forest cover. Even then it will not be as rich and diverse as the original rain forest.

## Saving/restoring the forest

The Rain Forest can be restored by:

★ Reducing or ending the grants and loans for clearing the rain forest

★ Encouraging mining companies to restore areas they have stripped for open-cast mines, preferably not with blocks of one type of tree

★ Creating National Parks and reserves such as the Xingu National Park, but very little of the Tropical Rain Forest in Brazil is actually protected

★ Demonstrating sustainable use of the forest without felling, for example, harvesting fruits, nuts, latex, rattan for export. The Body Shop, for example, has contracted the Kayopo Indians to collect Brazil nuts for use in making cosmetics, bath oils and body creams

### ASSIGNMENTS

1 What percentage of Brazilian's population lives in the Rain Forest? Name the two cities of more than a million people located in the TRF.

2 What was the first step in developing the Rain Forest in Brazil?

3 Study Figure 8.46. Give four reasons why so much of the Tropical Rain Forest has been cleared in Brazil.

4 Give four results of the clearance of large areas of the rain forest in Brazil.

5 Which solution to the loss of the TRF in Brazil do you think will be most successful?

6 Give two ways in which the methods used by new farmers differ from those used by the Yanomamo.

7 Between 1980 and 1990, the area cleared of rain forest in Brazil was almost twice the area of Scotland. Has Brazil done enough to protect its Rain Forest?

★ Developing a sustainable tourist industry which might help the native Indians.

# Ecotourism in Amazonia

*'Day 9: Fly to Manaus … Day 10: Ariua Jungle Lodge … a supervised jungle walk … later visit native houses; go alligator spotting and piranha fishing!'*
Extract from the itinerary of four-centre holiday in Brazil

Few tourists, even Brazilians, holiday in the Tropical Rain Forest, but their number is slowly increasing.

## Attractions for tourists in Amazonia

★ The wilderness of the unspoilt rain forest

★ The wildlife, both mammals and birds

★ The different lifestyle of the Indians.

## Problems in developing tourism in Amazonia

★ The vast areas and distances involved

★ Accessibility by i) road ii) river iii) air

★ Limited accommodation, except in a large city such as Manaus

★ Possible impact on the people and the environment

★ Providing opportunities to see glimpses of wildlife in dense rain forest.

Large-scale tourist developments would be out of place in Amazonia. They would damage the environment which people had come to see. The new highways provide better access than in the past, but the developments which have taken place along these highways would deter tourists.

## Ecotourism

This is a term used to describe small-scale tourist development which does not harm either the environment or the native people. An example of this is on Bananal Island (Figure 8.50). This is a very large, thinly populated river island between two branches of the Aruguia River. Most of the Tropical Rain Forest on the island is flooded during the wetter months.

Large areas have been cleared for dry-season grazing for cattle in the last 70 years. The Indians' traditional shifting cultivation, growing manioc and maize, has been badly affected. Many herders and hunters stay without permission on the island in the dry season.

### Saving the island and developing ecotourism

★ Cattle grazing is being phased out

★ Illegal hunters are being banned

★ A reserve for the Indians has been created; the northern part of the island has been made a National Park

★ A visitors' centre with accommodation for 40 people has been opened in the Park.

Brazilian, European and Japanese tourists come to see the abundant wildlife. The centre is also visited by trekkers on a long-distance West-East trail. The Indians at the moment do not benefit from the presence of the visitors.

### Other examples of holidays in the rain forest

★ an Amazon cruise by liner to Manaus

★ a study tour of dolphins by river boat

★ a visit to Manu National Park, a World Heritage Site, in Peru.

**Figure 8.51** Ecotourism in Manu National Park (Peru)

## ASSIGNMENTS

Visit the website: www.pantiacolla.com

1 On the four centre holiday mentioned above, there are flights from Recife to Rio; Rio-Iguassu Falls; Iguassu – Manaus; Manaus – Recife. Find the four places on an atlas map, and measure the distances between them.

2 Bananal Island
a) Make a list of ways in which the Indians might become involved in tourism.
b) Decide which of these are i) possible ii) impossible.
c) Would the Indians' way of life be improved or not by tourism?

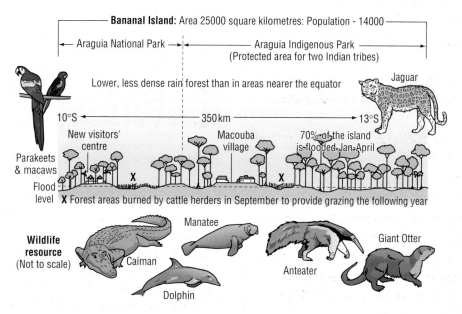

**Figure 8.50** Bananal Island: tourist development and wildlife conservation

## Population growth and decline

### World population growth

Figure 9.1 shows that on 12 October, 1999, the population of the world reached 6 billion. The graph also shows that:

★ in early times, population grew slowly, increasing and declining in turn. Wars, famines and disease slowed population growth. In the 1350s, around a third of the people of Europe were wiped out by plague during the Black Death (Figure 9.2)

★ from around 1750 population began to grow at an ever faster rate. In 1800 there were 1 billion people, by 1930 there were 2 billion, and this figure continued to rise. In fact, population was growing so rapidly that the term **population explosion** was used. More people were being born than were dying. This was the result of improved food supplies and new medicines that were spreading to many parts of the world. However, people worried about housing, educating, feeding and providing health care for the ever-growing numbers of people, especially in the poorer countries.

**Figure 9.2**   Print of The Black Death

### Birth rates and death rates

The rate at which the world's population increases or decreases depends on a 'balance' between birth rates and death rates (see Figure 9.3 A, B and C).

★ **Birth rate** is the number of babies born in a year for every thousand people in the population.

★ **Death rate** is the number of people who die in a year for every thousand people in the population.

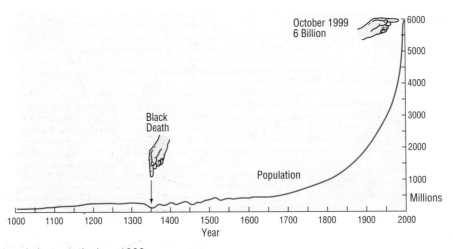

**Figure 9.1**   World population growth since 1000

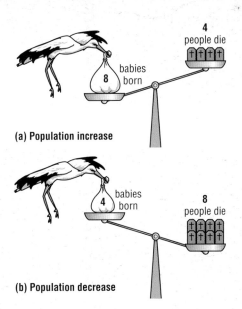

(a) Population increase

(b) Population decrease

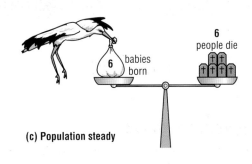

(c) Population steady

**Figure 9.3**   Population 'balance'

The difference between the birth rate and death rate is called **natural increase**. Taking the world as a whole, there has been a high rate of natural increase in the past 200 years. This is because the number of births has been greater than the number of deaths. This is shown in Figure 9.3 A. Figure 9.3 B shows population decrease, while in Figure 9.3 C population stays the same. It is all a matter of balance between birth and death rates.

## *Birth rates and a poor family in Bahar*

'We need our children to help us in the fields, to help us in the fields, especially with the rice planting and harvesting.'

'Its traditional to have a large family in this village'

'I'm not happy with birth-control, it goes against my Hindu beliefs'

'We need our daughters to help in our home'

'A large family is an insurance policy for our old age and when we are ill'

'We've already lost one child – we must make sure that some survive'

Figure 9.4A and 9.4B suggest why there are differences between the size of families in India and Italy.

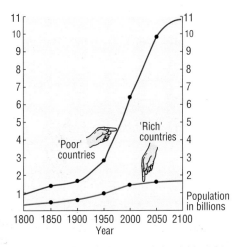

**Figure 9.4 (A)**   A poor farming family with five children from Bihar (India)

**Figure 9.5**   Population growth in 'rich' and 'poor' worlds

## Population growth in rich and poor countries

The rate of population increase varies around the world. The graph in Figure 9.5 shows that population is growing fastest in the 'poor' world and is slowing up in the ' rich' world. Look at the table in Figure 9.8. It shows that:

★ in the countries of the 'poor' world there is a big difference between birth and death rates, for example, in India the population is increasing rapidly

★ in the countries of the 'rich' world, such as the United Kingdom, there is little difference between birth and death rates so the population is growing very slowly

★ in some countries of the 'rich' world, such as Italy, the death rate is greater than the birth rate. Italy's population is expected to decline in the future.

## Birth rates and a rich family in Turin

'It is very expensive to buy a house in a nice part of Turin – we can only really afford one child' and pay our mortage'

'In spite of the church, contraception is used by many people'

'Like many women, we enjoy a good standard of living and enjoy our holidays abroad every year'

'I enjoy my career and can cope with one child. Two would make it impossible'

**Figures 9.4B**   A prosperous family with one child from Turin (Italy)

### ASSIGNMENTS

1 Look at the graph of world population growth since the year 1000.
   a) What was the population in: 1000, 1800 and 1900?
   b) After 1900 how long did it take the population of the world to double?
   c) When did the population of the world reach 6 billion?
   d) What happened to population in the 1350s and why?

2 Why do we use the term 'explosion' to describe changes in population since the 1950s?

3 Why do people worry about the population 'explosion'?

4 What is the meaning of each of the following terms?
   ◆ Birth rate
   ◆ Death rate
   ◆ Natural increase

5 Study Figure 9.4 and the text. Look at the reasons for differences in birth rates in Bihar and in Turin.
   a) Give three reasons why the family in Bihar have six children
   b) Give three reasons why the family in Turin have one child.

6 Describe and explain the changes in world population from 1000 to 2000.

7 Look at Figure 9.8.
   a) Make a copy of the first 5 columns of the table.
   b) Complete the missing figures for birth rates, death rates and natural increase.
   c) Is there a link between the rate of natural increase and Gross National Product? Explain your answer.
   You could draw a scatter graph to show the link.

**TO TAKE YOU FURTHER**

# Population decline

In 2002, experts identified the main population problem as the ever increasing number of **elderly** people. World population is expected to decline as people have fewer children and live longer. Instead of a population 'explosion', the world faces the problem of a population '**implosion**'. It is forecast that by 2050

◆ the number of people aged over 60 will increase from 629 million to 2 billion

◆ the number of people in the world aged 60 and over will outnumber those under 15.

According to a United Nations official, countries in the 'poor world' will follow the example of European countries such as Italy:

*'It is astonishing – the Mexicans, the Brazilians and even the Indians are saying their birth rates will fall within twenty years.'*

## Results of population decline

In a country like the UK what will be the results of this 'greying' of the population?

◆ there will be fewer people of working age to support the ever growing number of elderly people

◆ it will be more and more expensive to provide pensions and health care for elderly people as they live longer

**Figure 9.7**  Elderly people help with the harvest in India

◆ there will be more elderly people around. There will be more sheltered housing, nursing homes and hospitals caring for geriatric patients.

**Figure 9.8**  Population figures for sample countries

| Country | A | B | C | D | E | F | G |
|---|---|---|---|---|---|---|---|
| Afghanistan | 27 | 43 | 19 | 24 | 43 | 3 | <100 |
| Egypt | 70 | 28 | | 21 | 36 | 4 | 1290 |
| India | 1024 | 26 | 9 | | 42 | 4 | 440 |
| Italy | 58 | 9 | 10 | | 14 | 18 | 20090 |
| Finland | 5 | | 10 | 1 | 18 | 15 | 24280 |
| UK | 60 | 12 | 11 | 1 | 19 | 16 | 21410 |
| USA | 285 | 15 | | 6 | 21 | 13 | 29240 |

A: Population of the country in millions
B: Birth rate  C: Death rate
D: Natural Increase/ Natural Decrease
E: % of country's population under 15
F: % of country's population over 65
G: Gross National Product per person (in $).
(Gross National Product is the value of all the goods and services produced, divided by the country's population).
Figures are for 2001 ( Population Reference Bureau and *The World Guide 2001/2002*)

**Figure 9.6**  Sheltered housing in Perth

*continued* ➤

> ▶ **TO TAKE YOU FURTHER** *continued*

## Dealing with population decline

Here are some possible solutions to the problems of population decline.

People should

◆ as long as they are fit, work longer and retire later

◆ pay much more in taxes to pay for their pensions.

The government should

◆ encourage people to have more children

◆ allow more immigrants and refugees to work here

What do you think?

### ASSIGNMENTS *TO TAKE YOU FURTHER*

**1** What is meant by the term population 'implosion'?

**2** Is population decline a good or a bad thing for a country such as the UK?

**3** Form a small group. Discuss each of the possible solutions to the problems of population decline. How easy will it be to persuade people to carry out these ideas?

**4** For project work on the population of any country you can use the following website:

**www.odci.gov/cia/publications/factbook**

# Rich world, poor world

## Our divided world

One great difficulty facing the world's 6.1 billion inhabitants is the enormous difference in wealth between countries. Figure 9.9 shows one way of dividing the world into rich and poor countries:

★ The countries of **the North** are generally wealthy and contain 20% of the world's population. They include the rich countries of Europe and North America, plus Russia, Japan, Australia and New Zealand. Most of them lie north of the Tropic of Cancer and enjoy high standards of living.

★ The countries of **the South** are generally poor and contain around 80% of the world's population. They are mainly found south of the Tropic of Cancer and have low standards of living.

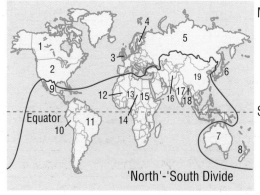

North
  Developed countries
  More economically
  developed countries
  (MEDCs)
  First World

South
  Developing countries
  Third World
  Less economically
  developed countries
  (LEDCs)

**Figure 9.9** North and South: rich world, poor world

If these 100 people represent the world's population -

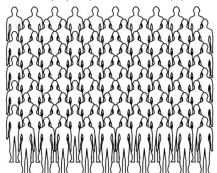

The richest 20 of them own 80% of the world's wealth
The poorest 20 own only 1% of it
50 of them do not have adequate sanitation
48 of them live on less than $2 a day
16 of them (all in Africa south of the Sahara) do not get enough food

**Figure 9.10**   Global gaps between rich and poor

Figure 9.10 shows some of the global gaps between rich and poor. These differences can be better seen by looking at Afghanistan, a poor country and Finland, a rich country (page 174).

**a**  Finland

**b**  Afghanistan

**Figure 9.11**   Contrasting work environments for rich and poor

## ASSIGNMENTS

**1**  Look at Figure 9.9. What are the various names that can be used to describe the 'rich' and 'poor' areas of the world?

**2**  With the help of an atlas, name the rich countries numbered 1 to 8, and the poor countries numbered 9 to 19.

**3**  Read about Afghanistan and Finland. Write out the four statements which are true from the following:
   ◆ Afghanistan is one of world's poorest countries.
   ◆ Finland has excellent health care services.
   ◆ Afghanistan's population is growing faster than Finland's.

   ◆ Almost everyone in Afghanistan, especially the women can read and write.
   ◆ Unlike Afghans, Finns have an excellent education system and most own mobile phones and PCs.

**4**  Either draw up a table to bring out the main differences between Finland and Afghanistan. or imagine that you intend leaving Afghanistan and are persuading a friend to come with you. What are the main factors 'pushing' you away, and what are the main factors 'pulling' you to a country like Finland?

# Afghanistan – a poor country

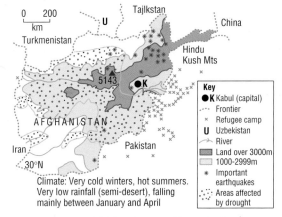

Climate: Very cold winters, hot summers. Very low rainfall (semi-desert), falling mainly between January and April

**Figure 9.12**   Map of Afghanistan and its neighbours

### Fact file

|  | Afghanistan | Finland |
|---|---|---|
| Population in 2000 | 27.2 million | 5.2 million |
| Population in 2050 | > 55 million | 4.8 million |
| Children per mother | 6 | 1.7 |
| Expectation of life | M46; F44 | M74; F81 |
| Access to clean water | 13% | 100% |
| People per car | 646 | 3 |

As in many developing countries, most people live in villages and work on the land. Figure 9.12 shows that most of the country is mountainous. Many villages are remote and roads are poor. Steep slopes make farming difficult in most areas. Severe droughts also occur, and then irrigation schemes fail. Thousands of farmers have been forced to flee to the cities and to neighbouring Pakistan. Frequent powerful earthquakes like the one in 2002, have killed thousands and made even more homeless.

There is much poverty and disease. Health care services are poor, and there are not enough doctors or nurses. Over 150 out of every 1000 infants die before they reach their first birthday. Education services are under pressure, for example, a secondary school in Kabul has over 9000 pupils, taught in three three-hour shifts. For religious and social reasons, the education of women and girls has been largely ignored until now.

War has made life much worse: many Afghans face death from warfare as well as hunger and disease. In the last 25 years:

★ Afghanistan was invaded and occupied by the former Soviet Union between 1979 and 1989

★ as a result, 2 million people died, and 6 million people fled to Pakistan and Iran

★ there has been civil war since 1989 between different groups of Afghans and involving foreign Muslims

★ in 2001, after the terrorist attack on 11 September, American, British and other foreign troops became involved searching for terrorists.

# Finland: a rich country

As in many developed countries, most people live in towns – especially Helsinki, the capital city. They work in factories and offices. With companies such as Nokia, Finland is a world leader in producing and using the latest technology. Finns have one of the highest

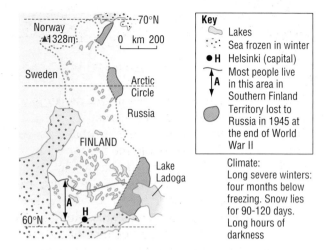

**Figure 9.13**   Finland and its neighbours

ownership rates of PCs and mobile phones in the world. All these developments have taken place in one of the most northerly countries in the world. Cold winters can be an expensive business: snow clearing, breaking the ice in the frozen Baltic Sea, heating costs and frost damage to buildings and crops.

There is little poverty and disease. Health problems such as heart attacks are often the result of too much food rather than too little. These problems are being tackled thanks to excellent health services. There are successful schemes to take more exercise, cut out smoking and improve diet. Schools and universities are excellent; huge sums have been spent on ICT.

In 1945, Finland was devastated after the war and had to give land to the former Soviet Union (Figure 9.13). As a result:

★ over 400,000 refugee Finns had to be resettled

★ enduring much hardship, they cleared new farms from Finland's northern coniferous forests.

Today, modern technology and a high standard of living make life comfortable for the vast majority of Finns throughout the country.

**TO TAKE YOU FURTHER**

# 'Development': measurement and meaning

Reading about Afghanistan and Finland should give you a good idea about the many differences between the rich 'North' and the poor 'South'. Other possible names for Rich World and Poor World are shown on Figure 9.19. Sometimes the countries of the South are called 'developing' and those of the North are called 'developed'. Choosing a suitable name is not always straightforward because of different ideas about the measurement and meaning of 'development'.

One way of measuring development is to use Gross Domestic Product (GDP). It is the total income earned by a country, divided by its population. Using this method: the average GDP in the USA works out at $33,000 per person, in India it is $440 per person. However, it is difficult to directly compare such countries because (i) these figures are only averages; no country divides out its wealth equally. There are poor people in 'developed' countries, and rich people in 'developing' countries. (ii) GDP does not take into account differences in prices and standard of living between countries.

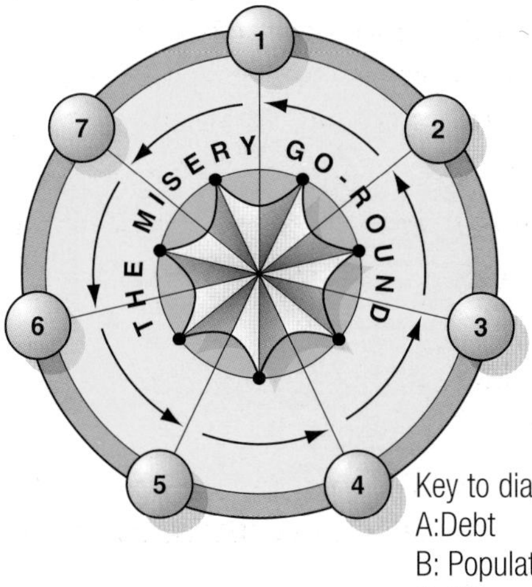

Development is about more than just money. Perhaps development means as many people (male and female, of all ages) having fair access to good health care, education, food, clean water, sanitation, jobs and decent housing. All these features, as well as GDP, need to be taken into account when discussing development.

Achieving fair shares for all will never be easy. Figure 9.14 shows some of the obstacles that face many of the poorest countries. They are caught up in a 'misery-go-round'. The challenge facing our world – and that means everyone, rich or poor – is how to stop the 'misery-go-round'.

## ASSIGNMENTS TO TAKE YOU FURTHER

1 Suggest why only using GDP per person is not the most accurate way of comparing development between different countries.

2 Match the numbers on the 'Misery-go-round' with the obstacles (shown by letters A–G) facing the poorest countries in the South.

3 Of the 7 difficulties facing the poorest countries, discuss which you think is the biggest obstacle to development. Give reasons for your answer.

Key to diagram
A: Debt
B: Population growth
C: Illiteracy
D: Unfair trade
E: Shortage of capital
F: Leaking profits
G: Natural disasters

**Figure 9.14**   The 'misery-go-round'

**Figure 9.15**   Depending on a single commodity: bananas

# Obstacles to development

★ Countries face huge interest payments to banks and countries in the North. This could be better spent on schools and hospitals.

★ Although natural disasters can strike both rich and poor countries, hurricanes, earthquakes etc. have a greater impact on the developing world.

★ There is a lack of money to invest in farming, industry, communications and hospitals.

★ In some parts of Africa and Asia, over 5 children per family is common. Although useful to their families as a labour force, large numbers of young people put pressure on schooling, healthcare, jobs and food supply.

★ Poorly educated people mean a shortage of skilled workers, teachers and managers. Women are more likely to have larger families if they have dropped out of school at an early age.

★ Many of the poorest countries in the South, depend on exporting one or two commodities such as cocoa, sugar, coffee and raw materials. The price of agricultural goods and raw materials can drop very quickly, for example, the prices paid to coffee farmers have fallen by 70% since 1997.

★ Many large American and European multi-national companies control many industries in the South. Most of the profits flow (or leak) back to the North rather than stay in the South.

# Introducing the United States

## The USA: a large country

Three countries – Canada, the United States and Mexico – make up the continent of North America. (Figure 9.16). All three countries were once ruled as colonies from Europe. In 1776, the USA became independent from Britain. A reminder of this event is the 13 stripes representing the original 13 British states on the east coast. Over the years, the USA expanded, and now consists of 50 states, shown by the 50 stars (Figure 9.16). These include Alaska and the Pacific Ocean state of Hawaii. Although not so large as Russia and Canada, the USA has to be divided into 5 time zones (6 zones if Hawaii is included).

## The USA: a varied people

Although the USA is described as a 'new' country, the original Native Americans have been there for 10,000 years. They were the start of millions of people who have migrated to the USA from all parts of the globe.

Figure 9.16 shows that the **Native Americans** originally came from Asia. Today, they are the poorest of all Americans, and about one-fifth of them live on reservations.

Millions of **Europeans** crossed the Atlantic, especially in the 19th century. Many were refugees looking for freedom. Others came to

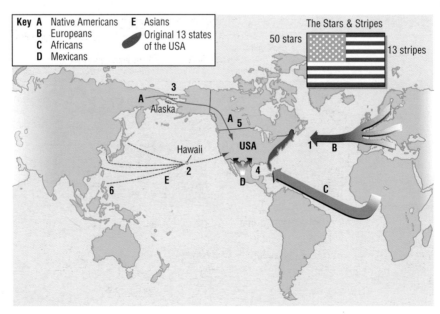

**Figure 9.16**   Migration flows to the USA

work in the rapidly growing cities such as Chicago (Figure 9.18), or to farm the available free land.

Some migrants had no choice at all. **Black Americans** (Figure 9.16) are descendents of slaves shipped to the southern states of the USA. They were forced to work on the cotton plantations.

Today, the second largest group of Americans are the Spanish-speaking **Hispanics**. Originally, the states of the south west USA, such as California, were part of Mexico. The number of Hispanics has continued to grow with migrants from Puerto Rico, Cuba and Mexico. Large numbers of Mexicans have settled in California and Texas. They are attracted by the jobs and high living standards.

Increasing numbers of migrants are **Asian**. Vietnamese, Koreans, Philippinos and Indians have all been 'pulled' by the opportunities offered by the world's most powerful country.

The 'Rustbelt' is the original industrial area of the USA. As these traditional industries closed down, many people migrated to the 'Sunbelt' states where new industries have grown up. Many older people also choose to retire to these warmer southern states.

**Figure 9.17**   Casinos bring in much needed income on Native American reservations

**Figure 9.18**   Chicago's Polish district

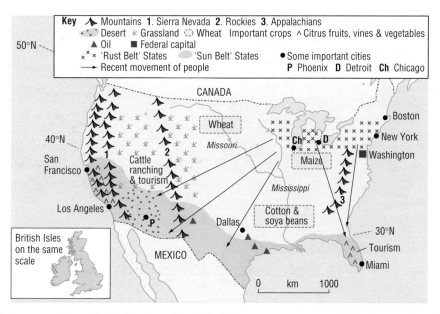

**Figure 9.20**   The USA: a general map (excluding Hawaii and Alaska)

## Overview of the USA

Why is the USA so important?

★ with a population of 287 million, the USA has the world's third largest population

★ thanks to its long history of migration, the USA is a multi-cultural and multi-racial nation

★ with an area of 9.4 million square km, it is big enough to contain 38 United Kingdoms!

★ it has enormous reserves of minerals, fossil fuels, water power, and forests. American farms produce a huge range of crops and account for 15% of world food exports (Figure 9.20)

★ the USA is one of the world's biggest democracies, the world's most important military power, and has very strong political influence

★ American multi-national companies such as Ford, General Motors, McDonalds and WalMart employ people worldwide

★ the USA is the world's biggest and most advanced manufacturing and high-tech country

★ the USA influences millions of people throughout the world who watch American television programmes and films, listen to American music, eat fast foods such as hamburgers, drink Coca Cola, and wear American style clothes and footwear.

★ **However**, not everyone enjoys the very high standards of living. Native Americans, Black Americans, Hispanic Americans and 'Poor White' Americans make up the 10% of the population who are poor.

★ not everyone is happy with the vast amount of resources that the USA consumes, or its enormous military power and influence, for example, the invasion of Iraq in 2003.

### ASSIGNMENTS

1   With the help of an atlas, name the following areas of water 1–4 and countries 5–6 on Figure 9.16.

2   What do the 13 stripes and the 50 stars represent on the American flag?

3   Who were the first Americans and from where did they come?

4   Why did millions of Europeans migrate to the USA in the 19th century?

5   What made the Black Americans different from other migrants to the USA?

6   Working in small groups, list those products, programmes, people, places etc. which come to mind when you think of the USA.

7   Draw two graphs to show the following figures for the different people who make up the USA.
   a)   Races of the USA: White 75%; Black American 12%; Native American 1%; Asian 4%; and Other/mixed races 8%.
   b)   People of Hispanic origin (millions): Mexican 20.6; Puerto Rican 3.4; Cuban 1.3; Other Hispanic 10.1.
   c)   Explain the patterns shown by the graph of origins of Hispanic groups.

8   Write a short account explaining which features of America makes it the world's most powerful country.

**Figure 9.19**   Los Angeles' Black American district

# Detroit: changing 'rustbelt' city

## Detroit: location and growth of Motown

Detroit is the 10th largest city in the USA. Figure 9.21 shows its location in Michigan, one of the Great Lakes states. From the 19th century, vast amounts of coal and iron ore were mined, and a huge range of products were manufactured. Detroit became a major centre of steel-making because of its lakeside location. It was an ideal base for local business men such as Henry Ford, one of the pioneers of car making. People flocked to the city, drawn the huge variety of jobs in steel, engineering and car production.

By 1950 Detroit city was home to 2 million people representing over 80 ethnic groups. It was also the world's biggest car producer. Nicknamed 'Motown', short for motor town, Detroit is home to three of the world's largest car making companies – General Motors, Chrysler and Ford.

## Why the car industry grew in Detroit

**A** Detroit is centrally located on the Great Lakes and is now linked to the St Lawrence Seaway. This allows the transport of raw materials and finished products.

**B** Car manufacture uses quantities of steel. It could be made from the rich resources of iron, coal amd limestone found around the Lakes area.

**C** Henry Ford was responsible for the development of the moving assembly-line method of car production. This allowed production of the Model T Ford at a cheap price.

**D** There was an increasing demand for cars from the growing American population.

**E** Thousands of people poured into Detroit to work in the car industry. Many Black Americans came from the southern states. All were attracted by the high wages, Ford paid $5/day when the average wage was $9/week.

## Detroit: 'Rust belt' city

By the 1970s, the traditional industries of the Great Lakes area were in decline. In Detroit, older car factories and steel works were closing down. With so many derelict factories, the Great Lakes area became part of the old industrial area called the 'Rust belt'. Industry declined because:

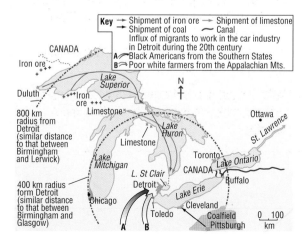

**Figure 9.21**  Detroit and the Great Lakes

**Figure 9.22**  The car industry grew in Detroit

★ Companies based in Detroit set up factories in the southern states of the USA where labour costs were cheaper

★ Large American produced cars used a great deal of fuel. They could not compete with smaller, cheaper cars from Japan and South Korea.

High levels of car ownership had already encouraged the growth of freeways in Detroit. This had encouraged the more prosperous, mainly white, families to move out into the growing suburbs or into other towns in Detroit's metropolitan area. They drove daily to their work. in the city. Unemployment then resulted in many more people moving out of the city. As more people lost their jobs it was worse for the Black Americans who remained in the inner city districts. With unemployment came poverty and crime. Parts of inner city Detroit were run down. with derelict buildings, wasteland and abandoned cars.

## Detroit in the 21st century

Detroit is now well on the road to recovery:

★ competition from foreign car companies is still fierce but companies such as Ford have invested in new techniques and models and amalgamated with foreign companies

★ new hi-tech firms have been attracted to the city, although many are located in the suburbs

★ tourism and business conferences are encouraged. Famous hit records (by Stevie

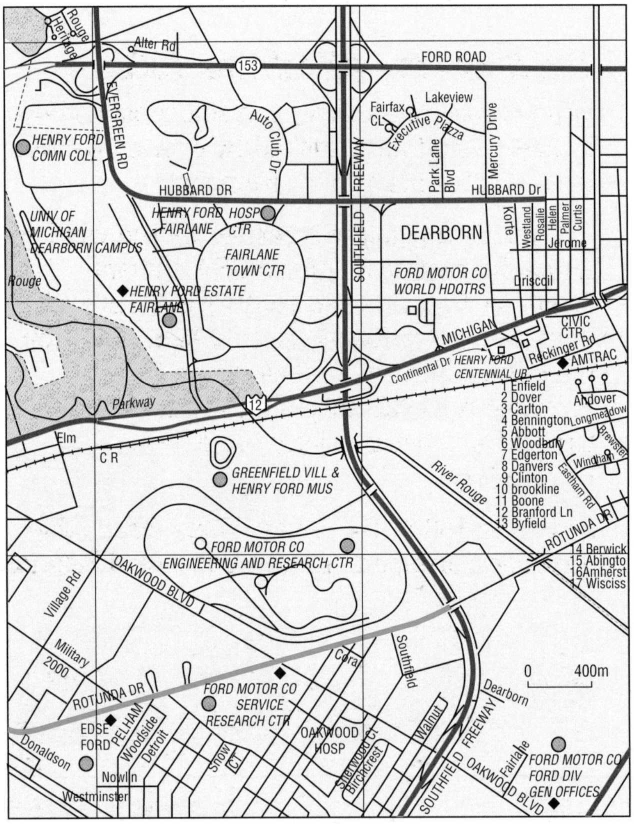

**Figure 9.23A**   Map of Dearborn (Detroit): a Ford landscape

**Figure 9.23B**   A redeveloped area in Detroit

Wonder, Diana Ross etc.) from the 1960s are celebrated in the Motown Museum. Cars are not forgotten either. Figure 9.23A shows the Dearborn district, where Henry Ford was born. The map shows not only Ford's world headquarters but the Henry Ford museum for those interested in cars and their effect on the American way of life

★ parts of Detroit's centre or **Downtown** area have been redeveloped. One huge building is the Renaissance Centre, headquarters of General Motors. The elevated rail system called the People Mover runs for 5 km round the perimeter of Downtown.

### ASSIGNMENTS

1 Copy the following, selecting the correct highlighted word:
Detroit is located in the **Great Plains/Great Lakes area**. It lies between **Lakes Superior and Michigan/Lakes Erie and St Clair**.

2 Five reasons are given for the growth of the car industry in Detroit. Match the following with the letters A to E:
labour force; raw materials; location; markets; business skill.

3 Look at Figure 9.23A. Name the landscape features showing the influence of Henry Ford on Detroit.

4 Write a short account about the rise, decline and recovery of Motown's car industry.

## The Great Plains

The Great Plains of the USA are located east of the Rocky Mountains. They are drained by the Missouri River and other tributaries of the Mississippi River (Figure 9.25). At the end of the Ice Age, when the climate was wetter, they were an area of mixed woodland and meadowland. As the climate became drier, trees only survived along the banks of rivers. The Great Plains became a 'sea of grass' which provided rich grazing for vast herds of buffalo and antelope. These animals provided food, shelter, clothing and equipment for the Plains Indians. The tribes survived by hunting and gathering. Their traditional way of life was

ended with the migration of settlers from the Eastern USA (Figure 9.24).

### Climate

These newcomers were faced with a harsh climate. The earliest explorers of the Great Plains had considered them to be a desert. Much of the area is semi-desert, with very unreliable rainfall. The result is a climate of alternate wet and dry cycles (**droughts**).

These droughts can last for a decade. The wet years encouraged people to settle on the Great Plains; the droughts resulted in depopulation. Figure 9.24 shows the cycles of drought over the last 100 years. In 2002, the Great Plains were in the middle of a drought which showed no signs of ending. It was thought to be as bad as the drought which partly caused the 'Dust Bowl' of the 1930s (Figure 9.24).

### The Dust Bowl (Oklahoma 1933)

Wind erosion blew away top soil, loosened by drought, and impoverished by over-cultivation, lack of nutrients and over-grazing.

The fertile top soil was carried by the wind as far as the east coast of the USA. Tenant farmers who paid their rent with a share of the crop they grew, for example, wheat or cotton, were forced off their small farms. Many migrated to California, and the farms on the Great Plains became larger and more mechanised.

Since the 1930s, there have been three other prolonged droughts. Expensive spray irrigation

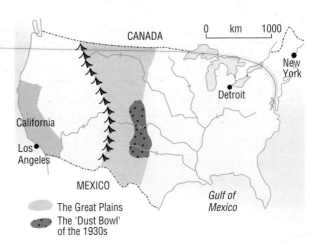

**Figure 9.25** Location of the Great Plains

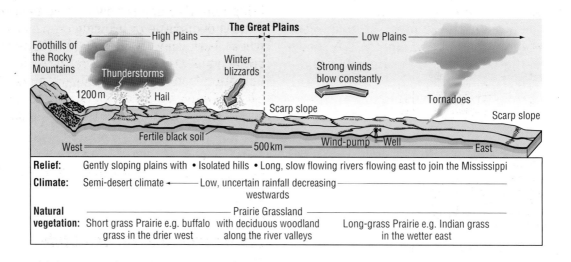

**The Great Plains**

| Relief: | Gently sloping plains with • Isolated hills • Long, slow flowing rivers flowing east to join the Mississippi |
| Climate: | Semi-desert climate ← Low, uncertain rainfall decreasing westwards |
| Natural vegetation: | Prairie Grassland |

| Short grass Prairie e.g. buffalo grass in the drier west | with deciduous woodland along the river valleys | Long-grass Prairie e.g. Indian grass in the wetter east |

**a. The Native Americans:** Until the mid-19th Century e.g. Comanche, Kiowa, Sioux, Cheyenne

The way of life depended entirely on the buffalo

Tipis made of buffalo hide

Antelope

The Indian tribes wandered in their large hunting territories following the vast herds of buffalo

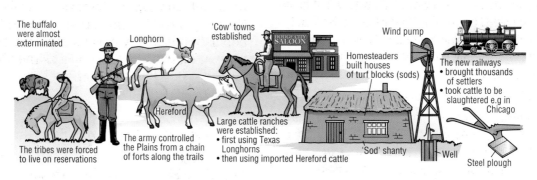

The buffalo were almost exterminated

Longhorn

'Cow' towns established

DODGE CITY SALOON

Wind pump

Homesteaders built houses of turf blocks (sods)

The new railways
• brought thousands of settlers
• took cattle to be slaughtered e.g in Chicago

Hereford

The tribes were forced to live on reservations

The army controlled the Plains from a chain of forts along the trails

Large cattle ranches were established:
• first using Texas Longhorns
• then using imported Hereford cattle

'Sod' shanty

Well

Steel plough

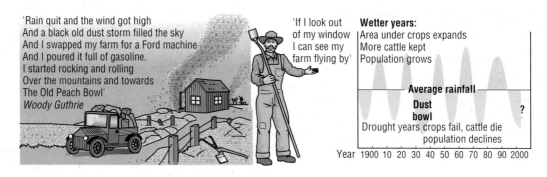

'Rain quit and the wind got high
And a black old dust storm filled the sky
And I swapped my farm for a Ford machine
And I poured it full of gasoline.
I started rocking and rolling
Over the mountains and towards
The Old Peach Bowl'
*Woody Guthrie*

'If I look out of my window I can see my farm flying by'

**Wetter years:**
Area under crops expands
More cattle kept
Population grows

**Average rainfall**

**Dust bowl**

Drought years crops fail, cattle die population declines

Year 1900 10 20 30 40 50 60 70 80 90 2000

**Figure 9.24**  The Great Plains

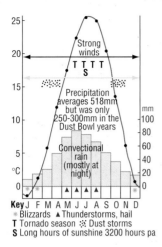

Key J F M A M J J A S O N D
✳ Blizzards ▲ Thunderstorms, hail
T Tornado season ⁖ Dust storms
S Long hours of sunshine 3200 hours pa

**Figure 9.26** Climate graph for Dodge City

schemes have helped, but they have also drastically reduced supplies of underground water. Cloud-seeding is often used to try and

## ASSIGNMENTS

1 Look at Figures 9.24 and 9.26. (i) Suggest reasons why the Native Indian way of life was suited to the Great Plains. (ii) List the features of the land and climate which made the Great Plains a) an easy place b) a difficult place for settlers in the mid-19th century.

2 Look at Figure 9.24. (i) Some settlers ordered windows and doors for their sod shanties by mail order. Suggest why they did so, explaining what a sod shanty was, and why it was necessary. (ii) The invention of barbed wire fences was a major innovation. List three other advances in technology which allowed the settlers to occupy the Great Plains.

3 Why has soil erosion been so common on the Great Plains since 1900?

4 The rainfall on the Great Plains is very variable. (i) How many periods of prolonged drought have there been since 1890? (ii) What has happened to the population during these droughts?

5 Find out (i) how strip cultivation and contour ploughing help to prevent soil erosion today (ii) the advantages and disadvantages of widespread irrigation on the Great Plains today.

bring rain. Farming is now on a large scale, rearing beef cattle or growing crops such as wheat, barley and sunflowers, but fewer people are needed. Drought is still resulting in migration from rural to urban areas like Dodge City or Denver, or again to California. The Great Plains are the most thinly populated area in the USA.

# California: people, water and power

## California – the 'Golden State'

Figure 9.27 shows some of California's main features. Of all the 50 American states, California has:

★ the largest population – over 35 million, and still growing

★ the biggest economy. California is the 5th strongest economy in the world, richer than many countries in Europe.

Once it was a poor, mainly farming area. Then, in 1848, at about the same time as gold was discovered, California broke away from Mexico. Its population rapidly increased as 'Forty-Niners' poured in. Since then, California's population has grown as its economy has prospered, and now is known as the 'Golden State'.

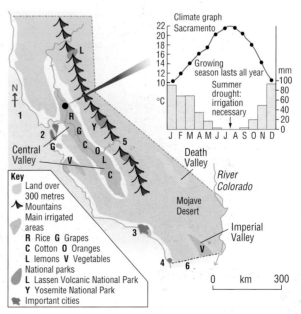

**Figure 9.27** General map of California

## People and California's economy

**Farming**: The native Indians were mainly hunters and gatherers. Farming really only began with the first Spanish settlers who introduced cattle, sheep, wheat and vines. Today, California has a larger farming output than any other American state. Areas such as Central Valley, Imperial Valley and coastal valleys produce:

★ a huge range of crops, including cotton, rice and wheat

★ about half America's fruit, for example, citrus and grapes

★ vast amounts of winter vegetables such as lettuces and tomatoes are supplied to colder parts of the USA.

In the 1930s, farmers escaping from the 'Dust Bowl' found work in California's fields. Today, up to a million Fillipino and Mexican workers (often illegal immigrants) provide a cheap labour force (see Figure 9.28).

They start picking in southern California, and move north where the harvest ripens later. The vegetables are then trucked in refrigerated lorries to the main cities of the USA.

**Transport, Industry and Services**: Chinese workers were among the earliest immigrants in the new state. First brought over to work in the gold mines, over 10,000 Chinese helped build the trans-continental railroads. These linked California with the eastern markets of the USA.

Industry was encouraged by:

★ World War II against Japan, and later wars in Korea and Vietnam

★ California's location – facing west for trade links with Pacific countries such as Japan and South Korea.

A wide range of industries from steel to aerospace developed. Cities sprawled, freeways grew, and services multiplied. A huge labour force was required. People attracted by these jobs included:

★ unemployed workers from the 'Rust belt' states, and cities like Detroit

★ Black Americans from southern states such as Arkansas and Alabama.

Since the 1950s, the area south of San Francisco has grown into the world's main high-tech centre called Silicon Valley (Figure 9.29). Where orchards once grew, hundreds of companies are concentrated because:

★ there are world famous research institutes and universities such as Stanford University

★ there is a huge pool of skilled graduates.

Highly qualified staff have been attracted from elsewhere in the USA, and from abroad, especially Asia. Many South Koreans, Taiwanese and Indians, for example, from Bangalore, have prospered in high-tech California.

**Figure 9.28**   Mexican workers in fields in California

**Figure 9.29**   Silicon Valley

## Water and California's economy

California's population growth and prosperous economy would have been impossible without water, and lots of it! California has two main problems with water supply:

★ most rain falls in Northern California where there are few people whilst the water is mainly required in the drier central and southern parts where most Californians live (Figure 9.27).

★ there is an ever-growing shortage of water. Irrigated agriculture uses most of the water, but California's population keeps growing. Industry and sprawling cities such as Los Angeles use more and more water. Lawns, golf courses, landscaped areas, and houses in prosperous suburbs with swimming pools and 2 or 3 bathrooms consume large amounts of water (Figure 9.30).

Figure 9.31 shows that large dams e.g. Shasta store water and produce hydropower. Water is then pumped through a network of canals, tunnels and aqueducts to the water-thirsty, semi-desert that is southern California. Water is led from the Colorado River to Los Angeles and the Imperial Valley.

**Figure 9.30**   Wealthy Los Angeles suburbs

## Energy and California's economy

As California prospered, it depended more and more on evergrowing amounts of energy. It is like a huge machine that depends on its own energy and imports from other states and abroad. Electricty is generated from hydropower schemes, geothermal stations, thermal power stations (using oil, coal and natural gas), and nuclear power plants. Since the 1970s, increasing use has been made of solar energy and wind power. However, these new energy sources only contribute a small amount to total electicity generation.

Without all this energy per person, Californians would not:

★ have homes with a wide range of domestic appliances such as dishwashers, PCs, TVs, DVDs, hi-fi equipment etc.

★ keep cool in the hot summer weather, thanks to air conditioning in homes, offices, shops, schools and cars

★ have one of the highest levels of car ownership in the world

★ live in the most productive agricultural and manufacturing state in the USA.

By 2001, there were occasional shortages of power. The amount of energy required was outstripping the supply.

### ASSIGNMENTS

1   Look at Figure 9.27. Use an atlas to name: Ocean 1, cities 2–4, mountain range 5 and country 6.

2   a)   What are the main agricultural products from California's Central Valley?
    b)   Look at the climate graph for Sacramento. What are the advantages and the disadvantages of this climate for farmers?

3   What is Silicon Valley, and why did it develop?

4   Write a short report about **either** Water supply in California **or** Energy supply in California

**TO TAKE YOU FURTHER**

# Cars and Californians

Perhaps more than anywhere else in the world, the car or automobile, and related forms of transport- trucks, bikes, ATVs (All-terrain-vehicles), and motor homes have affected life and landscape in California. Figure 9.32 shows that the automobile has

◆ allowed cities, especially Los Angeles, to sprawl over extensive areas, often wiping out once thriving fields, orchards and citrus groves (see page 185)

◆ created a daily drive-to-work way of life. Freeways are crowded with cars, often from two-car suburban homes, carrying commuters to work in Downtown offices, or industrial estates and science parks on the outskirts of the cities. At peak traffic times, congested roads can result in gridlock. Smog is common, especially in the cities of Southern California (see Figure 7.53)

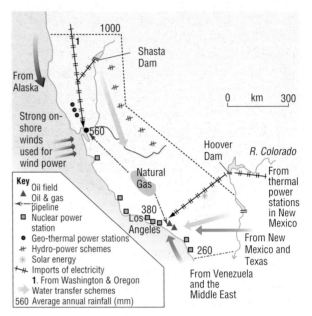

**Figure 9.31** California: energy sources and water diversion

*continued* ➤

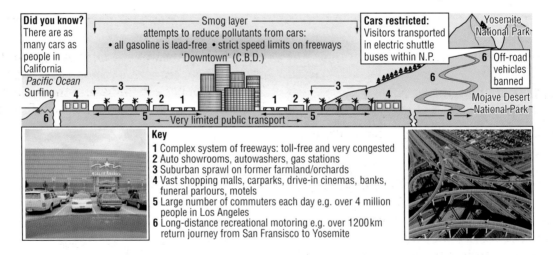

**Figure 9.32** The importance of automobiles in California

**Figure 9.33**    A tour bus in Yosemite National Park

◆  resulted in a drive-in way of life. Huge suburban shopping centres with enormous parking lots are located at highway intersections. Drive-in cinemas, banks, motels, restaurants (see Figure 9.32) are common landscape features. Even drive-in churches and funeral parlours are not unknown

◆  permitted Californians to drive to the Pacific coast beaches to swim and and surf. Alternatively, they can drive inland to ski in the Sierra Nevada mountains and visit National Parks like Yosemite (Figure 9.33). Roads to deserts, such as the Mojave, are popular at weekends. Unfortunately, unregulated driving by owners of trail bikes, recreation and four-wheel-drive vehicles can destroy vegetation like creosote bushes and kill wildlife.

### ASSIGNMENT *TO TAKE YOU FURTHER*

Write an illustrated report about 'Cars and Californian (or American) life and environment'. Carefully, work out the main sections for your report. You could refer to the information in this book about Los Angeles, Detroit and Phoenix.

**Remember: always have an introduction and a conclusion, and use maps/diagrams to illustrate your report.**

# Introducing India

## Countries and people of South Asia

Figure 9.34 shows the countries which make up South Asia. The largest is India which, along with Pakistan, Bangladesh and Sri-Lanka, was once ruled by Britain. From the 1500s, Europeans came to Asia to trade. They bought tea, cotton and spices. By 1914 large parts of Asia were ruled as colonies by several European countries. The colonial powers brought some benefits but they used the people and resources of countries such as India to make themselves more rich and powerful.

In 1947, after a long struggle and thanks to people such as Mahatma Gandhi (see panel), British India became independent. Britain had ruled over an area as large as Europe. It was a rich, colourful land with many languages and home to different religions (see Figure 9.35). The two largest religious groups were the Hindus and the Muslims. Over many years, they had become very suspicious of each other. The

Muslims did not want to be ruled by Hindus once India became independent. So the mainly Hindu areas became India and the mainly Muslim areas became what are now Pakistan

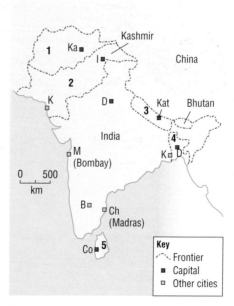

**Figure 9.34**    India and its neighbours

and Bangladesh. Millions migrated for safety. There was terrible bloodshed – at least a million people died. Mistrust between Muslims and Hindus continues to the present day (See Taking You Further). There are disputes between India and Pakistan over Kashmir (Figure 9.34).

## Overview of India

When India became independent, it was very poor, had little industry and was hardly able to feed itself. Today, India is a very important country because:

★ with over 1 billion people, India has the world's second largest population after China – every sixth person in the world is Indian

★ three of the world's major faiths – Hinduism, Buddhism and Sikhism – began here

★ over 200 languages are spoken in India with Hindi spoken by 40% of the population. English is used by many Indians

★ it is the largest democracy in the world

★ it is one of the biggest industrial countries with highly skilled people working in a wide variety of jobs including space engineering, nuclear power, electronics and computing

★ it has improved agriculture so that it now produces enough food, especially rice and wheat, to feed itself

★ over 250 million people (almost the population of the USA) enjoy a high standard of living

**However:**

★ there are still many millions who are amongst the poorest people in the world

★ although slowing up, India's population and its busy cities still continue to grow

### Mahatma Gandhi (1869–1948)

Gandhi was an inspiring leader. After working as a lawyer in South Africa, he returned to India to lead the campaign for independence from Britain. He always encouraged peaceful protests such as strikes. In 1947, Indians were finally given 'swaraj' or self-rule.

**Figure 9.36**   Mahatma Gandhi (1869–1948)

## Physical landscapes of South Asia

The countries of South Asia form a very large, sub-continent. It is cut off from the rest of Asia by the Himalayas, the highest mountain range in the world. Figure 9.37 shows that this diamond-shaped sub-continent has three main parts.

★ In the north (Figure 9.38) are the snow-capped Himalayas. Stretching for 2,700 km, they include Mount Everest. Located in Nepal, at 8,848 m, it is the world's highest mountain. Kanchenjunga (8598 m) is India's highest peak.

★ To the south of the Himalayas are the large plains. These are formed by some of the world's major rivers. such as the Indus, the Ganges and Brahmaputra. They rise in the

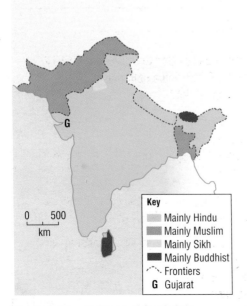

Key
- Mainly Hindu
- Mainly Muslim
- Mainly Sikh
- Mainly Buddhist
- Frontiers
- **G** Gujarat

0    500
km

**Figure 9.35**   Religions of South Asia

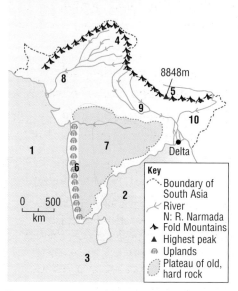

**Figure 9.37** Physical landscapes of South Asia

**Figure 9.39** A village on the base of the Ganga river

Himalayas and are fed by heavy summer rain and melting snow. Along with their many tributaries, they have built up huge plains with usually rich fertile soil. Millions of tonnes of such soil are still deposited. A huge, low-lying delta has been built up by the Ganga and Brahmaputra. Daily, it gets larger as new islands form. The plains and the huge delta are the most populated areas of South Asia (Figure 9.37).

★ South of the plains lies the Deccan Plateau. Figure 9.37 shows that it is shaped like a triangle. It is formed from very old, hard rocks and is about 1000 metres high. It tilts to the east from a range of highlands called the Western Ghats.

## ASSIGNMENTS

1 With the help of an atlas, name the following features on Figure 9.34.
Countries 1 to 5; cities shown by first letters.

2 a) What were the the cities of Mumbai and Chennai once called?
b) Name the capitals of India, Pakistan, Nepal, Bangladesh, Afghanistan and Sri Lanka.

3 Copy and complete this table

| Country | Main Religion(s) |
|---|---|
| India | |
| Pakistan | |
| Bangladesh | |
| Sri Lanka | |

4 a) Which country ruled South Asia until 1947?
b) Why did British India split into separate countries in 1947?

5 With the help of an atlas, name the following features on Figure 9.37
Seas/Oceans 1 to 3; Mountains/plateau 4 to 7; Rivers 8 to 10.

6 Write a short account describing the three main physical landscapes of South Asia.

7 Which of the three main physical landscapes supports
a) most people, and
b) least people.
Give reasons to explain your answer.

**Figure 9.38** A mountain village in the Himalayas

## TO TAKE YOU FURTHER

# Hinduism and India

India and Nepal are the main centres of Hinduism in the world (see Figure 9.40). The Hindu faith has influenced India in different ways:

**Landscape**: With its many gods, Hinduism is responsible for large numbers of ornate and richly decorated temples, sacred bathing places and roadside shrines (Figure 9.41). Hindus cremate their dead on large funeral pyres. They leave no monuments or tombstones to the dead. Often they re-use the same cremation site and it is then regarded as impure.

**Caste**: Hindus believe that people are born into a particular social group or caste. A person is born into a particular caste according to their actions in a previous life. Those who have lived badly will be reborn as an outcast Hindu or 'dalit'. There are about 200 million dalits (meaning the 'broken people'). Although the Indian government has passed laws to improve conditions of life for the dalits, they can still be discriminated against. Jobs such as cleaning latrines, raising pigs and cremating the dead are reserved for the dalits. In some Indian villages, the dalits have to live in separate houses. Children are divided by caste in some primary school classrooms,

## Hindu-Muslim tension

On three occasions since independence, Pakistan and India have gone to war over the disputed territory of Kashmir. There are still millions of Muslims who live in India (11% of the population). Unfortunately, Hindu-Muslim disputes can break out, for example, in Mumbai in 1993 and in 2002 in Gujarat the home state of Gandhi who urged non-violence and tolerance between people of all faiths.

## Global religious tension

India is not alone in having problems because of religion. Religious differences are responsible, directly and indirectly, for problems in many parts of the world. Some recent flashpoints are shown (Figure 9.40).

### ASSIGNMENTS TO TAKE YOU FURTHER

1. Match the five flashpoints shown on Figure 9.40 with: Northern Ireland; Afghanistan; Israel; Nigeria; Chechnya.

2. Draw a diagram to show the following figures for religious beliefs in India:
   Hindu – 82%; Muslim – 11%; Sikhhism – 2%; Christianity – 2%; Others (eg Buddhist, Jains) – 3%

3. What is a caste and why is it important in India today?

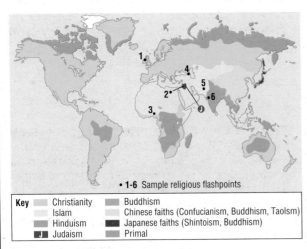

Figure 9.40    The world's main religions

Figure 9.41    A Hindu temple

# The monsoon and South Asia

## *What is the monsoon?*

Every year hundreds of millions of people in South Asia are affected by the **monsoon**. This is the name given to a very wet season which can last for some five months. The rains are very heavy and are brought by the south-west monsoon winds. Figure 9.42 shows the different dates when these warm, moist winds move across South Asia from the Indian Ocean. Advancing at roughly 20 km per hour, the monsoon rains soak the land, eventually reaching the north-west by mid-July. From November to May, the winds change direction and blow from the land outwards. During these months most of South Asia is dry.

As South Asia stretches from close to the equator northwards to the snow and ice of the Himalayas, there are big differences in climate. It is usual to suggest that there are three main seasons, as shown by the climate graph (Figure 9.43) for Mumbai:

★ June to October is the hot, **wet monsoon season**

★ November to February is the **warm, dry season** – in northern India, the nights can be cold, especially in January and February

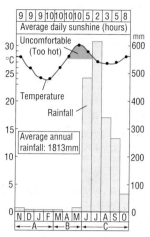

**Figure 9.43** Climate graph for Mumbai (India)

★ March to May is the **hot, dry season** – some years, temperatures can be unbearable and reach over 40°C. People look forward to the 'burst' of the monsoon and its welcome rain.

## *Seasonal descriptions*

### New Delhi, Early June

'With temperatures touching 46°C twice this week – the highest in 50 years – it has been like waking up in a sauna for Delhi's citizens. Thousands of people in affluent and poor neighbourhoods spent Tuesday night picketing power stations demanding restoration of their current. Housewives busied themselves storing water in buckets, drums and even saucepans before the trickle that came through most taps ceased as the day wore on. Dozens of tankers sold water as newspapers reported an alarming drop in Delhi's water table. The rich had sunk hundreds of wells, leading to a water shortage'

(*Scotsman* 9 June 1994)

### Countryside – Late June

"The rains normally break at the end of June. The first rain usually comes in the night. The skies seem literally to break open. The sound is like the crashing of cymbals in an orchestra. The rain comes down in sheets and splashes back in fountains from the hard earth. When a little of the top is softened, the ground begins to soak up the water.

Along with the first rain comes the welcome coolness. People who gasped for every breath they drew got up early to enjoy the difference."

(*Men and Monsoon* Jean Bothwell)

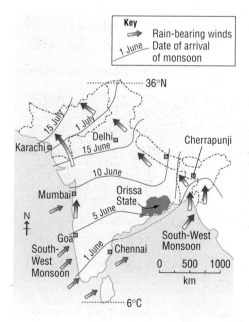

**Figure 9.42** The arrival of the South-West Monsoon

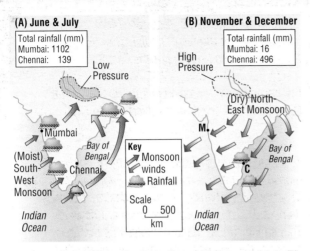

**(A) June & July**

Total rainfall (mm)
Mumbai: 1102
Chennai: 139

Low Pressure

•Mumbai

Bay of Bengal

(Moist) South-West Monsoon

Chennai

Indian Ocean

**(B) November & December**

Total rainfall (mm)
Mumbai: 16
Chennai: 496

High Pressure

(Dry) North-East Monsoon

M.

Bay of Bengal

C

Indian Ocean

**Key**
→ Monsoon winds
☁ Rainfall

Scale
0    500
km

**Figure 9.44**  India's climate between (A) June and July (B) November and December

**Figure 9.45**   Impact of the monsoon in India

## What causes the monsoon?

Map A (Figure 9.44) shows that in June and July, an area of **low/high** pressure builds up over a large part of **northern/southern** India. In this area, the land is very hot. The land heats the air causing it to **rise/fall**. This results in a large area of low pressure over the Ganges valley. The low pressure pulls in **dry/moist** air from the Indian Ocean. This air flows as the **south-west/north-east** monsoon and brings 70% of India's rainfall

Map B shows that in November and December the reverse situation occurs. The land is dry and cool so an area of **low/high** pressure grows over northern India. A mainly **dry/moist, south-east/north-east** wind blows from the land out to the Indian Ocean. Only a few areas receive rain at this time, for example, the coastlands around Chennai.

## The effects of the monsoon

The monsoon affects much of life and the landscape of South Asia as the photographs (Figure 9.45) suggest. It is all a question of how much rain falls and whether or not it comes on time. The monsoon rains can be described as unpredictable. Look at the graph in Figure 9.46. If the monsoon rains are late or fail completely, there will be drought and even famine, especially in the past. If the amount of rainfall is above average, there will be floods, as in Orissa in July 2001. The monsoon, therefore, is both help and a hindrance. It can be thought of as a mixed blessing.

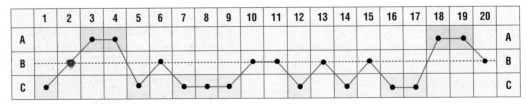

|   | 1 | 2 | 3 | 4 | 5 | 6 | 7 | 8 | 9 | 10 | 11 | 12 | 13 | 14 | 15 | 16 | 17 | 18 | 19 | 20 |   |
|---|---|---|---|---|---|---|---|---|---|---|---|---|---|---|---|---|---|---|---|---|---|
| A |   |   |   |   |   |   |   |   |   |   |   |   |   |   |   |   |   |   |   |   | A |
| B |   |   |   |   |   |   |   |   |   |   |   |   |   |   |   |   |   |   |   |   | B |
| C |   |   |   |   |   |   |   |   |   |   |   |   |   |   |   |   |   |   |   |   | C |

**Key**   **A** Flood years - rainfall much above average          **C** Drought years-rainfall much below average
**B** Years with enough rainfall                -------  Average rainfall

**Figure 9.46**   Variations in annual rainfall in Orisa

# The monsoon – a mixed blessing?

"*The monsoon brings water to millions of farmers. About 80% of India's farmers need the monsoon for irrigation.*"

"*The monsoon rains refill the reservoirs and provide water for cities and hydropower schemes.*"

"*Heavy rainfall can accelerate soil erosion in the foothills of the Himalayas.*"

"*If the monsoon arrives too late bringing below average rainfall, there will be drought. Animals die, fields and wells dry up and there are severe food shortages especially harming the poor.*"

"*Some tourist areas like Goa run 'Monsoon Holidays' which are very popular with tourists from dry regions like the Middle East.*"

"*Water from the monsoon is important in certain Hindu religious celebrations such as the HOLI festival.*"

"*Exceptionally heavy rain, caused by an early monsoon can cause rivers eg the Ganga to flood. As they burst their banks, crops are destroyed, roads damaged, and people and animals are drowned. Thousands can be made homeless as the mud bricks of the poorer houses are destroyed when settlements are flooded.*"

## ASSIGNMENTS

1   Look at the climate graph for Mumbai. Copy and complete these sentences:
    ◆ The maximum temperature is _____ in the month of _____.
    ◆ The minimum temperature is _____ in the month of _____.
    ◆ The range of temperature is _____. (Remember range of temperature is Maximum minus Minimum)
    ◆ The wettest month is _____ and _____ mm of rain falls on average
    ◆ The four wettest months are _____ , _____ , _____ , _____ .

2   In India it is possible to pick out three broad seasons. These are shown as A,B and C under the climate graph. Copy and complete the following sentences:
    ◆ Season A at Mumbai lasts from _____ to _____ and is cool and dry.
    ◆ Season B at Mumbai lasts from March to _____ and is _____ and dry.
    ◆ Season C at Mumbai lasts from _____ to _____ and is the _____ wet monsoon season.

3   Look at the graph showing variations in annual rainfall.
    a)   How many years had average, below average and above average rainfall?
    b)   What problems would result in years of above average rainfall?

c)   What problems would result in years of below average rainfall?

4   Read and think about about what causes the monsoon. Look carefully at the two maps to help you. Copy the first paragraph on page 192, selecting the correct word(s) from those shown in bold print.

5   Read the descriptions of the Indian countryside and New Delhi (on page 191). Which seasons are described in the passages? Pick out phrases that best describe the weather features of these two seasons.

6   Cherrapunji (1313 metres above sea level) is the wettest recorded place in the world.

|        | J | F | M | A | M | J | J | A | S | O | N | D |
|--------|---|---|---|---|---|---|---|---|---|---|---|---|
| T (°C) | 12 | 13 | 17 | 19 | 19 | 20 | 20 | 21 | 21 | 19 | 16 | 13 |
| R (mm) | 18 | 53 | 185 | 666 | 1280 | 2695 | 2446 | 1781 | 1100 | 493 | 691 | 13 |

Draw a climate graph for Cherrapunji – take care over the scale. With an atlas to help, try to explain the differences between Mumbai and Cherrapunji. Compare the rainfall of your home area/town with Cherrapunji. You could compare:
a) total rainfall b) seasonal rainfall pattern, and suggest reasons for the differences noted.

7   With the help of the extracts above, write a short illustrated account on the theme: 'The Monsoon – A Mixed Blessing?'

# Kerala – people, development and farming

## India's census: 2001

India held its 14th census in 2001. A **census** is a detailed survey which asks questions about a country's population. A census helps a government plan for future development by finding out, for example: how many people are there? how old are they? how many can read and write? how many are males/females? what differences are there from one part of India to another?

Conducting a census is never easy in India. It is very expensive – over 2 million people had to be employed because it is such a huge country with some very remote areas. There was disruption thanks to the earthquake in Gujurat (see page 89). Census forms had to be printed in 16 different languages, including **Malayalam**, spoken in the state of Kerala in the south-west of India (Figure 9.48).

## Development in Kerala

The figures from the census showed that, in some ways, life in Kerala is better than in India as a whole (Figure 9.49). Although it is not the wealthiest Indian state, Kerala has achieved:

★ very high rates of literacy, especially among females (Figure 9.47)

★ very high rates of life expectancy

★ very low birth rates

**Figure 9.47**  A girl's school in Kerala

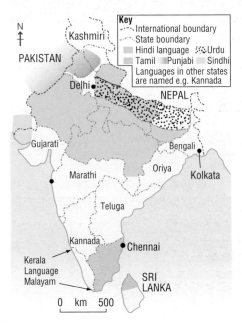

**Figure 9.48**  A land of many languages

★ very low infant mortality rates.

These measures of development show that Kerala has been very successful in improving the quality of every day life for many of its 32 million inhabitants. Kerala has succeeded because:

★ the state has encouraged spending on schools and colleges, and literacy classes for adults, especially women

★ a better health care service has been developed than in wealthier parts of India. Birth control measures are accepted and infant mortality rates have rapidly dropped. People accept that their children will survive infancy and a small family is seen as normal

★ women are treated differently. Unlike some parts of India, many women inherit land and are seen to be as important as men.

Kerala is in many ways a success story. Its population is slowing up so much that by 2050 over a third will be over 60. By that date, unless India's population growth rate drops to that of Kerala, India will have have taken the lead from China as the world's most populated country,

| | Kerala | India (including Kerala) |
|---|---|---|
| Population 2001 (millions) | 32 | 1027 |
| Population density (per square km) | 819 | 324 |
| Literacy % Male/Female | 94/87 | 76/54 |
| Life expectancy (Female) | 75 | 61 |
| Infant mortality | 14 | 70 |
| % of married women using contraceptives | 64 | 48 |

**Figure 9.49** Comparing Kerala and India

## Farming in Kerala

Figure 9.50 shows some features of a farm in the village of Ooruttukala in the south of Kerala. Kerala is a fertile state with the farms mainly found along the level land of coastal plain. Its southerly location means that:

★ it normally gets a plentiful supply of monsoon rainfall (see page 192), 2000-3000 mm per year

★ farmers are able to grow two to three crops of rice per year.

The farm is typical of farms in Kerala in that:

★ it is small, covering an area of only 1.8 hectares. Thanks to state rules, no farms are larger than 10 hectares in Kerala. This means that farmers in this crowded state try to get as much as possible from their small farms. This is called **intensive farming**

★ farmers often use 3 tier cultivation. The diagram shows that by intercropping coconut palms, banana trees and tapioca, farmers can make as much possible use of their limited land

**Figure 9.51** Farming in Kerala

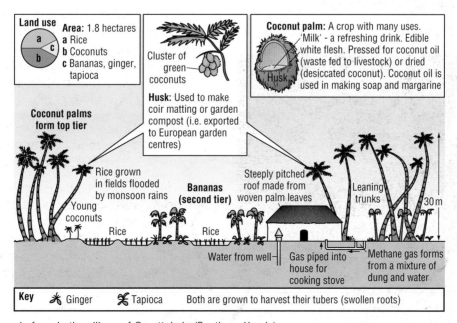

**Figure 9.50** A sample farm in the village of Ooruttukala (Southern Kerala)

★ little use is made of machinery (see Figure 9.51). Most of the work is done by the farmer. At rice harvest time (twice a year), however, he hires labourers who use sickles to cut the crop. His farm is so small it is not worthwhile buying a motorised harvester

★ the farmer receives money (subsidies) from the Kerala government for new rice seed, fertilisers and pesticides. He also gets advice an new techniques from TV farming programmes

★ some farmers are reducing the amount of land used for rice and switching to coconuts. Coconuts can be used for a variety of purposes and earn more money than rice (see diagram)

★ it is owned by the farmer. In Kerala, unlike many other parts of India, many farmers own their land. Often these owners are women who make important decisions about farming the land.

## ASSIGNMENTS

1 Copy the following sentences selecting the correct highlighted words:
   ◆ Kerala is a state in **south-west/north-east** India. **Hindi/Malayalam** is the main language spoken in Kerala.
   ◆ The birth rate in Kerala is **higher/lower** than in the rest of India.
   ◆ Compared to India, far **fewer/more** women can read and write in Kerala.

2 Suggest two ways in which the state government has improved life in Kerala.

3 Using all the information on pages 195–6, write a short description of the farm in the village of Ooruttukala. You should mention:
   a) farm size b) crops grown c) animals d) workers/machinery e) changes on the farm.

4 What are the different uses of the coconut palm and why are farmers growing more of them?

5 Give three reasons why Kerala has been able to improve the quality of life for its inhabitants.

6 Do you think that Kerala is more developed or less developed than the rest of India? Give reasons for your answer.

## TO TAKE YOU FURTHER

# The Green Revolution in India

The government of Kerala is worried about the switch from rice to coconuts. Rice and wheat are two of India's basic food crops. Fifty years ago, India could not grow enough food. Some areas suffered from famine, and India often depended on food aid from the USA and Canada, Today, India is self sufficient in rice and wheat production. India is now a grain exporter and, by 2002, had passed the USA to become the world's second largest grain producer after China. The key to success has been the Green Revolution.

**The Green Revolution** is the name given to the development of new varieties of crops such as rice and wheat. New varieties produce a greater amount or **yield**. Providing the conditions are right, the introduction of high yielding varieties (HYVs) into many developing countries such as India dramatically increased food production at a time of population increase.

## Essential inputs for the Green Revolution

To achieve the highest yields, certain inputs are essential:

◆ improved strains of rice and wheat, developed by plant scientists

◆ large amounts of fertiliser

◆ chemicals which are sprayed to control disease and pests to which HYVs are prone

◆ increased irrigation. A more reliable supply of water allows 2 or 3 crops per year of the quicker growing HYVs

*continued* ➤

**TO TAKE YOU FURTHER** continued

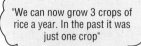

"We can now grow 3 crops of rice a year. In the past it was just one crop"

"I fancied the idea of the new rice crop but I could not afford it. So I borrowed money from a money lender. Even with the extra rice I can't pay off the debt. so I'll have to sell what little land I have and move to Mumbai"

"We can afford to buy the need HYV seeds and fertilisers. In fact, we're better off. My husband is buying a new tractor"

"We're producing more rice and wheat than ever but the rich are getting richer and the poor are getting poorer"

**Figure 9.52**    The Green Revolution: success or failure?

◆ machinery makes for quicker ploughing and harvesting. Using machinery also encourages larger fields.

**Figure 9.53**    Mechanised farming in the Punjab

### Assessing the Green Revolution

These inputs cost a lot. Better-off farmers in states such as the Punjab have been able to profit from HYVs. The Punjab is a state with a well developed irrigation system. Unfortunately, the success of the Green Revolution has been at the expense of poorer farmers and the environment as shown in Figure 9.52. Unless smaller farmers receive financial help as in Kerala, many sell their land and either work for larger farmers or migrate to the cities.

**ASSIGNMENTS** *TO TAKE YOU FURTHER*

1   What is the Green Revolution?

2   a)   Look at Figure 9.52. Draw up a table to show the good and bad results of the Green Revolution.
    b)   Do you think it has been worthwhile?

# Mumbai: a growing city

## Location and growth of Mumbai

*'I flew into Mumbai … The taxi driver kicked the engine of his battered three-wheeled auto-rickshaw into life and we set off down the highway … We entered a city built of tin (beaten oil drums) and hessian sacks. Thousands upon thousands of makeshift shacks. Children defecated in the open…we had to negotiate potholes…that*

**Figure 9.54**    Rich and poor housing in Mumbai

*was a signal to be besieged by begging children, or the maimed ... but beyond the poverty, men joked as they washed in muddy pools and women combed through piles of rubbish with a smile.'*
(R. Hoxham *The Great Hedge of India* 2001)

Mumbai is India's largest and busiest city. Figure 9.55 shows its location on the west coast, facing the Arabian Sea. With a population of 16. 3 million (and still growing), it is a compact and very crowded city compared to sprawling Los Angeles (see page 185). Once called Bombay, Mumbai in the 17th century was a small group of fishing villages on seven islands surrounded by marshy land.

Mumbai is now India's main port, its busiest international airport, and has the country's highest concentration of industry, banks and foreign companies. It is also one of the world's largest film making centres. This has earned for the city the nickname of 'Bollywood'.

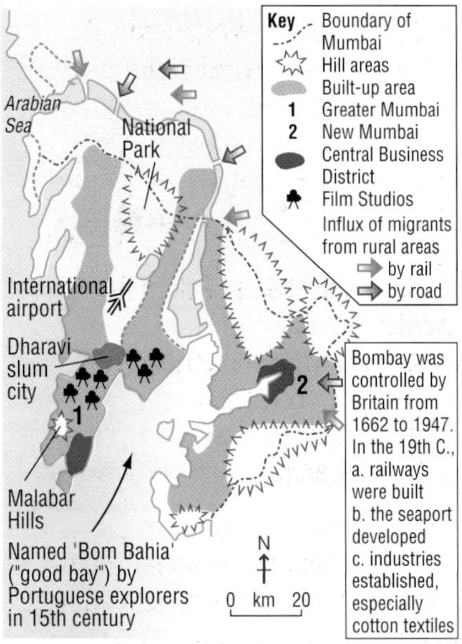

## Looking for work in Mumbai

### Tale of a young boy:

**Figure 9.57**   Ravinder Patel

Ravinder Patel is 12 and has decided to leave his village. His father has no land, and earns some money now and then as a farm labourer. But job prospects are poor as the richer farmers now use more machinery.

Ravinder arrives by train and he has to find a place to stay. Some family friends live in Dharavi (see Figure 9.56), so they agree to put him up in their one-roomed home. He's agreed to pay some rent but he needs to find a job. He only attended school for a few years so he has no qualifications. Possibly, Ravinder could start by shining shoes, selling nuts, or running errands in zone B. With a bit of luck, he might be given a job in one of the older cotton mills.

**Figure 9.58**   Romila Kaur

### Tale of a young lady:

Romila Kaur is 18 and has completed her senior school education. She comes from Kerala and has been offered a job in one of Mumbai's new call centres.

**Figure 9.55**   Greater and New Mumbai

Key
- Boundary of Mumbai
- Hill areas
- Built-up area
- **1** Greater Mumbai
- **2** New Mumbai
- Central Business District
- Film Studios
- Influx of migrants from rural areas
  - by rail
  - by road

*Arabian Sea*
National Park
International airport
Dharavi slum city
Malabar Hills
Named 'Bom Bahia' ("good bay") by Portuguese explorers in 15th century

Bombay was controlled by Britain from 1662 to 1947. In the 19th C., a. railways were built b. the seaport developed c. industries established, especially cotton textiles

N
0   km   20

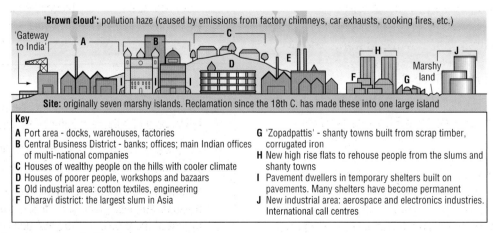

**'Brown cloud':** pollution haze (caused by emissions from factory chimneys, car exhausts, cooking fires, etc.)

'Gateway to India'

Marshy land

**Site:** originally seven marshy islands. Reclamation since the 18th C. has made these into one large island

Key
**A** Port area - docks, warehouses, factories
**B** Central Business District - banks; offices; main Indian offices of multi-national companies
**C** Houses of wealthy people on the hills with cooler climate
**D** Houses of poorer people, workshops and bazaars
**E** Old industrial area: cotton textiles, engineering
**F** Dharavi district: the largest slum in Asia

**G** 'Zopadpattis' - shanty towns built from scrap timber, corrugated iron
**H** New high rise flats to rehouse people from the slums and shanty towns
**I** Pavement dwellers in temporary shelters built on pavements. Many shelters have become permanent
**J** New industrial area: aerospace and electronics industries. International call centres

**Figure 9.56**   Land use zones in Mumbai

It is located in one of the new industrial estates. One of the reasons she got the job is her excellent English.

She is also lucky because the company has offered her housing at a reasonable rent in a re-developed part of the city.

## Problems of Mumbai

Like other cities in the world, Mumbai has to deal with many problems. Most of these are the result of its very rapid growth.

**Housing**: it is reckoned that every day 300 families come to Mumbai looking for work. However, there is a huge shortage of land, and land is very expensive. In fact, land values are amongst the highest in the world. For half the population, there is no hope of buying a house, so they have to live (1) on the pavements, living under canvas and wood covers, (2) in slums like Dharavi (Asia's largest slum with over 800, 000 inhabitants) or (3) in hastily erected shanty towns called **zopadpattis** on the outskirts on marshy land or close to roads and railways (Figure 9.56).

**Disease**: The poorer pavement and shanty town dwellers suffer from a range of diseases. Tuberculosis, cholera, typhoid and asthma are common among the young and the elderly. These are encouraged by poor sanitation and polluted water supplies. Matters are made worse in the swampy areas, especially during the Monsoon rains.

**Poor services**: In the poorer areas of Mumbai services are limited. Water supplies are available for only a few hours daily. People have to queue at standpipes. Power cuts are frequent. Huge amounts of garbage are produced daily, although youngsters help with recycling. Worst of all, over 2 million people have no toilet facilities. Raw sewage is discharged directly into the Arabian Sea.

**Traffic**: Buses and trains are very crowded. Daily, they carry over 6 million passengers. Passengers often can be seen clinging to the sides and sitting on the roofs of buses and carriages. Private cars, taxis and auto-rickshaws also compete for space on the congested roads. Perhaps the biggest problem is the pollution from the exhausts. Cities such as Mumbai are contributing to a vast brown

**Figure 9.59**    Traffic in Mumbai

pollution cloud that covers large areas of South and South-East Asia.

There are over 67,000 auto-rickshaws in Mumbai. Their engines run on a mixture of petrol and oil. Autorickshaws are estimated to contribute over 1 million tonnes of pollutants every year. An alternative is the battery operated rickshaw but they cost three times as much.

### ASSIGNMENTS

1   Copy the following sentences selecting the correct highlighted words:
    **Calcutta/Mumbai** is the largest city in **India/Bangladesh**. It is located in **west/east** India, facing west to the **Arabian Sea/Bay of Bengal**.

2   Attempt either this question or question 5. Write the heading 'Problems of Mumbai'. Match the following beginnings with the correct endings:

| | |
|---|---|
| Cars, buses and autorickshaws | water, electricity or sewage disposal |
| Many houses do not have | houses for the hundreds of newcomers every week |
| There are not enough | T.B., asthma, cholera |
| Many people suffer from | cause air and noise pollution |

3   Write a short account describing the first few days in Mumbai of either Ravinder or Romila.

4   Describe the different land uses you would see on a journey from zone A to J shown on Figure 9.56.

5   Summarise the problems facing Mumbai? Giving reasons, suggest which you think is the most urgent of the problems. Suggest possible solutions.

**TO TAKE YOU FURTHER** ▶

# Why Mumbai is growing

We have seen that most of Mumbai's problems are the result of the city's rapid growth. Mumbai is growing for two reasons:

◆ **natural increase** – most migrants are young (20 to 40 year-olds), and the birth rate is high.

◆ **migration** – is even more important. People are attracted to the city because Mumbai acts rather like a giant magnet.

Since the 1980s, migration has been the main reason for Mumbai's growth. Migration in, and around, the city is of two types.

## Rural-urban migration

Many people move from the countryside (or **rural** areas) to the cities (or **urban** areas). Like all migration, it involves:

◆ **'push'** factors: Figure 9.60 shows that these include few job opportunities, poverty and natural disasters

◆ **'pull'** factors: in the rural areas, city life seems very attractive. Television, films, posters and letters from relatives all suggest that life in the city is much better. And usually, in spite of all the problems, living standards, health care, educational opportunities and job prospects are better.

## Migration within the city

Migration also involves moving from one part of a city to another. Many people in Mumbai have chosen to move from the old part of the city to New Mumbai (Figure 9.55). New Mumbai was planned as a satellite city to accommodate

people and businesses from overcrowded Mumbai. Since the initial plan produced in the 1970s, New Mumbai has spread over an area of low-lying land which once had around 95 villages. It grew slowly at first but now there are almost 1 million people living there. Industrial estates, docks, schools, and a CBD have developed as well as private and public housing. Some of Mumbai's markets such as the vegetable market have moved to New Mumbai.

One attraction that 'pulls' families is the availability of planned plots of land. Laid out in a regular fashion, 30 square metres in size, they are provided with electricity, water and sanitary facilities. Each plot is shared beween 4 families. Initially each family build a house to their own design but they are given help to plan extensions and buy building materials at subsidised rates. These 'Sites and Services' plots are a good example of **self-help schemes**. Improvements can be carried out slowly, as and when families can afford it.

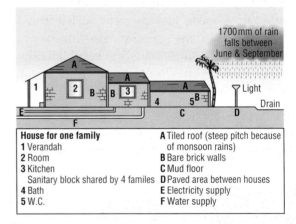

| House for one family | A Tiled roof (steep pitch because of monsoon rains) |
|---|---|
| 1 Verandah | |
| 2 Room | B Bare brick walls |
| 3 Kitchen | C Mud floor |
| Sanitary block shared by 4 familes | D Paved area between houses |
| 4 Bath | E Electricity supply |
| 5 W.C. | F Water supply |

**Figure 9.61**   Housing on a 'sites and services' scheme

**'Push' factors**

• Lack of jobs outside farming
• Natural disasters e.g. drought and earthquakes
• Poor eductation
• Poor health provision
• Restrictions of the village caste system
Push people from the countryside to the towns

**'Pull' factors**

The chance of
• A better way of life
• Improved housing
• A better education
• Improved medical care
• Paid work with regular wages
• A share of the 'good' life in the towns

rural drought

**Figure 9.60**   Rural–Urban migration

urban wealth

*continued* ➤

TO TAKE YOU FURTHER *continued*

**ASSIGNMENTS** *TO TAKE YOU FURTHER*

**1** Give two reasons why Mumbai is growing.

**2** What is a 'push' factor? Give three examples
What is a 'pull' factor? Give three examples.

**3** Why did Ravinder and Romila migrate to Mumbai? Try to group your answer into 'push' and 'pull' factors.

**4** **Either** write an essay on migrating to Mumbai **or** write two brief reports on the advantages and disadvantages of:
◆ encouraging self-help schemes to improve housing in Mumbai, and
◆ clearing zopadpattis and forcing people to return to their villages.

# Industry and tourism in India

## *Indian industry*

The Tata four wheel-drive car in Figure 9.62 is an example of one of India's newest industrial exports. Tata is one of India's largest companies with world-wide links, and produces a wide range of goods from steel and motor vehicles, electronics and computer software, to tea and chemicals.

Tata is unusual because it was founded during British rule. The British forced India to export raw materials such as cotton, and buy manufactured goods like cotton textiles from Britain. A few Indians saw the need for industry. In 1911 Jamshedji Tata established the iron and steel-making town of Jamshedpur in north-east India.

When India became independent in 1947, there was relatively little industry for a country with such a large population. Since then, however,

Indian industry has developed a great deal. India is an important manufacturing country with very varied output.

**Traditional manufacturing goods** include a wide range of products from cotton textiles to steel, from cars to foodstuffs. Most of the factories are found in and around the major cities. The Damodar Valley, in the north-east, is still the main area of iron and steel production (Figure 9.63).

**New High-Tech industry** has really developed in the past twenty years. A wide range of products is produced on new industrial estates and science parks. These are mainly located on the outskirts of the larger cities. The main high-tech centre is the southern city of Bangalore in the state of Karnataka. With over 6 million people, it is India's fifth largest city. Bangalore is home to almost a thousand high-tech companies and call centres, earning it the name of India's 'Silicon Plateau'.

**Figure 9.62** The young Ewings beside their Tata car in Scotland

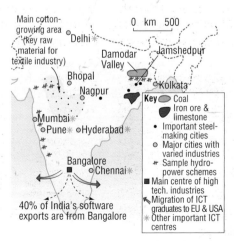

**Figure 9.63** Main industrial areas in India

## Why is Bangalore a major high-tech centre?

★ the Karnataka state government has helped to set up science parks such as Electronics City with over a hundred electronic companies (Figure 9.64)

★ Multi-national companies like IBM, have been attracted by the English speaking, well-qualified, highly skilled and cheap labour force – American and European companies contract out (outsource) specialist business to smaller Indian firms

★ Bangalore has a long tradition of scientific research with four universities and many colleges

★ Bangalore is an attractive 'garden' city.

**Figure 9.64**  High-tech industry in Bangalore

**Traditional craft industries** are still found in the villages and squatter settlements. Using raw materials such as cotton. wood and leather, many are involved in spinning cloth, hand-loom weaving, and other crafts, for example, making pots, leather sandals, and brassware. Craft industries were encouraged by Gandhi, who argued that such jobs improved the quality of life in the villages. A reminder of his belief in village crafts is the 'charka' – the spinning wheel on the Indian flag. Craft villages are also encouraged as part of India's growing tourist industry (Figure 9.66).

**Tourist attractions**: India is a growing destination for international tourists. It is a country which offers a wide variety of attractions. There is an interesting mixture of mountain scenery, beaches, wildlife reserves, and historic cities and world famous monuments. Some of these are shown in Figure 9.65. Most visitors to these destinations, however, are mainly prosperous Indians from cities such as Mumbai and Bangalore.

**Early tourism**: The earliest form of tourism began with pilgrimages to sacred religious sites. Hindus believe that rivers are sacred because water is so essential for life. Millions have visited sites on the River Ganga such as the city of Varanasi and the river's source at Gangotri, more than 4000 metres high in the Himalayas. In 2001, over 30 million pilgrims gathered for

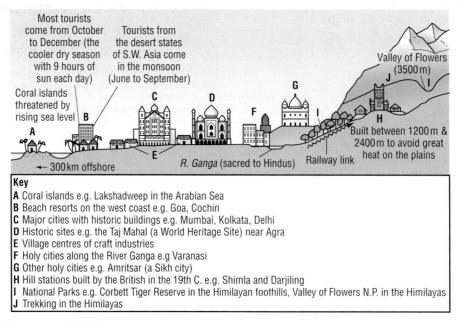

**Figure 9.65**  Tourist resources in India

up to a month to celebrate the festival of Kumbh Mela.

During British rule, mountain resorts or 'hill stations' such as Shimla were set up in the foothills of the Himalayas. They are still popular today, and retain many 'British' style buildings.

**Developing tourism**: The Indian government is keen to promote tourism. Tourism

★ brings valuable foreign currency into the country

★ creates jobs in cities, beach resorts and in villages where craft industries are encouraged

★ however, it can affect traditional ways of life, for example, in the Himalayas where incomers run the tourist trade

★ waste and litter cause problems on the tourist trails, and on the beaches

★ there is competition for water in the lowland regions between the resorts with modern hotels and golf courses, and local farmers, for example, in Goa

★ is easily disrupted by political problems and terrorism, for example, in Kashmir.

**Figure 9.66**   Village craft markets attract tourists in India

## ASSIGNMENTS

1   Which three of the following statements are true?
    ◆ Iron and steel are made in the Damodar valley.
    ◆ Bangalore is the main high-tech centre of India.
    ◆ The giant industrial company Tata was founded by the British.
    ◆ Craft industries employ large numbers in the villages.

2   Give four reasons why high-tech industry has developed in Bangalore.

3   Look at Figure 9.65. Either write a paragraph or design a poster to describe what India offers the international tourist.

4   a)   What are craft industries?
    b)   Why are they being encouraged in the villages of India?

5   Is tourism a good or a bad thing for a developing country such as India?

# Index